How to
TRAIN
YOUR DOG

Ryan and Jen Tate are a unique couple whose passion for animals is central to their work and lives. Between them they have almost 30 years of experience as two of Australia's most in-demand and respected dog and animal behaviourists, including several years at the famous Taronga Zoo. They hold a range of qualifications and their business, TATE Animal Training Enterprises, specialises in many areas of training, from puppy preschool all the way to training for conservation and scent detection dogs. Jen and Ryan live in Port Macquarie with their three young children and several highly skilled and affectionate dogs.

How to
TRAIN
YOUR DOG

*The complete guide to raising a confident
and happy dog, from puppy to adult*

JEN & RYAN TATE

EBURY
PRESS

EBURY PRESS

UK I USA I Canada I Ireland I Australia
India I New Zealand I South Africa I China

Ebury Press is part of the Penguin Random House group of companies whose addresses
can be found at global.penguinrandomhouse.com

First published by Ebury Press in 2021

Cover photography by Nathan Edwards
Cover design and internal illustrations by James Rendall
© Penguin Random House Australia Pty Ltd
Other images: page 44 Alamy (bottom); page 48 Newspix;
page 141 Pet Food Manufacturers' Association.
Typeset in Sabon LT by Midland Typesetters, Australia

Printed and bound in Australia by Griffin Press, part of Ovato, an accredited
ISO AS/NZS 14001 Environmental Management Systems printer

 A catalogue record for this
book is available from the
National Library of Australia

ISBN 978 1 76104 278 2

penguin.com.au

To Ari, the most brilliant and handsome dog who ever lived

Contents

Introduction

Why Train Your Dog?

Dogs are incredible companions: they have a sense of humour; they live in the moment; they show strength, courage, devotion and unconditional love.

Right now, there are more dogs in homes than there have ever been at any point in history. Access to a variety of different breeds and crossbreeds is incredibly easy, with almost any puppy purchase possible at the click of a button.

In 2020, when most of the world became restricted to their homes for a period of time due to the lockdown laws surrounding COVID-19, many people had the same idea: to adopt or welcome a dog into their lives. Pounds and rescue centres for the first time emptied out and breeders closed their books due to the overwhelming demand for puppies. But the fact that more people are living in smaller homes in denser, busier suburbs creates new challenges that can make living with a dog more complex than it once was.

Training your dog is the best way you can give back to these magnificent creatures.

When it comes to understanding and influencing dogs' behaviour, it's easy to underestimate the fact that most breeds have behind them hundreds of years of genetics driving their desire to perform a specific task, whether that's to herd sheep, fight lions, bait bulls, catch rats, guard land, pull sleds or warm the laps of royalty. We don't believe that any one dog breed is better than another, but the way you choose to raise and live with dogs of different breeds certainly needs to be tailored to them as individuals.

With this book, we hope to impart our knowledge and help you fully understand, appreciate and bond with your dog – and ensure that dog lives his best life.

We believe that training your dog is too important to be serious. For your sake, and your dog's, your training journey needs to be fun. Like good schoolteachers, dog trainers need to come up with fresh and exciting ways to communicate the syllabus. As your teachers for the next thirteen chapters, we encourage you, at the very core of everything you do, to have fun with your dog!

Who We Are and What We Do

We are a couple with a long-standing shared passion for animals. Ryan began his career at twelve years old, raising and training parrots for pet shops, and Jen's first job at age fourteen was in a vet clinic where, despite her short stature, she found a love for large and powerful dog breeds, bonding closely with an abandoned Rottweiler called Darcy. Between us we've got qualifications in dog training, zookeeping, marine science and more.

We met while working at the famous Taronga Zoo in Sydney. Ryan was the supervisor of the marine mammal department – presenting seal shows, training animals, supervising the keepers and overseeing marine science research. Jen worked as a keeper with a variety of different animals including ungulates (hooved animals like giraffes and zebras), carnivores (bears and big cats) and Australian native fauna. Alongside our zoo jobs, we ran our own business, training dogs.

In 2015, the dog training component of our business exploded due to a couple of well-timed television appearances, a new world record with our dog Ari, and some wonderful opportunities and mentorship from our dear friends, trainers Vicki and Steve Austin. So we dialled back our zoo work and invested our focus in the world of dog training.

Today, we run a business called TATE Animal Training Enterprises (you may notice that the letters of our business spell our surname, TATE – brilliant, we know). It's become quite a diverse company over time, but in a nutshell, it consists of:

- pet dog classes at a variety of locations in Sydney and the Mid North Coast
- training and handling detection dogs (for conservation and biosecurity)
- an online animal training school, the TATE Online Training Hub
- consulting to a variety of zoos, aquariums and fauna parks around Australia
- training animals for film, television and live presentations
- the Cynophobia Clinic (for humans with a fear of dogs) with psychologist Anthony Berrick, where our dogs help people overcome their phobia.

Our careers have already given us many memorable highlights (and we hope there are many more to come), including:

- working in Antarctica
- training animals as small as zebra finches and as large as leopard seals, and some that people rarely see, such as squirrel gliders and sharks
- working with our dogs in pristine natural environments such as Kosciuszko National Park, Lord Howe Island and the highlands of Tasmania
- training our dogs to help us find some of the rarest animals and plants on earth.

At home in Port Macquarie, our family of humans consists of three children: Lennox (aged six), Evelyn and Wren (one-year-old twins). Since becoming parents, we often discuss the similarities between raising both kids and dogs. Our goal as parents is to help our kids grow into independent individuals who feel confident and comfortable in social situations, teach them real life skills and resilience towards the unexpected twists and turns in life, and provide them with plenty of outlets and hobbies to allow them to work out what they enjoy. It's much the same with raising dogs.

Of course, when any family with children brings home a new puppy or dog, it's exciting and pretty chaotic, and our house is no different. Over the past six years, we've integrated many dogs into our family life. There is nothing more beautiful than watching our son play fetch with Spaniel puppies or our girls babble and coo at the presence of one of our mature dogs. We have some of the most energetic dogs in the country, yet they bring a sense of warmth and entertainment into our household that wouldn't otherwise exist.

So, on to our dogs. They are not only family but the backbone of the business and the best brand ambassadors we could hope for: diverse in personality and skill set, happy and impeccably trained.

- **Taylor:** A working line English Springer Spaniel who gained worldwide attention after her work during the 2019–20 Australian bushfires, searching for injured or displaced wildlife. She works full-time as a conservation detection dog predominantly in search of Australia's most iconic species, the koala. Still, to this day, she was without a doubt the 'naughtiest' puppy we have ever raised. Now she is our hardest working dog – wild, fearless and driven.
- **Finn:** A Shetland Sheepdog who was a very successful truffle detection dog in his youth, and now spends his days helping humans overcome their fear of dogs at Sydney's Cynophobia Clinic. He also assists our trainers in consultations for fearful or reactive dogs. Nothing fazes Finn – he is bomb-proof and kids absolutely adore him.
- **Rafa:** A Belgian Malinois, he works as a biosecurity dog and back-up detection dog on a variety of different projects. He is incredibly emotional and bonded to the family. He will work all day and does fierce aggression demonstrations and bite work on cue, but he absolutely requires cuddles inside the house every night.
- **Dash:** The youngest member of the Tate dog family (at the time of writing this book). She's a working line Springer Spaniel and another conservation detection dog who in many respects is the opposite of Taylor. Still very hard-working but sensible, affectionate and a very easy dog to live with. She was finding koala poo with 100 per cent accuracy at 5 months of age. The beauty of hardwired genetics!

- **Connor and Sally:** These Spaniels were initially selected as puppies and trained by our wonderful friend Steve Austin to do rare and invasive plant detection work. They now work full-time with our team on a variety of important conservation projects in some of the most beautiful parts of our country, from the tops of snowy mountains to coastal reserves.
- **Piper:** A Yellow Labrador who is in training to be a therapy dog for Ryan's sister's paediatric occupational therapy business, working with children with special needs.
- **Hugo:** Our Shepherd cross who is very much the retired 'office manager'. Hugo spends most of his days sleeping on the couch and getting completely spoilt by family.

We also have an extended family of special dogs owned by colleagues and family who join us on special projects, spending many months of the year working with our team. The English Springer Spaniels Tex, Becky and Tommy, Banjo the Kelpie, and the Labradors Phillip and Ernie.

Some of our dogs (clockwise from left): Rafa, Finn, Taylor, Ari (more on him later) and Hugo.

So that's us: passionate about animals, highly experienced in working with dogs – and excited to share our tips and advice with you.

How to Use this Book

Think of training a dog like building a house: beautiful features need to begin with solid foundations. So while it might be tempting to flick straight to the 'training' section (because let's face it, that's why you bought the book), we urge you to start from the beginning, a mere 40,000 years ago. An understanding of the evolution of dogs will be useful background once you get into the more practical stuff.

Then we'll cover, well, anything and everything else you need to know about your canine counterpart – how to find the perfect breed, how to train him, what to expect at certain ages and how to tackle behaviour problems in adult dogs, all mixed in with interesting facts and personal experiences along the way.

We encourage you to scribble, highlight and make notes in this book based on your unique situation with your dog. Just don't leave it within your puppy's reach while he's between the ages of 10 weeks and 8 months because, like most things in his path . . . it will be destroyed!

The Tates

Chapter 1

Understanding Dogs

The dog's position as 'man's best friend' is so entrenched that it is easy to forget the long and incredible journey they have taken from wild beast to becoming the domesticated pooch that shares our lives today. Dogs take many forms and play a role in every society on earth: some are lauded, others reviled, many are indispensable. The symbiotic relationship that has formed between human and canine has shaped the domestic dog we know now, and this understanding will be really helpful when it comes to forming the unique relationship you'll have with your own dog.

A Brief History of Dogs

Despite the enormous physical, behavioural and cultural variations between each breed, dogs all belong to a single species (*Canis lupus familiaris*, for the Latin fans). Relatively recent trait-focused breeding is responsible for the many distinct breeds we recognise today.

Though it may not be immediately obvious when you see a terrier being carried in a handbag, it is widely stated that 'dogs evolved from wolves'. This is not strictly true, as research suggests that grey wolves and domestic dogs in fact share a common ancestor, the two lines having split some 15,000 to 40,000 years ago, depending on which study you refer to (the evolutionary history is still not totally clear-cut and conclusive).

Dogs are not just man's best friend, but man's *oldest* friend. While scientists are still enthusiastically seeking the absolute oldest fossil or genetic example of the modern dog (at time of writing, this belongs to a 14,000-year-old skull piece from Germany), it is widely accepted that they have been domesticated for at least 10,000 years. Dogs were the first animals to be domesticated, in a process that would revolutionise the way humans traversed, used and inhabited the earth. Over the next 5000 years the domestication of animals continued with sheep, goats, pigs, cattle, oxen and buffalo. It is hard to overstate the impact that such developments had in the formation of structured societies: for the first time, animals could be kept close at hand for milk, meat and clothing, and could be used to carry goods and till the earth. Right from the start, dogs would have been key to helping humans catch, herd and protect many of these valuable animals. It is also worth noting the head start that dogs got on cats regarding domestication. The human–cat bond can be traced back a mere 5000 years to Egyptian times – no wonder cats are so unruly and ill-tempered!

So we know from fossil evidence that dogs have lived alongside humans for thousands of years, mirroring their dispersal and patterns of inhabitance on Earth. Yet we can't be sure exactly how and why their bond initially formed. As stressful as caveman life might have been, it's unlikely in the early days that cavemen were seeking emotional support from their dogs the way we do today! However, you can imagine a scenario where the less adept hunters in a pack of wild dogs, possibly those who were tamer by nature, might linger on the outskirts of a camp and seek scraps. This move would have been fraught with danger: any carnivore lingering that close would likely be deemed a threat. Perhaps the puppy-dog eyes were an early and critical evolutionary trait?! Highly unlikely – more likely these less-imposing dogs had a practical appeal for humans: the ability to see off – or at least alert humans to – greater threats. In this way, once these ancestral canines had remained on the outskirts of the camp without eating any children and demonstrated their worth to the group by barking at, or even chasing off, other carnivores in the night, you can imagine why they may have been allowed, or even encouraged, to stay.

The journey had begun: dogs had moved from the shadows to the fireside, earning their place beside humans. Then came their real moment to shine. A look at the most ancient dog breeds (those with the least divergent DNA from the ancestral wolf) reveals that they were originally used by humans for hunting. While dogs are commonly used for this purpose today, the initial realisation of this role that dogs could play – the mutual benefit of working together – would have been an absolute game-changer. The Guinness World Records names the Saluki as the oldest domestic dog breed – there are mummified remains in Egypt from 329BC! This breed was utilised by nomadic tribes for its strength, speed and endurance to hunt prey species from squirrels to deer. Other records suggest that the origins of ancient breeds, including the Akita Inu, Basenji and Afghan (good hunting and guarding dogs) could go back as far as 8000 years.

Another breed with ancient heritage believed to go back as far as 3000 years is the Alaskan Malamute. Along with this breed came a new use for dogs: with their great strength, they were put to use to pull sleds. Such an advancement would have been invaluable to the nomadic Mahlemut tribe, for whom the breed was named, and it signifies a broader evolution in the way in which dogs became incorporated in human life.

From here, dogs would take on a guardianship role with livestock, which would evolve to herding. For this purpose, dogs were bred to be smaller and swifter, which meant humans could still use their hunting instinct (for herding), but the dogs would not need additional bulk to 'take down' livestock.

So the origin of the dog–human relationship was one of functionality. But thanks to so much time spent working alongside one another with a shared purpose, it has gradually evolved into true companionship. Dogs again followed us from paddock to pillow to become leg warmers, confidants and comforters-in-chief. The broad title of 'pet' dog now covers a range of unofficial duties, from personal trainer to therapist, hot water bottle to beach buddy, accessory to entertainer. This spectrum of roles results from thousands of years of shared experience and a relationship based in symbiosis.

SYMBIOSIS: a relationship between two organisms where either or both benefit.

Reading Each Other

Anyone who has had a dog in their life will be familiar with the deep emotional connection that can be formed with these intelligent, social creatures. There is a connectedness between dogs and people that has formed over thousands of years and a recognition of fine social and emotional cues in both humans and canines that has allowed this relationship to flourish.

That said, it is important that we draw a distinction between true human emotion and the emotional displays of our canine friends. They play such an integral part in our lives that it can be easy to forget that they don't experience our *full* range of human emotions. It certainly feels like they love us and the bond that they form with specific people may be akin to an interpretation of that human emotion. But what is really happening when we interact? That's what we'll look at now.

Many of a dog's behaviours are learnt, a result of the operant conditioning that shapes an animal's natural existence (more on this in Chapter 12). And other things occur because of evolutionary usefulness. For example, we mentioned earlier about the role that puppy-dog eyes may have played in the ancestral wolf being invited into the camp. While this may not have been the first evolutionary step, science has revealed that it *has* played a part since! There is a unique forehead muscle, with the catchy name *levator anguli oculi medialis*, which is found in the majority of modern dog breeds (though, interestingly not in more 'ancient' or 'wolf-like' breeds, such as the Husky). The use of this muscle allows them to perform that mournful puppy-dog gaze. This suggests that it is a trait that has been actively bred into the dogs of today and speaks to the way that we have perceived dogs through their evolutionary history: we are drawn to a recognition of our own emotions in their behaviour and appearance.

It would be truly cynical to suggest that the dog who puts her head in your lap when you are struck by emotion has simply recognised a moment of weakness when she might earn an extra scratch or treat. However, sometimes it is easy to forget that dogs are not, in fact, four-legged people. Terms such as 'fur baby', while accurately capturing the care and regard that we have for our beloved pets, can also do a great disservice. It is nearly impossible not to anthropomorphise our dogs!

ANTHROPOMORPHISE: to attribute human characteristics or emotions to non-human entities.

The intertwined nature of our existence with that of dogs allows us to get an accurate read on their response to different stimulus and scenarios: we learn where they are comfortable and when they are anxious. But projecting our complex thoughts and emotions on dogs in these situations creates unnecessary confusion and can affect our ability to respond in the most appropriate way.

From the dog's perspective

As pack animals, dogs are social by nature. Their place in the hierarchy is formed through their ability to read and respond appropriately to innumerable cues from their pack mates. Some are subtle: a slight change in posture, the blink of their eyes. Others are more obvious: a growl or a snap. With thousands of years of shared history, dogs have effectively transferred this social awareness to people. The fact that dogs have managed to do this in a way that other species have not likely reflects the amount of time they have spent in our presence as a result of their proven usefulness.

And humans are relatively easy to read. Yes, our individual personalities mean we might display our feelings a little differently and sometimes we actively conceal our emotions in social situations. However, most people feel no real need to do this in front of their pets: dogs see us as we are, and they get to know us and recognise our moods and behaviours. Every fidget, subtle eyebrow raise and sigh we make is being closely read and interpreted by our dogs. Even things we can't see, like spikes in cortisol from feelings of stress or anxiety, they can sense. In other words, it's difficult to fake how you are truly feeling in front of a dog . . . they are the ultimate living lie detector!

It is important, though, to distinguish between the dog's ability to recognise *our* emotions and the dog experiencing these emotions herself. More precisely, dogs have learned the behavioural response their human counterparts are likely to elicit when displaying certain emotions.

Here are some common ways humans can misread dog responses and anthropomorphise their needs.

Guilt

'She knows when she's done the wrong thing!' is a phrase we've all heard (perhaps even declared) in relation to dogs. It seems so obvious to the owner who returns home to find a cushion has exploded in the living room! And then they're faced with those pinned-back ears, that bowed head, the expert application of the *levator anguli oculi medialis* . . . but does this pup really feel shameful and guilty about her crime?

More likely she gleefully lost herself in the act of destruction, wore herself out with the effort and collapsed in the debris with satisfaction. Then she rose hopefully at the sound of the key in the lock but suddenly realised, as her owner entered the house and caught a glimpse of the carnage, that the owner's mood was (strangely enough) not one of delight to see her – and immediately made the switch to appeasement mode. It is the ability to accurately read their human companion and *adjust their behaviour appropriately* that has enabled dogs to embed themselves in our society.

In order to prevent future destructive behaviour, we must first understand the dog's perception of the scenario and how anthropomorphising the dog can confuse the response. If we were dealing with a human in a similar circumstance then sitting down, assessing the damage, discussing the disappointment it caused you, determining an appropriate way forward and hugging it out could all be very effective.

Unfortunately, in the case of this dog, she stopped thinking about her crime at approximately the same moment she dropped the last cushion. When the owner arrived home several hours later and saw the destruction, the owner's changes in facial expression along with a host of other subtle cues were what indicated the owner's unhappiness to the dog. The dog is *only* responding to the human's display of uneasiness. This triggers appeasement behaviour, which to us looks like 'guilt'. Scolding the dog at this point would be unfair, as she will make no association between the punishment and the destruction. What's worse is that you're likely to make your dog confused or anxious and therefore possibly more prone to destruction when left alone.

So don't confuse an outward appearance of guilt with the genuine emotion!

Socialisation

We can often let a human perspective interfere with what is best for our dogs in the area of social interaction. For example, there is a broad assumption that dogs all want to run together in dog parks. But a dog park is effectively a music festival atmosphere for dogs, complete with the jacked-up meatheads muscling their way through crowds, the tongue-lolling clown with no sense of personal space, the public hook-ups and the first-timer cowering in the corner. Just do a quick poll of your friends and family and you're sure to find that this scene isn't for everyone!

Dogs perceive their meetings much differently from us. 'It's okay, he's friendly!' is a phrase that is commonly stated (if not yelled from afar) by an owner, as their dog tows them across a park to greet you and your pooch. The reality, though, is that our interpretation of 'friendly' sets a pretty low bar for dog interactions. If you and your partner were having a picnic and a teenage boy ran over, stood leering between the two of you, flexed, then helped himself to a cupcake and sauntered off, you would be unlikely to share his parents' assessment that he was 'friendly'! Yet somehow the broadly-held belief is that if a dog's mouth is closed and teeth aren't bared when they approach, no matter how fast or intrusive they might be, they're basically friendly. This is too simplistic.

In the world of dog communication, this interaction (to anthropomorphise) is rude and (from the dog's perspective) potentially threatening. A polite dog greeting actually means approaching slowly, averting eye contact, then sniffing each other's rear end (if ever you needed a reminder that dogs and people are different!) before engaging in any other kind of social interaction or play. Such interactions will only take place if both are comfortable with the approach and satisfied with the sniff. A dog who's allowed to rush wildly into a situation could be on the path to an altercation with an unsuspecting or less accepting dog. (We'll come back to dog parks in Chapter 11.)

Creature comforts

The environment in which our animals will be most comfortable is often very different to the one that we would choose for ourselves. Our perception of the most appropriate animal environment is often skewed by our human biases: while *we* would be pleased to see chickens enjoying a large, grassy field, the preference of most chooks would be a dust bath beneath trees that provide protection from predators and attract grubs for a snack.

Likewise, zoo visitors would typically say that an exhibit that uses a river moat to contain monkeys is much better than a similar-sized exhibit with metal bars containing them. This is an opinion formed from our negative association with cages, ignoring the fact that bars would provide a better climbing structure for many monkeys and thus dramatically increase the space they have to use.

Similarly, we can be led to make decisions regarding our dog's environment based upon human emotions that may not – if we were honest with ourselves – even apply to our own preferences. Take sleeping arrangements, for example: there can be a perception that crates are cruel, confining a dog who would rather be running free. However, anyone who's had a puppy can attest to how much they love to wedge themselves in tight spaces! We humans may romanticise resting in open spaces with the vast sky as our ceiling, but the reality is that we generally sleep best in the familiar comfort of our own bedroom, protected in our enclosed setting where our bodies are trained to relax, and the wider world is closed out. The effect of a crate (when well introduced to a dog) is much the same.

There is an instinct for us to give our dogs maximum space during the day: the biggest yard possible or full roam of the house. After all, these are pack animals that might run tens of kilometres daily across a territory in search of food, right? Well, as we know, the dogs who share our lives are a far cry from the ancestral wolf that roamed wide and fought hard for survival. If anything, their predisposition towards the easy life is what brought dogs out of the forest and into the lives of people!

A dog's perception of her yard and home life can be much the same, particularly any dog breeds with guarding instincts. Too much space can feel like a lot of responsibility for the dog to guard, and a screen doorway in a busy apartment block might cause them to develop guarding obsessions. Adjusting the areas of your property your dog has access to can do wonders for her mental health and behaviour. Of course, there are things that dogs need in order to be fulfilled, which vary greatly between breeds and individuals, but the amount of space they have is far from the most critical. Rather, the stimulation your dog receives both from her interaction with you and the environment you provide will have more impact on her wellbeing. Ensuring that your dog is comfortable in her home space and is provided with adequate appropriate outlets will see her far more settled and fulfilled.

Food

Dogs are the ultimate opportunists when it comes to food and will always be ready and waiting for their next snack, whether it's putting those puppy-dog eyes to work to negotiate a portion of your pizza, hoovering the mess from beneath the highchair, or risking a roasting to raid the barbecue. Table etiquette aside, a dog's willingness to consume anything on offer should not be taken as a guide to healthy living! The dietary needs of canines are entirely different to our own, as is their ability to process certain foods. Just as you would find yourself hugging the porcelain if you joined your hound at hoeing into a deceased beastie she found in the bushes, many of the delicacies that you enjoy cannot be processed by your dog and could render her very unwell. A good rule of thumb is: if it's a treat for you, it's a no-go for them. But there are also many other examples, such as avocado, onion and grapes – food we would consider healthy – that are toxic for dogs (for a comprehensive list see Appendix A at the end of the book). From your dog's perspective, a dried dog treat or piece of leftover meat is an absolute delight, so there is no reason to compromise her health by sharing your every meal with her. By all means, give your dog the silver service – just ensure that her food is healthy and safe.

The amount of food that dogs receive also play a big factor in their overall health. It is impossible to give an accurate guide for how much a dog should be eating based solely upon breed or size. Like people, dogs' metabolisms are unique to the individual and are affected by their genetics, age, sex and, to a large degree, physical activity. However, your dog's physical condition, rather than her behaviour around food, will give you a good idea as to whether she is eating too much, too little or just the right amount. It is very easy to overfeed a dog. A dog with healthy eating habits will leave nothing in her bowl and will typically come looking for more (particularly if history has taught her this is a worthwhile ploy!).

There can also be a tendency for people to compensate for a lack of attention or (ironically) exercise with more food, the result of which is an overweight dog. Obesity in dogs shortens their life expectancy and is linked to poor behaviour and a broad range of health issues, including joint strain, major organ diseases and various cancers. While it may seem loving to share your dessert or give them an extra scoop of food, a balanced, appropriate diet is a far kinder option (more on this in Chapter 8).

How to read dogs' body language

Sometimes your dog's emotions and intentions are very obvious: when she is watching you eat something she'd like to try, you will notice her eyes are wide and pleading while she licks her lips, or she will bounce around with sheer joy and lean in asking for pats when you get home.

But that is just the tip of the iceberg. Dogs communicate their emotions and intent through different parts of their body. If you know what to look for, you will soon realise your dog is constantly communicating with you and everyone around her; she just does most of it with her body.

Depending on your dog's breed, coat and shape, the signals you need to look for can vary greatly. For example, you can tell a lot from what your dog does with her tail and how it wags, but that isn't much help to someone with a French Bulldog. (Frenchies lack le tail.) So be mindful that subtle dog body language can be more difficult to read with dogs who have the following physical traits:

- very thick coats like the Newfoundland
- very curly coats like the Lagotto Romagnolo
- excessive wrinkles like the Shar Pei
- tiny legs like the miniature Dachshund
- fewer facial muscles like the Husky.

The easiest types of dogs to read are those that have a more 'traditional' dog shape and have been domesticated for a long time, such as the Kelpie or German Shepherd.

The tail

Subtle changes to a dog's tail offer big clues to the dog's state of mind.

A tail tucked between the legs is usually a sign the dog is scared, nervous, or in pain (with the exception of Whippets and Greyhounds, who usually keep their tail tucked while resting or running).

A 'loose' side-to-side wag indicates a happy dog.

A high or stiff tail means your pooch is on alert and focused – which, depending on the situation around her, could be a potential precursor to aggression.

Stiff tail   Tucked tail

Ear position

A relaxed dog generally holds her ears forward and to the side. When your dog hears something of interest the ears may twitch from side to side or even directly forward.

A dog who is scared or in a submissive state will usually pin her ears back.

A very alert and focused dog will usually hold the ears as high and forward as possible.

Scared ears

Relaxed ears

The eyes

Dogs aren't fans of prolonged direct eye contact with strangers or unknown dogs, so those that avert their eyes are simply being polite. If we want extended eye contact from our dogs it's something we usually have to train.

An intent stare at another person or animal therefore means the dog is in a very heightened state and is weighing up her options of how she should behave.

A dog showing the whites of her eyes (often called a 'whale eye'), particularly during a close interaction with another person or dog, is incredibly threatened or scared. She is seconds away from biting as she feels she has no other choice. This dog needs immediate space and help.

A happy or relaxed dog is often described as having 'soft' eyes and may even have some visible wrinkles or softening of skin/fur around them.

Whale eye

Soft eyes

The mouth

When a dog is happy and relaxed, the mouth is loosely closed or slightly open, giving the impression of a smile.

Yawning isn't just a sign of being tired. If your dog is fresh from a nap and is still yawning, it could be an indication of stress, fear or pain.

A dog licking her lips in the absence of food can indicate she perceives some kind of conflict, which she is trying to calm.

Baring teeth can be interpreted in several ways, depending on the situation. It can be a sign of a submissive dog or, if accompanied by growling, a signal of aggression.

Relaxed mouth   Bared teeth

Posture

A dog's overall body posture is the final and most important aspect to consider that gives you the whole picture of how your dog feels.

A happy dog's posture will regularly transition between sniffing, moving, and looking around. We often refer to it as 'fluid'.

A dog who appears to be making herself look tall, large, stiff and still is often threatened or trying to be threatening. Or, at the very minimum, she is on high alert and trying to decide what she will do next.

A scared and/or overly submissive dog will be low and wriggly.

Relaxed   Scared   Alert

The whole picture

We really want you to look at the whole picture: not just your dog's body language, but the entire environment she is in and what it might mean.

When we hold a tennis ball in front of Rafa, our Malinois, he looks incredibly serious – mouth firmly shut, eyes locked on, ears forward, tail stiff and high – and his body is presented like a brick wall of muscle. Which is totally fine: 'fetch' is serious business for Rafa. But if he looked at us like that while we were holding a newborn child in our arms, we would be very concerned about what he would like to do to that child! Fortunately, Rafa was raised around children so he knows those squirmy little toy-sized things are not for him to squeak.

So observe the whole body of the dog and the context of the situation she's in, too.

Here are some broad examples:

A happy dog – loose, fluid body, relaxed mouth, soft eyes, loose wagging tail.

A nervous or unsure dog – yawns, licks lips, scratches, averts eye contact, shakes body.

A scared dog – shows the whites of her eyes, bares teeth, growls, head low, hackles (fur on back) may be up, tail tucked or low.

A submissive dog – low and wriggly upon approach and rolls on her back at greetings.

A boisterous dog – pins other puppies down, jumps, humps, barks, mouths, body slams.

An aggressive dog – stiff body, intent gaze, facial features appear firm, hackles might be up, may growl, teeth may be shown, tail high and stiff.

With Great Knowledge Comes Great Responsibility – and Greater Outcomes

Many of the once-critical roles that shaped the specific breeds we identify with today are no longer as prevalent or necessary as they once were. However, the breeds remain, and so too do the instincts of hundreds of years of selective reproduction. Recognising these unique and hardwired characteristics is critical in choosing the right dog for your lifestyle and living arrangements, and in Chapter 3 we'll help you to make the best choice for you.

None of this is stated to scare you away from welcoming a new pet into your family. There is a dog suited to most people and most lifestyles, so don't worry! We have worked with countless dogs and learned from a few mistakes of our own, and our goal is to equip you with the knowledge you need for you and your furry friend to have the best possible life together. We love to see dogs living fulfilled lives alongside happy owners, and this starts with truly understanding our canine friends.

Chapter 2

What Makes a Good Dog?

If you've ever been lucky enough to share your life with a 'good' dog, you would have experienced firsthand his unrivalled love and companionship. Such dogs can make a bad day better, offer support when you are feeling down and have an uncanny ability to do something comical at the right time and make you laugh. Dogs live in the moment – a constant reminder for humans to be more present in our own lives.

However, the fact that hundreds upon thousands of dogs are surrendered to the pound every year suggests that not everyone who sets out with this dreamy idea of dog ownership finds a happy ending with their pet.

Bringing a dog into your life is a big and important decision. From your dog's perspective, this is a lifelong relationship, so it should not be rushed into! Too often, dogs are selected on impulse and the owners have not considered whether they can meet their dog's needs. It is in these circumstances that a good dog ends up in the wrong situation. In our experience, dogs who seem dominant, highly strung, bossy, stubborn, pushy or naughty are just dogs who are poorly trained or don't have a lifestyle suited to their genetics.

So ending up with a good dog isn't about luck. In fact, people often tell us, 'You're lucky to have such good dogs!' which is hard for us to swallow when we've invested a huge deal of research, effort and dedication into raising every dog we've owned. There are so many underlying factors that play into whether a dog is pleasant and well-behaved *beyond* its natural temperament. The upside is most of these are within our influence, and a happy and confident temperament can absolutely be fostered over time.

In this chapter, we will introduce you to some of the golden principles that will underpin much of the content in this book, giving you a great launchpad into your dog training knowledge.

The Happy Dog Pyramid

We would like to introduce to you the Happy Dog Pyramid. Much like the very popular 1980s food pyramids (which you might remember seeing on the back of cereal packets), we've developed this for clients to help them visualise the necessary building blocks in order to achieve a happy, well-adjusted, well-behaved adult dog. Most people might assume that training alone creates a happy and easy-to-live-with dog, but training is only effective if the dog is emotionally happy and stable to start with. Getting the foundations right is crucial.

Genetics and health

Genetics matter!
Genetics have the potential to directly affect health, behaviour and everything else in the pyramid more than any other single factor in your dog's world.

The Happy Dog Pyramid

It's better to think of some behaviours as genetic gifts rather than 'behavioural issues'. A Labrador who runs around with random things in his mouth, a Jack Russell who loves to chase small animals, a German Shepherd who guards your property with great vigilance – these are all things informed by genetics.

Instead of trying to suppress a dog's natural desires and instincts or passing them off as problematic, we need to consider embracing these genetic traits and harnessing them into positive outlets – which is why it's important for owners to choose the right breed for themselves and their lifestyle from the outset. It's the reason we acquired a Belgian Malinois for bite work, Springer Spaniels for scent work, a Labrador for therapy purposes and an Aussie Shepherd for TV and trick work. We can then play to their natural strengths – what they were born to do.

Here are some examples where, regardless of the environment or the way a dog is raised or trained, the genetics (both in relation to a dog's breed and parents) will dictate the outcome:

1. If the mother and father of a litter of Pugs have difficulty breathing and both needed corrective surgery, you can bet the whole litter will also have difficulty breathing by the time they turn one and will need surgery.
2. If a Cattle Dog comes from a long line of hard-working farm dogs, chances are he will want to nip the heels of anything that moves quickly past him, even if he's raised on a couch in the city.
3. If you buy a German Shepherd puppy whose parents are both nervous, vocal and aggressive towards strangers, even with brilliant training and careful socialisation this dog is highly likely to display overzealous property guarding by the time he is 2 years.
4. If you buy a Rottweiler from parents that both have poor hip and elbow scores, the dog will almost certainly have joint issues early on in life, even if you keep exercise to a minimum.

We will continue to highlight genetics in various ways through-out this book, but it is never for the purpose of shaming any breeds or putting others up on a pedestal. Our aim is to give you a greater understanding of the puppy you are contemplating acquiring, or the dog who is in front of you. There is no single perfect dog or breed: they all have their strengths and weaknesses, and suit different people and different tasks.

Health checks above all else

If you've ever had a skin rash, a broken toe or a toothache, you'll understand how these ailments affect your mood and behaviour. Your patience, tolerance and performance all tend to suffer. It's the same for dogs.

Whenever anyone comes to us with a dog who is displaying sudden aggressive behaviour, we always insist the dog gets a full health check by a vet before a trainer sees him. It's not safe or fair to train a dog while he's experiencing any pain or discomfort. In many cases, a health issue is found that can be resolved, and hey presto: the good dog is back.

TRAINING TALES

We made a mistake many years ago with a family friend's Kelpie who occasionally nipped people. Some dogs do nip during over-excited greetings, and the owner described the light bites as something that happened every now and then when the dog was giving them or friends an enthusiastic greeting when they arrived at the house.

On the first consult the dog was a model student: very happy and playful and showing no signs of wanting to nip or bite when we arrived. So we progressed with some exercises that would help with settling down the excitement around the greetings of family and friends.

At our second visit, about a week later, the dog still hadn't bitten anyone and things seemed to be going well – until Ryan gave her a rub on the side of her face while she was leaning in for a pat. Bam: a little nip on the hand.

The penny immediately dropped for Ryan: the dog was actually in pain and we had made a rookie error. When we very gently inspected her face, we noticed a slight discolouration on one of the top molars. A quick visit to the vet revealed a tooth infection that required an extraction. Once that was sorted, the dog never nipped again.

Management

Managing a dog's environment while he is still a puppy (or even an older rescue dog) is a key component in raising a well-behaved adult dog and will prevent him from experiencing or rehearsing undesirable behaviours. You will be in a better position to succeed with training if you go to greater lengths early on to provide safe and secure management options.

For example, we recently knocked up a temporary 'puppy-raising enclosure' at the end of our balcony outside the main bedroom for our puppy, Dash. This has multiple benefits:

- We can offer Dash a range of enrichment options (see Chapter 7) within the enclosure that will allow her to chew and explore the right things.
- We can leave her alone without supervision, comfortable in the knowledge she can't race up and down the fence line chasing the neighbouring dogs or practise barking at people walking past the front of the property.
- Our kids can play safely and happily in the backyard without being jumped on or bitten.
- Visitors can enter the house without being jumped on. This means we can also choose the right time to introduce them to Dash when she is calm. We have treats to reinforce 'sit' when she's greeting people.

Socialisation and environmental exposure

Socialisation and environmental conditioning refers to how we expose a puppy to the world around us during his early months of life. Overexposure can be just as detrimental as underexposure (we will explain this more in Chapter 6). A dog with good socialisation and environmental exposure is generally very comfortable and confident with his surroundings, and will have a stable headspace for training and fun . . . which leads us closer to the top of the pyramid.

Obedience training

Training is the obvious path for teaching good behaviour. Most dogs thrive when given clear instructions they understand. The more a dog learns to understand, the more confidence he gains.

Our tips for good training:

1. Set your dog up to succeed. Is he food motivated? Is the environment you are training him in too distracting for him to learn a new skill? Is it worth having him on lead to prevent him running off and ignoring you?
2. Small, successful steps are much better than big leaps of failure.
3. Less is more. When we are teaching a puppy a new skill, we keep words and movement to a minimum.
4. Use treats! They are such a clear and easy method of communication with your dog. We've never found a dog who didn't eventually like treats, once we tinkered with diet and motivation (discussed in Chapter 5). A lot of our clients are initially concerned that if they use treats they will be stuck using them. The reality is, once good behaviour is established, fading away treats for other 'life rewards' is very easy – but if you don't have good behaviour to begin with, treats are the easiest way to make that happen!
5. Repeat the same behaviour in the same environment a handful of times with success before changing things up.

When you are experiencing a problem with your dog, focus on teaching him what you *do* want him to be doing instead of trying to stop or constantly and continuously reprimanding him for what you *don't* want. It's said that the definition of insanity is doing the same thing over and over again and expecting different results. If a puppy is nipping at your heels as you walk around the house and you yell

'No!' but the puppy continues to bite, he is just learning to ignore you and you are, no doubt, losing your sanity. Meanwhile, nothing is changing. Instead you could teach the puppy to 'sit' for your attention and affection, and place the puppy in a contained location with enrichment between training while you are not focusing on him.

Here's how you can flip a few common problem scenarios:

1. 'I want him to stop jumping on me when I get home' becomes 'I want him to keep all four paws on the floor when I get home'.
2. 'I want her to stop roaming the house and stealing the kids' toys' becomes 'I want her to stay on her bed when inside'.
3. 'How do I stop my dog from pulling on lead?' becomes 'How do I teach my dog to walk beside me?'

One of our favourite animal training mottos is: 'If it's not working, it's either too hard or the dog isn't motivated by what is on offer.'

We often say this when people are stuck at a particular point in their training, such as trying to get a dog to come when called. What we want to highlight is that either the dog doesn't understand what his owner is saying, or maybe he does, but would rather play with his friends than come for the same old dry treat. So the two keys to successful obedience training are clarity (for understanding) and motivation (for engagement). Keep these in mind and you'll be sure to have greater success.

Outlets

Outlets are a way of providing your dog with specific training and exercise opportunities that directly relate to his genetic requirements. We have written an entire chapter on this subject because we believe it is so important in raising a fulfilled adult dog. Outlets play a crucial role in changing poor behaviour patterns.

Creating effective outlets requires an understanding of the motivation behind your dog's behaviour. Yes, you can use management strategies to prevent your dog from escaping by building a taller fence – but *why* does your dog feel the need to escape in the first place? Is he bored, under-stimulated or afraid of being alone? If you can hit upon the underlying reason, you can then think about which outlets (and perhaps training opportunities) you can give your puppy or dog to make him feel more comfortable and content.

Putting the pyramid into practice

If you are faced with a problem and are not sure how to tackle it, ask yourself the following questions:

- What was my dog **bred** for and does he have a clean bill of **health**?
- What **management** options do I have to prevent my dog from rehearsing undesirable behaviour?
- Does my dog need **confidence building** or **desensitisation** towards a particular stimulus?
- What can I **train** my dog to do that will counteract the undesirable behaviour?
- What kind of **outlets** can I provide my dog with that may fulfil his desire to perform certain behaviours?

Consistency, not Routine

There are some differences between consistency and routine that need to be considered and thought out with dogs – particularly young ones – to help get the best out of them. Owners that are *consistent* with what they will provide and accept in terms of life rules will create a happy and stable dog, whereas owners that follow strict *routines* can unintentionally make dogs bored or sensitive to change.

Consistent activities that can create good outcomes include:

- using the same cues and commands for an activity
- rewarding consistently
- having clear expectations.

Routine that can create bad outcomes include:

- walking your dog at the same time every day, on the same route

- feeding your dog the same food every day, at the same time, in the same location
- having your dog sleep on your bed every night.

Humans are creatures of habit, so it's only natural that some basic routines will form. Honestly, that's fine, but we want you to be mindful that if you follow a strict routine you may create problems. If you establish a long-running routine with a dog and that routine suddenly changes, this can create extreme anxiety in the dog.

For example, a dog who has always slept on the bed with his owners will feel like his whole world has come crashing down when one day a new baby appears and he's no longer allowed to sleep there. We *sometimes* let our dogs sleep on the bed, particularly when we are on the road and the dogs have been working. But our dogs are also fine sleeping in crates, in our ute, outside, on couches, on towels and anywhere we park our butts!

Or consider a dog who is always walked within 20 minutes of the owner waking up. He is likely to be restless, or even vocal, if his owner has a headache or is not feeling well enough to walk him one day. He is likely to bark and add to the headache because the routine has been broken. We exercise our dogs very well, but because we do this at varying times, they are completely fine if they don't go for a walk every day.

The good news from a lifestyle perspective is that you can be relaxed and don't need to worry about sticking to a schedule every single day with your dog. As the saying goes, variety is the spice of life.

The Role of Emotions

As you embark on your relationship with your canine friend, it's good to be aware of the influence of emotions – you're both sentient beings, after all! There are a few key things to remember.

1. Emotions between you and your dog are contagious

Dogs are brilliant at reading our emotions. Being mindful of your own emotional state is particularly important if you are training your dog or are trying to help your dog overcome a fear of his own. We advise people not to train dogs when they are feeling highly stressed or anxious, because your emotional state is likely to be contagious and might send your training backwards. We advocate for a fun and light-hearted approach to training for the welfare of the dogs as much as owners. We want our clients laughing, smiling and feeling welcomed in our classes and consultations, as it makes training their dogs *so* much easier. If you feel good, your dog is likely to feel the same and vice versa. We believe dogs have a bullshit detector too, which means they can sense when you are not enjoying yourself. The good vibes must be genuine in order to have a dog who loves his owner and is engaged in the training.

2. Dogs will make assumptions about people, places and experiences based on our emotional state

This is particularly relevant when your dog is in a state of fear. If your dog is frightened of a particular object (e.g. a vacuum) or event (e.g. fireworks) and looks to you for information or safety, how you respond will really affect your dog's long-term perception of that object or event.

In our opinion (and there is some literature that supports this), giving your dog comfort when he is scared isn't a bad thing, *but* the way you do it can make all the difference.

Some people think picking up their scared dog will help him, but some dogs feel restrained and more anxious when held. Others think talking to their dog in a high-pitched baby voice will soothe him. However, to many dogs, that high-pitched tone is the equivalent of another whimpering dog, so your dog may think you fear the fireworks as well, in turn potentially reaffirming their original fear.

When a dog barks aggressively at the neighbours and the owner comes out and yells aggressively at the dog to 'Shut up!', the owner may think it works because the dog momentarily stops. But we've seen many dogs who we are sure really think the owner is angry at the neighbour as well – therefore reinforcing their response to the neighbour and actually making the barking more likely to occur in the future.

What is the solution? Communicate with your dog in a way that you'd like your dog to behave. Be warm, calm, friendly and upbeat.

Provide information or instructions in a clear manner that your dog understands, and avoid giving him new instructions he's not been trained in when he is scared or anxious – it's useless.

3. You cannot reward or punish your dog's emotional state

The latest scientific research regarding animal behaviour indicates that you cannot reward or punish *emotions*, or how dogs feel. You can only reward or punish *behaviour*, or what they do.

Let's look at a couple of examples:

- A dog barks or growls aggressively at children. Every time the dog does this, his owner yanks on the leash or hits the dog with a stick. The owner believes they are punishing the dog for being aggressive and with a few repetitions the dog will probably learn not to act in this way. Problem fixed? No – unfortunately, it's worse. The dog still hates kids, possibly even more, but he's now learned that he shouldn't show this with a bark or growl. The behaviour (vocalisation) has been punished and may cease, but the underlying emotional state (a hatred of children) will remain. This means we've now lost a very clear warning signal from the dog and he is also more likely to bite instead of bark or growl next time.

- A dog runs around the house like a frightened lunatic every time there is a thunderstorm. Owners in this situation often worry that if they give the dog any attention or rewards, they will reward him for being scared. However, if they give the dog a few treats for lying down on his bed, the dog may learn, 'If I go to my bed during a thunderstorm, I get treats and attention.' There is a bonus here: the dog may start to *feel* calmer as a result of the training and the act of lying down. When the dog feels good, the fear that was driving the behaviour of running around fades, which means you have made your dog less scared.

Put Money in the Bank

Think of your relationship with your dog like a bank account: you want to have a positive balance rather than be in debt. This is achieved through repeating the experiences your dog likes, to build up good associations.

You can also 'put money in the bank' for other people, places and experiences. We take all our new dogs (particularly puppies) to the vet on a regular basis purely for some fun. They get treats from the staff, maybe have a game of tug and generally end up liking the place. This means we are putting money in the bank for the vet clinic. Why?

Well, at some stage in our dog's life they may need to be desexed, have an operation, be groomed or, at the bare minimum, have injections. These experiences will no doubt take a bit of money *out* of the bank, but because our dogs have already had a few good experiences there, they will handle this process much better and the account never goes into debt. Emotional states affect the way animals respond to pain – particularly mild pain. We are the same! If you are willing, happy and having fun you can tolerate much higher levels of pain than you can when you are nervous or scared.

Confidence is More Important than Obedience

For us, a dog who is confident is playful, happy, willing to learn, has some level of independence, is capable of overcoming challenges and has an ability to chill out. A dog who displays those characteristics – even if he has zero obedience training – is going to be a dog trainer's delight!

On the other hand, a dog who lacks confidence is less playful, is cautious, potentially clingy, reluctant to try new things and struggles to settle and learn. This is a much harder and more complex dog to work with.

Obedience is easy to establish once you've achieved confidence in your dog. Of course, it's possible to build obedience and confidence at the same time, but your dog's training regime and exercises need to be carefully considered to be successful.

Building confidence can be achieved through many fun and simple ways. It might involve toy-based games, climbing simple obstacles, getting the dog to find treats or jump into ball pits. Confidence building will be discussed in more detail in Chapter 6.

So now that you know what a 'good' dog looks like and the key principles that will enable you to raise one yourself, let's get into the fun part of choosing the right dog for you. We'll come back to many of these ideas again later in the book and you'll probably see it all a little differently once you've had your dog for several months! If you hit a bump in the road at any stage, come back and read this chapter again.

Chapter 3

Choosing the Right Dog

At least once a week a friend or relative asks us, 'What kind of dog should I get?'

We always do our best to give them an abridged version of what we'll expand on in this chapter. Depending on their circumstances, we might suggest they get something family-friendly and lower energy like a King Charles Cavalier.

And then we wait for them to ignore our advice and get a Kelpie.

We get it, aesthetics are important. The two of us certainly didn't fall in love because we thought the other person was a 'suitable fit' to our lifestyle! If you think a Kelpie or a Jack Russell is the most divine-looking creature in the world and your life won't be complete without that particular breed, don't let us stand in your way. But *please* do the dog the courtesy of researching and understanding what *you* must do in order to keep her safe, healthy, emotionally stable and out of the pound.

A Few Key Questions

Before making up your mind on a particular breed, consider asking yourself the following questions:

1. Why do you want a dog?

We've owned several dogs over the years, all fulfilling different facets of our lives and business: family pets, dogs who help us with puppy school, and dogs who do film and television work, cynophobia (fear of dogs) workshops or conservation detection jobs.

Ari – the first dog we owned as a couple – was an Australian Shepherd who we acquired for film and television work and to fulfil the family pet role. He would have made a hopeless conservation detection dog – he just didn't have the desire or interest to do the same job for several hours a day. Taylor, on the other hand, our brilliant 'koala dog', would be a terrible couch-cuddler as she hates sitting still. She's not great at learning new things quickly, but ask her to survey vast landscapes for the same scent over and over and over again and she couldn't be more in her element. So ask yourself:

What are you hoping to gain by adding a dog to your life?

Would you like a lazy companion? An active family pet? A guard dog? A farmhand? A service dog? If you can answer that one question, you will be ready to start researching appropriate breeds that will match.

Choosing a second dog

If you already have one dog and are considering adding another dog to your family, read the graphic below. Often, people think a second

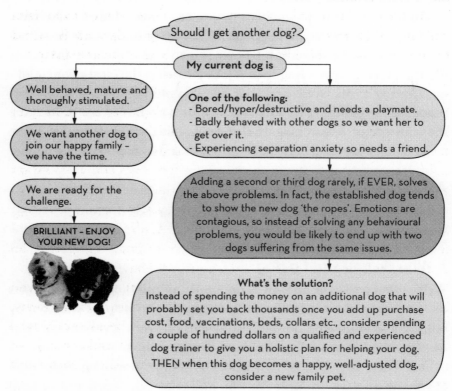

Should I get another dog?

My current dog is

Well behaved, mature and thoroughly stimulated.

We want another dog to join our happy family – we have the time.

We are ready for the challenge.

BRILLIANT - ENJOY YOUR NEW DOG!

One of the following:
- Bored/hyper/destructive and needs a playmate.
- Badly behaved with other dogs so we want her to get over it.
- Experiencing separation anxiety so needs a friend.

Adding a second or third dog rarely, if EVER, solves the above problems. In fact, the established dog tends to show the new dog 'the ropes'. Emotions are contagious, so instead of solving any behavioural problems, you would be likely to end up with two dogs suffering from the same issues.

What's the solution?
Instead of spending the money on an additional dog that will probably set you back thousands once you add up purchase cost, food, vaccinations, beds, collars etc., consider spending a couple of hundred dollars on a qualified and experienced dog trainer to give you a holistic plan for helping your dog.
THEN when this dog becomes a happy, well-adjusted dog, consider a new family pet.

dog will help fix behavioural issues in their first dog. This is rarely, if ever, the case.

2. How much time will you have for this dog over the next 10–15 years?

It's important to think about time. Do you work long hours away from home? Are you retired? Do you have a busy schedule that the dog will just have to accommodate? Or do you want a dog who you can seriously stimulate and work with on complex tasks on a daily basis?

This question should determine your choices. Greyhounds, for example, love to be couch potatoes and are reasonably independent, so they can survive if their owners do the odd long day out at the office and only have time for a shortened amount of exercise. If they are well-fed and warm, and get some affection and social interaction they are pretty happy, even in apartments.

On the flip side, if you want a dog to run several hours a day with you and dabble in some dog sports, a Greyhound might not be suited to you. You may instead lean towards a herding or retrieving dog.

3. What kind of house do you live in?

Space isn't everything, and many apartment dogs lead much happier lives than dogs on a large suburban block, because their owner takes them out for more activities. Dogs generally won't use a huge yard unless the owner uses it with them! A big yard does help if you want to train your dog in your yard, but apart from that the main concern is whether your property will safely and humanely contain your dog. Some breeds (Beagles, Staffies, Huskies and Cattle Dogs, to name a few) are escape artists, particularly if they are under-stimulated. So consider the living arrangements the pooch will have before buying.

We often get called to see people having a hard time with dogs who escape. They usually want us to train them not to leave the property. But there could be many different reasons for this behaviour. Maybe the dog is anxious and needs more human contact and training, or perhaps she has high hunting instincts and enjoys escaping to sniff or chase wildlife.

In the case of dogs who have a lot of fun while escaping, our advice to the client is that they may need to spend more money on builders than they do on dog trainers! Particularly if their yard has low fences and they have an agile, motivated dog.

Consider preparing your property as best as possible before acquiring a dog. If changing your containment arrangements isn't possible, you should really consider what kind of dog is suitable for your living arrangements.

Breaking Down the Seven Dog Groups

There are over 400 acknowledged breeds worldwide, and hundreds more that may not be officially recognised, as well as many popular crossbreeds (particularly hypoallergenic varieties) that are very common. Understanding dog groups, their history and genetics will *really* help you choose the right breed for you and/or your family.

The seven major groups differ slightly from country to country, but in essence they are pretty similar. In Australia, the dog groups are broken down as follows:

1. Toys

The word 'toy' refers to this dog group's small size. They have been selectively bred over the years to be smaller and smaller, predominantly for aesthetics or, in some cases, for a particular function (from lap warmers to ratters).

Popular toy dog breeds include: Chihuahuas, Silky Terriers and, our favourite, Cavalier King Charles Spaniels, literally bred to keep the laps of royalty warm and thought to protect their owners from fleas and the plague. They were bred to be small, soft and content with chilling out on your lap for hours on end!

Well-bred toy dogs (i.e. those bred from healthy, confident parents) truly make some of the best family pets and companion animals for a variety of households. Most of these breeds have fairly low energy requirements, which is attractive for a lot of people.

But have you ever heard of 'Small Dog Syndrome'? The phrase tends to get thrown around as an 'affectionate' term for a cranky little dog. Let's dig a little deeper into why these small breeds get labelled with this syndrome.

Due to the toy dog's small size, they can have a higher proportion of physical ailments compared to dogs of a 'medium' size. Combine these physical ailments with selective breeding for size rather than for temperament, and we tend to see a bit more *fear-based aggression* in toy dog varieties than in larger dog breeds.

Another label that small dogs get is the 'Handbag' dog. This is because they tend to get carried around in people's arms or bags instead of walking on the ground. For an impressionable puppy, this can be detrimental to the way she learns to perceive the world. For an owner, it's more difficult to read the dog's body language. As a result, the dogs are more likely to be thrust into situations they are not comfortable with or prepared for, resulting in an adult Chihuahua or equivalent who snaps or snarls when someone comes in for a pat. This is not her way of 'protecting the owner'; it's her way of communicating 'I'm not comfortable with your advances'.

Pros:

- A great choice for families or perhaps a single person seeking a companion.
- Low energy requirements – ideal for smaller homes.

Cons:

- Some lack confidence.
- Health problems are more common in very small breeds.

2. Terriers

The terrier dog group were all bred for a desire to hunt vermin through the earth. The name 'terrier' has nothing to do with the word 'terror' (despite what you might think if you've ever met a very naughty Jack Russell). It is actually connected to the terrier's ability to hunt through the ground – in Latin, *terra* means 'earth' and in French, *terrier* means 'burrow'.

Terriers are broadly considered to be very sociable with people, physically robust and fearless when they want something.

Popular terrier varieties include: Airedales, Bulls, Staffordshires, Cairns, Borders, Foxies, Jack Russells and the particularly striking Irish Terrier.

Most of these dogs are small or medium-sized, but it is crucial that we don't confuse their small size with low energy requirements or a laid-back personality. This is far from the truth with this dog group. Take the Lakeland Terrier, for example, which would generally weigh about 7 kg. This dog is one of the fittest on the planet and can run rings around most medium and large-sized dogs all day, every day. The word 'fearless' would also be an understatement.

Because of their extremely social nature, most terrier dog breeds don't do well being left alone for long periods of time. We see a significantly higher proportion of terriers with separation-related issues compared to other dog varieties. Due to their fearless nature and 'big dog' attitude, no terrier will tolerate being pushed around by other dogs, so if you own a terrier and your local dog park has a lot of rowdy, poorly behaved dogs, don't go there. It's not Small Dog Syndrome with terriers; it's more that they don't tolerate fools and don't mind a scrap if they believe it's required – which can land you both in a lot of trouble!

People interested in terriers also need to be mindful of their very strong hunting instincts, particularly for small animals. If you want a dog to keep away rats and mice, then a terrier would be a great option, but if you want a dog to get along with your prized collection of show guinea pigs, we suggest you look elsewhere.

Pros:

- Incredibly human-social.
- Usually very confident.

Cons:

- Not suited to being left alone for more than a few hours a day.
- High prey drive towards small mammals (a problem unless you want a ratter).

3. Gun dogs

Gun dogs are a group of hunting dogs that were specifically bred to assist hunters in either finding or retrieving birds or small mammals. Unlike terriers, they have a low desire to grab or shake their prey. They typically have a 'soft mouth', which has been bred into them so when they retrieve shot game it is not further damaged.

Gun dogs are generally considered the most 'light-hearted' and dog-social group of all dogs. Over the years they've had to work with large numbers of other dogs, often while crammed into small boats or waiting quietly together in large numbers for their 'turn' to find or retrieve. Dogs in these situations who started fights or were pushy with other dogs were unpopular and rarely bred from.

Popular gun dogs include: Labradors, Golden Retrievers, Springer Spaniels, Cocker Spaniels and Pointers.

Within this group, there is significant variation in size, energy levels and desire to 'work'. All of the popular gun dog breeds have two separate genetic lines which we refer to as 'working line' or 'show line'. The working line dogs have typically been bred to maintain their finding and retrieving abilities above all else, which means they will generally have shorter coats, be more athletic and have a higher desire to work. The show line dogs have been bred for the physical attributes described by the kennel clubs (organisations that maintain the rules and standards for breed conformation and records of pedigrees). They usually have very specific dimensions, colours and shapes. Most good show line breeders will also consider temperament and the desire to find and retrieve.

If you want to see how dramatic the difference can be between working line and show line, consider the pictures overleaf of Springer Spaniels from each line.

There are good reasons why gun dogs like Labradors are some of the most popular family pets, as well as the most popular for service roles such as detection dogs, therapy dogs and seeing eye assistance dogs. It's not that they are comparatively brighter than other dog varieties – it is really because they are social, a suitable size, can handle adversity and have a nice balance of being either determined or

Working line: a very short coat, smaller ears and extremely muscular body.

Show line: a longer coat and ears, softer features.

laid-back when required. Their robust nature makes them very resilient. The retrieving and finding instincts come in handy when we want
a dog to retrieve items for blind people or if we want to teach a dog to

sniff out contraband: gun dogs find these tasks intrinsically reinforcing. While some dogs from other groups can do this, very few will be as reliable or willing to do this task over and over again in a variety of different locations.

The most common complaint we get with gun dogs is a 'prolonged' puppy period. They seem to take a very long time to mature, but that is part of their light-hearted nature. Also, if you don't utilise their retrieving instincts they will find things to pick up *constantly*. As we were writing this chapter, we had Piper, an autism assistance Labrador in training with us in the same room. In the space of five minutes she picked up a remote, a nappy, a baby's teether, our notepad, a packet of corn chips and finally a mobile phone before we decided we should probably put her on lead!

Pros:

- Make great active family pets.
- Socially robust and forgiving (capable of handling more chaos than other breeds and shrugging it off).

Cons:

- Prolonged puppy period.
- Very prone to picking up everything in their mouths due to strong genetics.

4. Hounds

Hound dogs are fairly distinctly split into two main categories according to how they were bred for hunting: 'sight' hounds and 'scent' hounds. Sight hounds are generally designed for incredible speed and the ability to visually track a small moving target, whereas scent hounds have an unstoppable desire to follow a scent trail, even if it is many hours old.

Popular hound varieties include: Greyhounds, Beagles, Bassets, Wolfhounds, Dachshunds, Whippets, Borzoi and Bloodhounds.

Unlike gun dogs, most hounds were bred to work independently of the hunter. That means when they either spot something they deem to be a target or find a scent trail, they can seem disobedient or hard to control. This shouldn't be a negative reflection on the breed; rather, it means we need to appropriately manage the kind of environment we put these dogs in and provide them with plenty of suitable outlets to make these instincts feel utilised. Anyone who has owned a couple of Beagles will know that if they are off lead and find a scent trail that interests them, they can switch from a devoted, loving companion into a single-minded sniffing machine who has apparently lost all hearing!

Like gun dogs, hounds were generally bred to be socially tolerant and laid-back in the presence of other dogs. Many of them do seem to genuinely enjoy the company of other dogs and a pair of Greyhounds loves nothing more than to cuddle up on the couch together. This doesn't mean they are socially bomb-proof but they certainly value companionship.

In terms of 'complaints' or issues with hounds, we generally get a lot of phone calls from pet owners whose hound won't come when called. We also hear complaints about scent hounds being rather vocal or trying to escape when home alone.

At the end of the day, they all need to be treated as individuals. Anyone owning a hound will need to consider the housing or containment of their dog specifically: some will need extra warmth and access inside year-round (e.g. Whippets have a short coat, relatively thin skin and very little body fat), while others will need a fortress to keep them in if living near wildlife.

Pros:

- Most hounds have low grooming requirements.
- Socially laid-back.

Cons:

- Some of the scent hounds are notorious escape artists who require a lot of training to come when called (see Chapter 9).
- Sight hounds will usually need extra warmth.

5. Working dogs (also referred to as herding or sheepdogs)

If ever there was a group of dogs that we say can 'do it all', it would be the working dogs. It's probably why so many people are drawn to them. This group has been primarily bred for herding work, which requires stamina, cooperation with humans, problem-solving, agility and strong nerves. What a tremendous task for dogs to do for humans – and largely using their own instincts!

Some of the popular working dogs include: Border Collies, Cattle Dogs, Kelpies, Old English Sheepdogs and German Shepherds.

Intelligence or IQ in canines is a somewhat arbitrary and difficult concept to consider fairly. Generally speaking, we judge intelligence by a dog's ability to learn a new skill or concept in as low a number of repetitions as possible. Without a doubt, the working dogs have this category covered: they learn obedience commands in a fraction of the time it takes every other dog group.

For example, we train all our detection dogs with a 'Stop' command while working off lead. Our Belgian and Australian Shepherds learnt this skill with reliable perfection after four repetitions on one day, in one training session, and have remembered it ever since. In comparison, our Springer and Cocker Spaniels took at least thirty repetitions over a week before the penny started to drop, and if we take them to new environments even now, they often need reminders of how to perform this behaviour.

Now, to quote Spider-Man: 'With great power comes great responsibility.' Working dogs are not only the smartest dogs, but also the most agile, and their endurance is only matched by sled dogs. If you get an Australian Kelpie, you are essentially signing up for a dog who would love to run a 30 km obstacle course every day and problem-solve and work out puzzles along the whole way. That's no joke. When working on film sets, our Shepherds have happily worked longer and harder than anyone else on set, and they love every single minute of it. They'll nap in between takes but they thrive at learning new things on the spot.

Naturally, if these dogs aren't mentally and physically challenged five to seven days a week, and you live in the suburbs, things can go a bit pear-shaped. A quick walk before and after work with a throw of a ball at the dog park won't cut it.

If you don't fulfil those problem-solving and herding instincts, herd dogs will find their own way to use them. Trying to stop these instincts is like trying to hold back the tide. Chasing cars, bikes, skateboards and scooters is extremely common among unfulfilled working dogs, as well as rounding up (and nipping) children and other dogs.

ARI: A SPECIAL DOG

Our Australian Shepherd, Ari, was the most beautiful dog we've ever seen and came everywhere with us. He was proficient in the following tasks:

- narcotics detection
- truffle detection
- competitive obedience (first place in every event he entered)
- performance in television and movies
- herding sheep.

Ari achieved a world record for the most dog tricks in under a minute (38, which was later bettered by a Border Collie). He understood approximately 1000 words and 100 hand signals, and could follow entire sentences. If we said to him, 'Ari, will you grab some toys and jump in the truck,' he would promptly do exactly that and be waiting in the truck for his next adventure. His many skills were the reason why our work became so diverse.

Ari, our Australian Shepherd

With all this in mind, working dogs require the greatest investment of time and energy in order to keep them happy and relaxed. If you're willing to put in that time and get involved in sports or activities on a farm with your dog, then you won't find a better companion. When they have an owner who is willing to appropriately invest in them, the working dog's sensitivity, intuition and loyalty is unrivalled.

Pros:

- Usually very healthy and fit.
- Considered the smartest of all the dog groups.

Cons:

- Have strong herding instincts that may result in rounding up children or chasing vehicles if not fulfilled.
- Do not cope well with long days at home alone. This can encourage excessive barking, digging or stereotypic behaviour (pacing and repetitive behaviours).

6. Utility dogs

Utility dogs are a diverse group of dogs which, despite having a variety of different physical traits, all have one thing in common: they were bred for a fairly specific job or set of skills. Many utility dogs were bred for their property- or people-guarding instincts while others may have been bred for pulling carts or working in water.

Popular utility breeds include: Akitas, Bullmastiffs, Rottweilers and Saint Bernards.

Guard dogs are the best known from this category and are also likely to be considered as pets these days.

Depending on the neighbourhood you are in (guard dogs are far more common in rural and industrial suburbs), this may affect how your neighbours and friends behave around your utility dog. If you're considering owning a guard dog, you must be mindful that even with the best socialisation, the dog will almost certainly display property guarding behaviours towards visitors.

We have good friends with three Cane Corsos (also known as Italian Mastiffs). The dogs have known us since they were puppies and are well-trained, happy and fulfilled dogs. The family lives on an acreage with lots of wonderful animals and expensive machinery. The dogs provide their property with a high level of security and generally scare off foxes and wild dogs that try to kill their chooks and sheep. This is an appropriate and ideal setting for these dogs. So, what should we expect when we visit once every couple of months? Charging, barking giants!

We know the drill. We don't sneak up on them. We don't try to get in the house without being seen. We allow them to go through the motions of protecting their property – it's their purpose. Then their owners come outside and say 'Good dogs', welcome us in, and everyone is safe and happy. Their owners put a lot of effort into socialising them with family friends and neighbours, which means even though we get the barking welcome, once the dogs recognise who we are, they are very safe to be around.

Where people often go wrong is in encouraging too much guarding behaviour or leaving the dog in a very busy spot where she is left barking at things that are not a real threat. This is dangerous and stressful for the dog, particularly if she ends up spending all day chasing pedestrians who are just going about their lives. We've actually been to see a client whose guard dog was so busy watching pedestrians on the street that a car was stolen from the garage mere metres away from the dog – not a good guard dog!

Also in the utility category are breeds like the Alaskan Malamute and Husky, great sled (or mushing) dogs who generally won't guard; the Newfoundland, a water rescue specialist; and the Portuguese Water Dog, which can help fishermen herd fish. As you might have guessed, these dogs have very thick coats, need regular grooming and can overheat if vigorously exercised in warm climates.

If you like the sound of a utility dog, do some research on their history and what they have been bred for in years gone by before getting too excited, because it might be that their specific traits and strong instincts won't suit your needs.

Pros:

- Unrivalled loyalty.
- Very task-oriented.

Cons:

- Some instincts such as mushing, pulling or guarding can be inconvenient at times.
- Generally have a shorter life span than most other dog groups.

7. Non-sporting

The non-sporting category is a pretty difficult group to summarise. As the name suggests, this category contains all dogs who were not bred for a specific sport, although the definition of 'sport' is a bit subjective. Safe to say dogs in this category are a real mixed bag.

The majority of dogs within this group have low energy requirements, as generally speaking they have not been selectively bred for fitness or agility.

Popular breeds in this group include: British Bulldogs, Chow Chows, Dalmatians, Shar Peis and Poodle varieties.

Some of these dogs were initially used for tasks such as terrier-like roles and bull-baiting (a barbaric practice of the 1800s where dogs were set upon a tethered bull with the object of immobilising it, creating such high levels of stress in the bull that the meat took on a unique flavour upon consumption – thankfully, it was outlawed in 1835). As the years have gone on, most non-sporting dogs have been largely bred for specific aesthetics. Breeding may have focused on coat patterns, colours and textures, or wrinkles such as in the Shar Pei. In our opinion, sometimes (but not always) these traits are prioritised above the temperament, health and welfare of the dogs.

This is particularly relevant when it comes to brachycephalic dogs (dogs with short faces). Again, we don't suggest that all breeders are doing the wrong thing, but in Australia, it is common practice for French and British Bulldogs to need surgery to help them breathe before they turn one. This problem is directly created by selectively breeding dogs with shorter and shorter faces.

As a general and very rough concept to keep in mind, non-sporting dogs who look more like wild dogs (think wolf, dingo, dhole) will move better and often have fewer health issues, whereas those who look far removed from wild dogs may be prone to things like skin irritations or breathing difficulties.

If you like the look of a non-sporting dog, ask for veterinary advice, do some research and visit and view the parents of the litter if possible to see how they move. Ask for health checks from the breeder – this is something the breeder can have done when the puppy receives her first vaccination. Some of the common corrective surgeries required are incredibly expensive and you may need to budget for them.

Having said all that serious stuff, some of the best family pets reside within the non-sporting group and we have dozens of friends with well-put-together (i.e. they have good anatomy and are not likely to have ailments and pains), happy and well-adjusted non-sporting dogs. They usually have lower energy requirements than working, gun and terrier dogs and are mostly quite social with people and other dogs. Again, as with the utility category, this group is incredibly broad and difficult to summarise, so you really do need to be motivated to research the individual breeds and the breeder prior to acquiring one.

Pros:

- Generally low energy.
- Usually highly social and affectionate.

Cons:

- Prone to health problems (particularly short-faced breeds).
- Temperaments are sometimes less predictable due to a long history of breeding for aesthetics.

Mixed Dog Breeds

This group covers designer dogs to mutts and everything in between. Up until this point, we have referred to specific breeds or dog groups. But mixed breeds are also very common and popular. The physical and behavioural traits of mixed-breed dogs will usually be a blend of the dog's predecessors' traits. So it's useful to have a sound understanding of the combination of breeds that are within your dog so you can be prepared for a potentially wider variety of outcomes.

Oodles of oodles

There is a worldwide phenomenon around dog breeds that are crossed with poodles:

- Labradoodle (Lab × Poodle)
- Groodle (Golden Retriever × Poodle) – the two puppies featured on the front cover of this book
- Cavoodle (Cavalier × Poodle) – the most popular mix in Australia right now
- Bordoodle (Border Collie × Poodle) – outrageously smart and energetic; not a good first-time dog
- and basically every other dog breed you've ever heard of with '-oodle' added in there somewhere.

The major appeal is that most of these dogs have a good chance of being low-shedding (thanks to their poodle coat) and are likely to reduce allergy issues for people sensitive to fur. Currently in Australia there is no 'breed standard' for any of the 'oodle' varieties, which means great variation is possible. Provided the parents are well bred, well cared for and the prospective buyers know what they are getting, we have no complaints and have seen many lovely examples of family pets come out of the 'oodle' phenomenon.

Other mixes

There are also dozens of other popular mixes. One we've seen on many occasions is a Beaglier, which is a Beagle × Cavalier. These are often bred because the owner likes the look of a Beagle but wants the chilled-out personality of a Cavalier. Sounds lovely. What we usually see, though, is a dog who looks like a large Cavalier and has the hunt and food drive of the toughest Beagle alive. Not quite what they were hoping for!

Regardless of what the cross or mix is, we believe it is vitally important that you get as much information about the parents of your dog as possible and that you gain an understanding of the myriad of likely genetic outcomes you could end up with.

Rescue Dogs

Many people are drawn to the idea of providing a loving home to an abandoned dog, and it's a great thing to want to do.

Over the years we've purchased and helped rehome brilliant dogs from pounds and rescue organisations, with limited information on the dogs' genetics. Often the best we can do is take an educated guess at the genetics based on the aesthetics and the information we have at hand, and suggest a home or a lifestyle that approximately fits in with what we believe will suit this dog.

Above all else, we love dogs and our main motivation behind writing this book is to improve the welfare of dogs around the world. Of course we want to see all pounds and rescue organisations free of dogs who need homes, but we also want people to be informed and educated when selecting dogs from pounds or rescue organisations. If you are looking at a dog in a shelter or pound environment, try to decipher her genetics and then weigh that up against your lifestyle and what you can provide this dog.

What's worse than a dog being in a pound is a dog coming out of a pound into an unsuitable home environment and doing something dangerous that lands the dog back in the pound – or even worse, causes them to be put down.

So please check out what is available in your local shelter, pound or rescue organisation and use all the information in this chapter to help you select the right dog for you and your family.

For anyone rescuing a dog, your initial instinct might be to make up for lost time and try to provide that dog with all of the comforts and pleasures in life that she may have missed out on in her past. However, from the dog's perspective, too much too soon can be overwhelming or overstimulating, and can lead to undesirable outcomes. In our experience, most rescue dogs who move to a new home take about three to four weeks to settle in before their true personality starts to shine through and great training can commence.

While a rescue dog may require extra considerations or time to settle in depending on her past and experiences, if you do choose to go down this route, the training advice in this book should still be relevant and helpful.

Ethically Sourcing a Puppy

Possibly the hardest task, after finally deciding on the breed, is the process of finding your beloved puppy. There is a minefield of information out there and it's hard to know where to start.

When discussing the breed groups, we talk a lot about genetics and the role 'nature' plays in the overall behaviour of an adult dog. When it comes to sourcing your puppy, the breeder and breeding environment play a huge role in contributing to the 'nurture' side of things.

From the moment a puppy starts developing in utero, she can be directly affected by stresses placed upon her mother. A pregnant bitch under high levels of environmental stress will release hormones into the bloodstream that cross over into the placenta and will alter the pups' response to stress later in life. Happy mum = happy pups.

Then, of course, your puppy will be in the hands of the breeder for her first eight weeks of life. Puppies are absorbing the world around them at a rapid rate. The whelping environment (the box or pen area in which a litter spends the first few weeks of life), the home environment and the way each puppy is handled during this time will also affect their behaviour as an adult, so finding a breeder who knows what they are doing (as opposed to a 'puppy farm') is well worth it.

A 'puppy farm' is considered an unethical environment where dogs are bred at an unhealthy rate and kept in small, dark, unclean conditions. The dogs' only contact with humans is usually when they are washed just before they are sent to their new home. These dogs can be very nervous, difficult to train, have worms, sensory issues and can struggle with toilet training as they have been desensitised to living in dirty conditions.

Be sure to visit

When reaching out to breeders, it is absolutely key to ensure that that they allow you to visit the property and meet the bitch and litter. You are about to invest in a family member for the next 12 to 18 years! Knowing how they are cared for at the beginning of their life should be your prerogative and in our eyes there isn't any valid excuse they could make as to why you can't visit. By going there in person:

1. You can establish that they actually exist. We've had cases of clients booked into our puppy school who have cancelled because their puppy never arrived – an unfortunately common scam that occurs, even when the pup is bought from professional-looking websites that provide regular updates of beautiful pups.
2. You can see the bitch (and possibly the sire/dad) and consider their health, behaviour and personality. This will provide an insight into what your puppy will be like as an adult. Do the parents move well (in other words appear healthy, agile and well-put-together)? Are they happy and confident?
3. You can view the conditions the puppies have been raised in to ensure they align with your values.

Some other points to consider that, to us, suggest a breeder is doing the right thing would be:

- The breeder takes the time and care to get to know you and what your lifestyle is like. They should make an active effort to pair you with the right puppy.
- The breeder starts to individually help each puppy develop confidence and independence in the world through gentle exposure to sounds, sights, textures, people and environmental changes from 3 to 8 weeks of age. Most breeders are happy to discuss this if you ask. The difference between a factory-farmed puppy and one from a highly experienced breeder is huge! Factory-farmed puppies might not even see the light of day until they leave the farm, which can create all sorts of long-term sensory issues.
- The breeder won't encourage or allow two dogs from the same litter into a pet home. While it may seem like a good idea to take home two puppies so they have a playmate while the family is at school or work, raising littermates can be fraught with difficulties and long-term behavioural issues if you are not invested in raising them as individuals early on.

- The breeder is happy to provide a full health check report from the vet. This is usually done when the puppy receives her first set of vaccinations around 6 to 8 weeks of age. Vets can usually identify any congenital or hereditary health issues at this age.

Last of all, prepare to wait for your puppy. Good breeders don't breed willy-nilly. They take time to pair good genetics, choose the right time for their bitch to fall pregnant and ensure there is a demand for the puppies prior to breeding.

Personality Types Within Breeds

So you've considered your options from the pedigree and mixed-breed categories and managed to narrow it down. The other thing to now bear in mind is that *within* breeds and even within litters, there is usually a bit of personality variation. And sometimes your urge to choose a puppy because of certain traits it displays will set you up for failure later on!

As a general rule, when we are looking at puppies or even adult dogs in shelters, we try to fit them into three categories:

1. High drive

These are the dogs who are full on: they might be barking, jumping, stealing toys, constantly looking for food, annoying the other dogs, and seem to have no obedience, fear or boundaries. These are the kinds of dogs we look for as detection dogs, because we can harness that crazy behaviour into work, and lots of it. However, they wouldn't be suited to people who have limited time, expensive furniture or no experience with tough dogs.

2. Goofy and laid-back

Most people who want a pet dog should be looking for this personality type and, to be honest, this 'should' be the most common type of puppy you see in pet breeds. These dogs probably have a few flaws – maybe some poor manners – but they seem loving, compliant and cuddly. They appear happy and interested in life, but also don't mind if they miss out on some action. They don't have to be the first to the ball or the treat. These dogs are generally well-suited to an active family and can handle a bit of chaos and adventure but are equally as happy chilling at home.

3. Shy or reserved

These dogs hang in the corner: they're the last to greet you, won't make eye contact and seem nervous of new things. In many respects, this meek nature can be mistaken for 'calm' and 'easy to live with', but these dogs generally don't cope well with change. If you have a variable lifestyle, lots of friends and visitors and want to go camping with your dog, this kind of pup might find your lifestyle stressful. Therefore, they are often suited to people who live a quiet life with no kids or are retired, have plenty of space and not too many visitors.

When you go to visit a puppy or dog in person, try to identify which of these three categories she would fit into – this is another helpful way to select the dog best suited to you.

Whether you've just realised a whole lot of new things about the dog who is already in front of you or you now have a clearer sense about what kind of dog is suited to you, the important message is that dogs vary a lot! Nature and nurture are intertwined, so if you understand that all dogs are unique and have their own special requirements, strengths and weaknesses, you can adapt the way you train, house and raise your dog to set her up for a lifetime of success.

Chapter 4

Preparing and Puppy-Proofing

Before those four paws even step foot into your home, there is plenty you can do to prepare for the arrival of your new puppy. This chapter will help you feel a little more organised and in control so you can focus on enjoying the first weeks together with your new pet. How you prepare your home environment will play a big role in building independence, preventing undesirable habits from creeping in and setting your puppy up for success rather than chasing your tail, or his, the whole time!

Essential Items

Below are some essential items to consider purchasing before your dog arrives. There are some things you'll need immediately and others that may be able to wait a few days or weeks. What you need will depend on the age of your dog, where he has come from, and what the previous custodian (breeder, rescue, owner) provides you with and suggests you might need.

A space for your puppy

Crates

Some people don't like the idea of crates, but dogs are actually creatures that seek out smaller, enclosed areas to rest. If they are shown that a crate or a kennel is a safe and comfortable space, they will retreat to it when they are stressed or tired. A crate provides them with their own space in which to relax. Crates are also the safest way for dogs to travel inside cars (for the driver and the dog). Have a metal one for home use and metal or material one for car travel.

Shopping list

Crate

Kennel

Play pen

Bed

Collar with tag

Lead

Water bowl(s)

Food bowl(s)

Food

Treats

Treat pouch

Toys

Medication

Dog poo bags

Pooper scooper for the house

Disinfectant and paper towels for toileting mistakes

We will expand on this in greater detail in Chapter 7, but we can almost guarantee that crate training your puppy or dog will pay off at some stage down the track. It's much easier to crate train a puppy than an adult dog, but even training an adult dog is achievable with patience and time. As we'll explain, there are just too many benefits not to crate train.

Shopping for a crate can be overwhelming, as the market is flooded with options. We suggest hard crates over soft crates, such as the plastic travelling ones or metal wire ones. Yes, we know – they're ugly! But they are far more functional, and you can pretty them up by draping a towel in the colour of your choice over the top. There are even companies out there that make washable linen crate covers to hide the 'cage'.

The idea of a crate is to teach your puppy to relax, switch off and have some downtime. The problem with a soft crate is that it has stitching, seams and zippers. These distractors provide puppies with a fantastic learning and problem-solving experience: 'How do I escape?' You end up with a puppy that isn't resting at all, and instead is on his way to being the next Houdini!

The crate should be just big enough that the puppy can comfortably stand up, and lie down stretched out. If you don't want to be continuously buying crates as the puppy grows, we suggest looking for a crate that comes with a middle divider, or you could find another way to divide the space and prevent the puppy from having access to the whole area. You can research your dog breed to find your dog's approximate size when fully grown.

Why? The smaller the space, the more secure it feels for the puppy. Puppies are clean animals (if whelped correctly), and don't feel comfortable toileting near where they eat, drink or sleep. The bigger the crate, the greater the opportunity for the puppy to toilet at one end of the crate and sleep at the other.

Finish it off with a comfy bed, a toy or chew and the bedroom is complete!

Kennels

A kennel is essentially an outdoor crate without a door. If your dog is likely to spend a lot of time outside, a kennel is necessary for him to retreat to and stay warm or dry, especially if you have limited undercover areas outside.

When sizing a crate or kennel, you want the internal dimensions to be just a little bit bigger than the dog: this means the height and width of the kennel is slightly larger than the dog is tall and the length just a little bit longer than the dog measured from nose to rear. We say 'just a little bit bigger' because if the size is too large, the dogs don't seem to settle as well. This means if you have an 8-week-old Great Dane puppy you may need to initially fill in some of the empty space with cardboard boxes to make it more snug until the dog grows into his house.

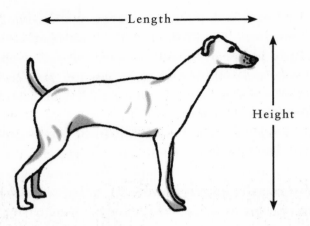

Measuring your dog for kennel size.

Beds

Dog beds are super handy for inside the house, for training exercises (like 'go to your bed') and, obviously, for making pens and crates more comfortable. A bed can quickly become a favourite chew toy for a puppy or adolescent dog, so if you have gone out and bought the fluffiest, comfiest bed and your dog is showing interest in destroying it, remove it immediately and purchase a more indestructible one to stop the behaviour from developing any further. We are big fans of the TuffMat by Rover Pet Products (which is like a sturdy mattress) and we also like the Lilcracka dog bed, which is a trampoline bed suitable for outdoors (and which, we might add, has *never* been destroyed by any of the dogs in our house – amazing!).

Puppy pens

A space for your puppy, such as a puppy pen, is essential. Having one or two areas ready to go before you bring your puppy home means you have a safe puppy-proofed space that will also protect valuable household items from being chewed, carpet from being peed on and ankles from being munched on, right from day one. Exposing a puppy to puppy pens from the beginning with daily feeds, enrichment and rest time in these locations creates a positive association with time separate from the family. Seek out a strong and sturdy puppy pen instead of a flimsy one, especially if you are bringing home a large or agile breed. The minute a puppy learns to jump out of, or knock over, a puppy pen, the space is almost immediately rendered useless. That one successful escape attempt will inspire many more to follow! We like the Pawever Pets Premium 8 Panel Metal Playpen, which you can accompany with heavy-duty gym floor matting to reduce the likelihood of the puppy chewing the floor. Puppy pens are also useful in helping to build a dog's independence (see Chapter 7).

Puppy pens: Our home set-up.

Baby gates

Baby gates are good for allowing your puppy time in a larger section of the house but still preventing them from having access to 'off limits' areas. For example, they may help in preventing your puppy from going upstairs, into a carpeted room or down the hallway. We also use baby gates to stop our puppies from ever having access to the front door. As with puppy pens, baby gates are also useful in building independence (see Chapter 7).

INDOOR OR OUTDOOR DOG?

Some owners have firm ideas on whether they want their dog to be an 'inside' or an 'outside' dog. This isn't something you need to decide straight away. What does need to be at the forefront of your mind is the safety and welfare of the dog. This means that for most dogs in the early stages, having them inside will generally be better for them emotionally and for supervision. We raise all of our new dogs indoors – it assists with desensitisation to children and noise, and helps the dog bond with the family. We gradually build their confidence with being left alone, and within a few weeks or months, they can live outside if we need or want them to. Most of our dogs are generally 'outdoor' dogs, but it's important to acknowledge we live in a very stable climate and spend most of our lives outdoors in our yard or on our verandah with the dogs so they aren't left outside alone. Having said that, because they've been raised indoors, if any of them gets sick, if we have wild weather, or if we just want a cuddle, any of our dogs can come inside and be trusted around the kids, furniture and carpet!

The climate you live in and your dog's genetics will also influence how suitable it is for him to sleep or spend time outdoors. Dogs with short coats in cold climates and dogs with thick coats in hot climates must be allowed indoors. Some dog breeds are also more needy and social than others (like our Malinois, Rafa) and for them, regular physical contact with the family may be as necessary to them as water and air, so keep an open mind.

Collar and name tag

Hopefully, if you are bringing home a puppy, your breeder has already started desensitising him to a collar and he has been wearing one for a few weeks now. If not, it's worth putting a well-fitted flat collar on as soon as he arrives home (no matter his age). Lost dogs who have a name tag and phone number are much more likely to be reunited with their family. As we have a lot of dogs with us and quite a few people in our team, we have lots of spare collars and tags with two to three mobile phone numbers on them. If one of our dogs is missing a tag, even for a moment, we replace it immediately. So make sure your dog has a collar with an ID tag containing at least two numbers and probably your dog's name on it too.

You might decide to upgrade to a fancier collar eventually, but a young puppy is likely to grow, so buy something simple that will fit now. When it comes to sizing, as a general rule you want to be able to fit a couple of fingers under the collar but not be able to pull it over either ear of the dog.

Lead

Choose a lead that is long enough to be loose when your dog is walking beside you, but not so long that he can go wherever he wants (more on this in Chapter 10). We usually suggest a lead length of 1.2 to 2 m. Please don't get a stretchy or bouncy lead, or a cheap extendable lead. It may feel like you are offering your dog more freedom, but you will also teach him bad habits, such as pulling or lunging on the lead. What we want is for our dogs to be happy and enjoy just walking beside us. If you want to give your dog more freedom, we suggest getting a long line (this is an oversized dog lead, from 5 to 10 m in length) and going to a park to allow the extra-long stretch and sniff, rather than having your dog associate neighbourhood walks with this equipment. We see many dog owners walking around with extendable leads, allowing their dog all the freedom in the world, until they suddenly 'snap' the lead down and reel their puppy back in response to a person, dog, or perhaps a cyclist approaching. From the dog's perspective, this may cause him to perceive the forthcoming person or dog as 'scary' by way of association with the uncomfortable pressure he feels down the lead.

Water and food bowls

Get something sturdy and appropriately sized for your dog. You might want one of each inside (with a mat underneath it to protect your flooring from spills) and one outside for water if your dog is likely to be an 'inside' dog. On average, we have two water bowls and one food bowl per dog at home, and one food and one water bowl per dog for our work cars.

Food

Your dog's previous owner may give you some of their food when you pick him up, depending on where your dog has come from. If you are happy with the dog's health and physical condition, you may wish to keep up the current feeding regime, so it will be handy to have some ready to go.

Treat pouch and treats

As we've already mentioned, these are a must! Generally speaking, a variety of treats is the way to go – not just dry treats but some with moisture as well. We therefore suggest buying a silicone-based treat pouch which is generally the cleanest and easiest to use. The best one on the market at the moment is The Trainer's Pouch. Okay, full disclosure: we're biased because we designed it ourselves! As trainers working with treats every day, we couldn't find a pouch that ticked all the boxes so we decided to produce our own. It allows easy access to treats (which is important when training), is comfortable to wear, and at the end of the day you can pop it in the fridge or dishwasher, which is important for hygiene.

Toys, toys and more toys

As a minimum, we suggest seven toys that the puppy can either chew or that are some kind of puzzle out of which they can get their food. The best types of toys and enrichment items will be further discussed in the 'Behavioural enrichment' section of Chapter 7. You will almost certainly want some kind of tug and/or retrieving toys and, for the committed, a flirt pole! All of these will be discussed at length in Chapter 11 on play, but trust us: they are a worthy investment in keeping your dog happy and calm.

Medication

Depending on where you are located, you'll probably need to pick up some kind of worming and tick/flea treatment for your new dog.

Check in with the prior custodian of the dog as to what they've been using and when they last applied it so that you don't accidentally double dose. They might even be able to give you some good insights into what has been effective for that dog. If you are in any doubt, book a consultation with your local vet clinic.

Setting Up the House

As people who have raised many a puppy, let us tell you: a good house set-up is everything! We have three kids and a busy lifestyle, so our dogs can't go with us everywhere. While your specific circumstances may differ, your dog will typically need to be left unsupervised at least some of the time. Here is how we recommend you set up your house for a new pup:

1. **A puppy pen inside the house**
   This usually has a bed, crate and water bowl down one end, some newspaper for toileting on up the other end, and a tub of toys close by.

2. **A puppy-safe area in the yard**
   We have an area outside our room where the puppy is still out in the yard but has plenty of shelter under a cover and is connected to the house. In this area we put a kennel with a comfy bed, a water bowl and some toys.

3. **A specific sleeping spot for the puppy**
   We let new puppies sleep in a crate right beside Ryan's side of the bed for the first three to seven nights. This may sound over the top, but by following this routine we've been able to get every single puppy we have ever raised into a predictable and easy sleeping routine within one week (this is discussed in great detail in Chapter 7). It's short-term pain for long-term gain. Yes, you will need to get up throughout the night and let the puppy out to toilet, but he will learn much better sleeping habits in the long term. We think it's easiest to designate the role to one person for the first few nights to give the puppy some predictability.

4. **A tie-up point and bed in the loungeroom**

We want our dogs to be part of the family, or at least to be exposed to the chaos of what happens inside the family house. So we always have a short lead and a bed available for the new dog to be tethered to in the loungeroom. This way the dog can be part of the family, but the lead will prevent him from roaming and stealing children's toys or (for a puppy) roaming and peeing everywhere.

5. **A separate pen in the back yard (only necessary if you have multiple dogs or pets)**

When we bring a mature dog home, we put another pen in the yard that will have a kennel, a comfy bed, a water bowl, shelter and a nice view of the house from only one side. We usually have three to seven dogs at our house and new mature dogs require a separate space to make sure they aren't overwhelmed by our existing dogs. Additionally, our property has a lot of stimuli around it: sheep, cows, horses, neighbours and their dogs. If dogs haven't been raised around that level of activity they often get overstimulated and bark, whereas by having a slightly smaller, quieter area to put them in for short periods, we allow them to gradually acclimatise to everything around them. Many dogs just simply can't cope with being left alone in a front yard, or a yard with clear fences where they can see people and animals moving past all day, so a separate pen for when you aren't supervising them can be the most comfortable option.

Whether your new family member is a mature, high-energy working dog or a cuddly puppy, physical structures like these will allow you to smoothly transition him into your home. We find that the initial expense is worth it for minimising the potential stress!

Setting Up the Car

Preparing your car for transporting your dog will ensure a safe and comfortable ride for everyone. It is possible that your dog's first car ride will be when you pick him up to bring him home, so you want to make a good first impression! Subsequent journeys may be visits to the vet, or adventures to parks, beaches, friends and family, so it is important that he is settled and secure. We have utility vehicles with secured crates in the back with comfy beds, plenty of airflow, fans, temperature sensors and water. But this set-up is fairly unique to professional dog trainers – you may wish for your dog to ride in the back seat or elsewhere in your vehicle. What we strongly suggest is that no matter where the dog is, he is not able to access the driver – this is law in Australia. Ideally the dog should be in a crate or a harness that is attached to a seatbelt. Both of these options are considered safe and effective in the event of a motor vehicle accident and will provide you with a consistent, safe way to travel on regular trips.

Some dogs get carsick or stressed if they haven't been in many cars before, so if your pooch looks worried during the first car ride to your house, prioritise some time to just hang out in the car over the following weeks, without driving anywhere. (This is a prime example of putting money in the bank!) Give the dog some treats and make the car a pleasant place to hang out in before going for your next drive. He should be more relaxed next time.

Designating House Rules

Before the dog comes home it's a really good idea to set out ground rules for everyone to follow and make sure you're all in agreement. If some family members let the dog jump up on the couch whenever he wants but other family members scold the dog when he climbs up, your dog will be receiving conflicting information – which is not fair on him.

So make a group decision on the list of questions below. You can even pop the rules up on the fridge:

- Can the dog come inside?
- Is the dog allowed on the couch?
- Will bedrooms be dog-friendly areas?
- Is the dog allowed on your bed?

- Will the dog be near the table during human mealtimes?
- Who will feed the dog?
- Who will walk the dog?
- Who will pick up the poo?
- Where is the dog's safe space (i.e. the space where the kids need to leave the dog alone when it is inside)?

In our home, our dogs can come indoors. We are flexible about things like dogs being on furniture, jumping in the bed for a cuddle or roughhousing on the ground, so long as they aren't associated with or create behavioural issues. To ensure this is the case, we start with some ground rules.

For example, with couches, we have a 'no jumping on the couch' rule until the puppy is about 6 months. During this period, we spend a lot of time on the floor with our puppy and get him used to their bed or tie-up exercise (explained in Chapter 7). If the puppies are unsupervised in the loungeroom, we pop them in the play pen so they can't jump up on the couch whenever they feel like it. Once they hit 6 months or thereabouts, we train them with an 'up' cue and an 'off' or 'down' cue. This way, we can pick and choose when it's couch cuddle time and they won't just jump up whenever they feel like it. Friends and family members who aren't such dog lovers appreciate that our dogs naturally relax on their own beds when guests are over.

With our bed, if any dogs jump up uninvited, we usually guide them off, or, if they know an 'off' or 'down' cue, we tell them to get down. As we have small kids, we cannot have our 35 kg Belgian Malinois jumping up on the bed whenever he feels like it! The important thing is that he knows he needs an invitation, doesn't expect it all the time, and when we say 'Off', he is happy to comply. If your dog starts to jump on beds and couches uninvited, we suggest you work on reinforcing that he stay in his own bed. In addition, do not invite him up onto your bed for at least four weeks, or until the uninvited behaviour has completely ceased for a few weeks consecutively.

RESOURCE GUARDING

A behavioural issue that appears particularly in Spaniels is the guarding of beds or surfaces. This means a dog will jump up on valued resources like a bed or a couch and growl, bare teeth or bark if someone comes near him or tries to remove him from the space. If your dog seems to 'guard' or 'protect' a piece of furniture from another person or dog, you need to consult a suitable dog trainer to help you work through this, as this is a serious issue. As a start, immediately put in place some management strategies to prevent the dog from gaining access to this spot.

Puppy School and Training Options

If you're acquiring a puppy, it is best to start looking into options for puppy training as soon as you have a confirmed date to bring him home, which should be when he is around 8 weeks old. The reason we recommend getting a head start on this is because most good in-person puppy schools and programs (like those we offer!) book out weeks to months in advance. The ideal time to start your puppy in pre-school is between 8 to 10 weeks of age, so thinking ahead will mean you won't miss that optimal window.

These days, there is a variety of training options to suit any situation. This book is designed to be comprehensive and tackle most facets of puppy raising and dog training, but we also recognise that people can find it helpful to remember and learn from visual and tactile experiences too. So combining the two is a great way to go.

Face-to-face puppy school

Puppy schools are the most popular and obvious learning experience for new puppy owners. A puppy is at its most vulnerable learning point (between 8 and 12 weeks old) when he attends puppy school, so the instructor holds great responsibility in providing a safe learning environment and ethical training options. Given that you don't *need* any qualifications to teach puppy school, there is a huge variation between trainers. Here are our tips on questions to ask to find a puppy school that will benefit your puppy's development and learning:

- What is the focus of the puppy class? If it has a nice balance of confidence building, basic obedience, problem prevention and controlled socialisation, then it sounds great. If it sounds like it's about dominating your puppy or, at the other extreme, a complete free-for-all off-lead play session for most of the class, we'd suggest looking elsewhere.
- Does the instructor have relevant experience, qualifications within the animal industry and are their own dogs well-trained? If that person ticks all the boxes that's another good sign.
- Is the class conducted in a safe and secure location? Puppy classes conducted in areas where stray or off-lead dogs can approach your puppies are a disaster. The environment should be clean and appropriately contained.

In-home training packages

This option is, for some owners, probably even more valuable than group puppy school, though it can be slightly more expensive than a class. An experienced trainer can help you set up your home to manage your puppy and prevent undesirable habits from arising. They can talk you through independence building in a way that is tailored to your home and lifestyle. They can talk you through correct socialisation and how to achieve a calm adult dog in the presence of *all* social creatures (people, dogs, wildlife, other pets, etc.).

Online puppy school

There are now options for online puppy pre-school that are just a click away. Some online options offer live video classes while others are self-paced and designed for you to have access to them before you even bring your puppy home, to prepare you for the journey ahead. We also have our own online puppy school, called the TATE Online Training Hub. So there really is no excuse not to have some form of training assistance while your puppy is young!

The beauty of in-home or online training, from our perspective, is that owners are able to fully absorb the information being provided, because they are not being distracted by a dozen other cute, sometimes barking, puppies. Likewise, their puppy can feel more confident and keen to participate in training because he is in a known and comfortable environment.

Training Options for a New Adult Dog

If you are acquiring an adult dog, whether it be from a breeder, shelter, pound or rescue organisation, we usually suggest taking it easy for the first three weeks. We don't believe taking that dog with a brand-new owner into group training settings is fair or realistic, particularly for dogs who may have previously been in high-stress situations. In those first three weeks, keep life pretty simple, avoid overwhelming environments or activities, and take note of the dog's behaviour. Some things that were initially a problem might disappear over the first few weeks and new problems may rear their head. In this situation, giving your new dog too much freedom too soon can be stressful, not advantageous for your pooch!

Where should you seek your training advice if you've got an adult or teenage dog who is too old for puppy school? Well, apart from this book, you have lots of options:

1. Find a trainer – If you have specific problems or specific goals, you could get a trainer in to your house. Try to choose a trainer that has skills relevant to your dog and what you hope to achieve. Within our team of trainers, we all have special skills or breeds that we have more experience with, so if a client has a certain dog with a particular goal, we will pair them up with the best trainer for the task. You may not have access to a variety of trainers, but if you do, ask them about their experience, their dogs and their qualifications. If they have well-trained or accomplished dogs, years of relevant experience and qualifications other than just 'growing up around dogs', then it is a good start. Again, we always advise you steer clear of anyone who suggests you need to

'dominate' your dog: it's a red flag for someone who uses outdated methods.

2. Dog clubs – If you have access to one, give it a go! Particularly if you want to be involved in some kind of dog sport (see Chapter 11) or you want to get to know more people in your community. Dog clubs are fantastic places for training.

3. Teenage and adolescent dog classes – This is one of our most popular services in Sydney and there are so many benefits to teenage dog classes. First, almost everyone has similar problems – usually that their dogs won't come when called reliably and/or pull on the lead. So the instructors are usually very well-prepared and experienced in helping to resolve those two issues. Plus, by splitting the cost with a group of other people, you tend to get good bang for your buck! As with puppy school, make sure the setting is appropriate and your instructor knows a thing or two about dog training.

4. Doggie boot camps – Also called 'board and train' facilities, they are an option to send your dog away for a period of time for intensive training. This may seem like a quick fix but the reality is that if you don't put in the hard yards in your home environment too, boot camp and 'board and train' options won't 'fix' your dog. Dogs are living social creatures, so sending your dog off to a facility for two or three weeks might help him learn some good new behaviours and curb some undesirable ones. But training really does need follow-through. If a board and train option you're looking at does not involve ongoing support, multiple follow-up consultations or weekly classes, it's unlikely to be effective long term.

Vaccination Schedules and Planning Vet Visits

Depending on where you live there are certain diseases your dog needs to be vaccinated against. For puppies in Australia they generally need vaccinations at:

6–8 weeks: the C3 vaccination, which protects against parvovirus, distemper and hepatitis – all potentially fatal to puppies. This should be done by the breeder.

12 weeks: the C5 vaccination, which is the C3 with the addition of a kennel cough vaccine. Kennel cough is incredibly contagious – it's not usually fatal but can lead to further complications in any dog. On acquiring your puppy, you should plan this vaccination with your vet ASAP.

16 weeks: C3 booster. Two weeks after this shot, puppies are considered 'fully vaccinated'.

12 months: annual vaccination.

Other treatments worth talking to your vet about are worming, flea and tick treatments. The east coast of Australia has plenty of paralysis ticks, which can be fatal to dogs of any age.

Registration and Desexing

Registration

Before bringing your dog home, it's a good idea to check out your local government regulations with regard to pet ownership, to check your responsibilities. Usually some form of registration is required. This should be done as soon as possible so that if your dog does go missing in the first 48 hours and ends up in a local pound or vet clinic, he already has the correct details. Some councils won't charge you a pick-up fee if your dog is registered with the council and has a collar with a name tag on it. If your dog isn't registered and goes missing, you could be up for hefty fines, and it also makes it harder for anyone who finds your dog to reunite him with you.

Desexing

Some local governments have strict rules or incentives around desexing dogs by the time they are 6 months of age, to prevent unwanted litters in the neighbourhood.

In our opinion, the decision to desex your new dog shouldn't be rushed. The timing of desexing can have significant behavioural and physiological consequences. This is an evolving area, with new research on the impact and age of desexing continuously emerging.

There are some valid arguments for delaying desexing, particularly for larger dogs. We now know that desexing large breed dogs before they are physically mature is likely to increase their risk of experiencing joint-related injuries.

We also know that dogs with fear-based reactivity or sensitivity to touch and strangers should be kept intact for as long as possible – particularly male dogs, as the testosterone helps build their confidence. It is common for some pet professionals to suggest that young male dogs displaying any aggressive behaviour be desexed. But if the behaviour stems from fear or sensitivity, the chances of that dog overcoming the behaviour after desexing are reduced.

There are a few trade-offs with early desexing and, depending on who you speak to and their motivations or concerns, opinions will vary. If you're not sure what to do after reading this chapter, we suggest talking to your breeder/rescue organisation, vet or dog trainer. If they understand your dog breed, its behaviour and the up-to-date research on desexing they should be able to give you reliable guidance. Based on our research on this topic, we would definitely suggest delaying desexing where possible if you have a large breed or a timid or nervous puppy who isn't fully mature yet.

People often ask what we did with our dogs. We have a real mix of dogs of differing ages at the moment, so we will briefly outline the dog, their breed, age, sex, desexing status and the reasons behind each decision.

1. **Rafa,** Belgian Malinois, 4, male, intact. Rafa is a large and perfect specimen of a Malinois. His breeder wants to breed from him one day and he also is required to work long hours each week. Data suggests intact males have more stamina than desexed males. So for now, he will stay that way.
2. **Taylor,** English Springer Spaniel, 5, female, desexed at 6 months. Taylor was a very small, well-put-together fearless puppy. We had a few intact males in our smaller house with her when she was young. We made the decision to desex her based on her low risk for any joint diseases and we also wanted to minimise any chance of unwanted breeding.
3. **Finn,** Shetland Sheepdog, 8, male, desexed at 3. Around sexual maturity Finn was the perfect dog, except that he worked very

hard to escape whenever he sensed an intact bitch nearby. None of our other intact males have done this. When we desexed him, this behaviour stopped, and he is still a perfect dog otherwise.

4. **Piper**, Labrador, 1, female, intact. Her breeder is a very well-respected Labrador breeder and service dog trainer. She advised us to keep her intact until she is physically mature (meaning when she has reached her full size and won't grow anymore) and we are going to listen to her. We have no desire to breed from Piper, and nowadays we can safely manage her intact without any risk of our male dogs getting to her.

5. **Sally**, Cocker Spaniel, 7, female, desexed at 1. The decision to desex her was based upon physical maturity, good temperament and no desire to breed from her.

6. **Connor**, English Springer Spaniel, 6, male, intact. Connor is a workhorse in the field but also a very sensitive dog. He used to be scared of some people (for no obvious reason) and needs to work very long days. For those two reasons we decided to keep him intact. He will most likely stay that way, at least until retirement.

7. **Banjo**, Kelpie, 4, male, desexed at 4 months. Banjo is Jen's sister's pet dog who we often use for film and television. He is a very laid-back puppy from a rescue organisation we knew well. Their policy was to desex dogs before sale.

Whatever the age or history of the dog you are bringing into your home, a smooth transition into your family starts with preparation. Planning the approach you will take with training, preparing the space where they will be living, acquiring supplies, fitting your car for pick-up and formulating a plan in your household for how you are going to receive this new addition will set you on the best path for success in this exciting adventure. If you've worked through this list, you're as ready as you can be. It's time to bring your dog home!

Chapter 5

The First 48 Hours

Regardless of the age or breed of the dog you bring home, the first 48 hours are particularly important for making a good first impression and helping your dog to feel immediately safe and comfortable. An 8-week-old puppy who has just left her mother and litter for the first time is likely to be very shy and will need a lot of emotional support. A 10-month-old dog who has just been rehomed might also be feeling out of sorts and unsure of her new surroundings and may possibly even look for an escape route. Either way, the dog is generally going to be experiencing some level of stress: she is likely to be confused and won't understand any of your cues or instructions. Therefore, the first 48 hours should really be focused on the safety and emotional needs of your new dog.

Tips for Success

Here are our rules of thumb for the first 48 hours:

1. Always supervise the dog when kids are around

This rule should be followed for the entirety of the dog's life when around small children. Obviously, as the years go on and relationships develop, the rules may change according to the child's and the dog's age, maturity and relationship with one another.

From a dog's perspective, children are unpredictable compared to adults. Statistically speaking, more adults are bitten by dogs, but in the reported cases where children are bitten, the proportion of cases with severe injuries is much higher. Most of these bites happen around the home environment and could have been avoided with good management and appropriate supervision.

We want the first few interactions between the dog and children to be smooth. There is no rush or need for the dog to immediately be on the couch watching TV with the kids while Mum and Dad are distracted elsewhere. This takes time. Use crates and pens and ensure the children know that when the dog is in one of these areas, they are to leave her alone.

2. Keep the new dog separate from other dogs or pets

We recommend waiting until the new dog has settled into the new environment before introducing her to other dogs and pets. The new dog has enough going on, being in an unfamiliar place, without needing to try to work out where she sits in the social hierarchy. A new dog can potentially be stressed and anxious so she might give your existing pets an unpleasant greeting, which could start their relationship off on a sour note. The previous owner might have told you the dog is fine with birds, cats or pocket pets (mice, guinea pigs, hamsters etc.), but these rules may only apply to certain animals or to a certain location. First impressions do count, so there is no need to rush these introductions – there is absolutely nothing to gain and everything to lose. Managing the new dog separately for the time being will give you the best chance of a successful introduction once you know her a little better and she trusts you more.

When you do decide it's the right time to introduce your other dogs, or your friends' dogs, do it outside your property, on neutral territory and on lead. Walk the dogs past each other; see how they respond. We cover this in detail in Chapter 6.

3. When you take the dog outside, do so either on a long line or on lead

There can be some flexibility on this point, but it's best to really look at your settings and the containment of your yard. Some backyards contain a lot of distractions, and a stressed or motivated dog might try to jump the fence the first time they see a kangaroo or sheep.

We've lost count of the emails and phone calls we've had from distraught families whose new dog has caught and killed chickens. If you keep chickens, remember they have feelings too, and if a brand-new dog comes charging, barking and snapping at them they are likely to become very stressed and flighty. As soon as the chooks behave like they're stressed (or like prey) they instantly become much more interesting to all dogs, whereas confident chickens are boring chickens. Ideally, the first time you expose any new dog to chickens, the dog will be on lead, the chickens will be in the distance feeding and it will all be very relaxed. We have always been able to get our dogs to the point of co-existing with our chooks without any barriers, and we firmly believe a huge part of that comes down to that first introduction.

The same principle applies to all other pets too (cats, guinea pigs, etc.). If, on their first introduction the dog is under control, you are really starting off on the right foot.

If you have your dog on lead and she spots your other pets and starts lunging, barking, growling, or even intensely staring at them, you are probably too close to them. And even if the dog doesn't scare the other animal, if she's hitting the end of the lead or practising any kind of aggressive or predatory-type behaviour while looking at the other animal, she is almost certainly building frustration and prey drive towards that animal. So keep moving the dog away until she settles right down and isn't fixated on the other animal. If the dog is so aroused or fixated that you cannot be in the same area as the other animal, you'll probably want to contact a dog trainer ASAP.

4. Always have treats on hand

Try to keep treats nearby whenever you interact with your dog, particularly when outside. You won't need to use this many treats forever, but it is a great way to start creating some obedience and confidence, and establish your positive relationship with her.

If the dog or puppy gets spooked or frightened by something she previously has no or limited experience with, you can use treats to change her mood and make a potentially scary experience into something more positive. For example, you may have a new dog in your loungeroom and decide to vacuum. The sound of the vacuum may cause the dog to flinch, bark, or hide. If you pair the sound of the vacuum (in the distance to begin with) with some praise and treats, you can quickly prevent the dog from developing a habit of barking or freaking out every time you decide to use it. This may happen with a variety of household appliances and stimuli in the home environment. (We'll cover this in much more detail in Chapter 6.)

Treats can also come in handy for 'luring' the dog outside, inside and into a pen or crate. Luring is an important part of teaching the dog where you want her to be. Through repetition and training, the dog will learn these life skills around your house, but in the first 48 hours (possibly longer), throwing a treat or using a treat in your hand to move the dog around is a much nicer way to start the learning process, compared to physically handling or moving the dog every time you want her inside or outside.

5. Crate the dog at night

This idea may not suit everyone, but trust us: when it comes to safety and toilet training, a crate at night is the best tool, hands down.

At night, an unattended dog (particularly a puppy) is likely to do something that we find unpleasant (or even dangerous), whether it be toileting in the house, barking for attention or chewing electrical cables. Having her in a crate nearby is the best way to create desirable night-time routines.

Dogs are social obligates: they cannot help but seek companionship. If they have just come from their litter or a home environment where they slept with other animals or people every night, an immediate transition to a new backyard or a laundry on their own will likely cause significant stress, often accompanied by barking or howling. Even if the dog is immediately quiet in your laundry when by herself, it's possible she is in some form of 'shut down', which isn't a good sign and may create longer-term behavioural issues.

SHUT DOWN

'Shut down' – or what may also be described as learned help-lessness – is when a dog is quiet or compliant, not because she is happy or content, but rather because she has experienced a high level of stress and has been forced to cope with events for which she is not emotionally ready. She does not protest or bark because she feels helpless and therefore shuts down. Dogs who regularly shut down are difficult to train and often develop physiological problems like weight loss and diarrhoea.

Our recommended set-up for the night routine is to place the crate next to a spare bed or mattress where the dog feels physically very close to the person sleeping in the bed. This may mean elevating the crate. By creating this proximity, we allow the dog to feel connected to another living creature without the possibility of getting up to any phone charger chewing!

We cover crate training in much more detail in Chapter 7.

NIGHT-TIME ROUTINE

Here is an example of a night-time routine for an 8-week-old puppy who has just been brought home. (This can be applied equally well to adult dogs too.) We find that by following this, we can settle a new dog into a consistent sleep routine within seven days. This means a settled night's sleep for all parties after just a couple of disrupted nights.

6–8 pm: Give dinner in the crate. When the dog finishes the dinner, let her out for some playtime and a toilet opportunity.

8–10 pm: Relaxation time with the family.

10.20 pm: Let the puppy out on lead for a gentle walk and toilet opportunity.

10.30 pm: The puppy is put in the crate and a family member goes to sleep next to it.

10.30 pm–1.30 am: If the puppy whines, barks or cries during this time, it can be helpful to stick a hand through the crate, talk to the puppy and let her know she's not alone. (As a general rule, we say puppies should be able to easily hold their bladder/bowels for 1 hour for every month they are old, plus one additional hour. So in the case of a 2-month-old puppy we can safely assume that any barking or whining within three hours is unlikely to be related to the physical need to relieve herself.)

After 1.30 am: Any whining or unsettled behaviour, such as moving around in the crate, can be dealt with by a calm trip outside. If possible, take the puppy somewhere with an absorbent, familiar surface such as short grass or a mulch garden bed and wait five minutes for her to go to the toilet. It almost always works. If it doesn't, we would usually set an alarm for another hour and try again.

Three hours after last toilet break: Take another toilet break outside for any whining or unsettled behaviour after another three hours. Sometimes this won't happen until 6 am, which is a good sleep for a puppy.

Anytime after 6.30 am: Start the day by letting the puppy outside again. Try to keep the puppy relatively calm until 7 am. When we say 'calm', this means no food, no toys, no training, no adventures. We want to condition the puppy so that when you wake up she doesn't expect to party immediately. Our theory is (and our experiences would suggest) this encourages a more gradual rise from sleep. As opposed to the hundreds of cases we see where puppies wake earlier and earlier because their owners either immediately feed them or take them for a big walk.

Anytime after 7 am: Take her for a walk, do some training or give her some enrichment (this will be explained further in Chapter 7).

Breakfast: If you are leaving the house to do the school run or run errands where the puppy won't join you, save the bulk of her breakfast to give her just a moment before you leave the house, so the puppy has something positive to do when you depart.

SLEEP AIDS

We don't habitually use or refer to sleep aids. We find that with the right initial sleep routine, they don't tend to be necessary. However, we do know that restless dogs can be helped by some or many of the following: white noise machines, music, heartbeat sounds, dog-safe heat packs, thunder shirts (a snug shirt for your dog who applies deep pressure, which can be soothing), DAP (dog appeasing pheromone) sprays and collars, flower essences, toys or bedding from their previous home in the crate with them, or clothes from the current owner.

We are usually fairly sceptical of devices or products that claim to calm dogs down. However, so long as it doesn't cause any harm to the dog, feel free to give it a go. There is also the possibility of the placebo effect on the owner: if you believe in a product and think it will make your dog calmer, there is a very good chance that you will be displaying behavioural signals and pheromones that indicate a new, calmer disposition, and this in turn can have a positive effect on your dog. Remember, emotions between you and your dog are contagious, so if you have an anxious dog, do whatever you can to make yourself calmer. You will not only help yourself, but you'll definitely help the dog.

6. Watch your dog eat

Some dogs will have unusual, unhealthy or unsafe eating habits, so supervising their first few meals (particularly if you are feeding any raw food items that may be a choking hazard) is advised.

If you find your dog eats outrageously fast and then ends up with some kind of upset stomach, there are lots of things you can do to slow her down. It's worth trying food puzzles, special bowls, scatter feeds or delivering food during training (see Chapter 7 for more details on enrichment). Some dogs who we have rescued seem to slow down once they realise that they aren't on the verge of starving, but others maintain the habit for life. Chances are, if food was scarce during the first 16 weeks of life and the dog was always hungry, she may maintain this attitude towards food forever, which may also mean you need to keep a close eye on her for food guarding (discussed in Chapter 8).

7. Avoid high-stimulus environments

Say this out loud: 'I will not take my new puppy or rescue dog to the dog park.'

You've got potentially another 14 years to visit the top ten dog beaches and dog-friendly pubs and cafes, so resist the urge to do it in the first 48 hours!

Let your new pup get familiar with your house, stairs, yard, family, appliances, floor surfaces, grass, water and every other thing she will be seeing, smelling and tasting for the first time.

As mentioned, the most important thing for your dog to start developing during her first 48 hours with you is a sense of safety. You must be your dog's custodian and keep her safe. Your dog won't be able to bond with you if she is constantly distracted or concerned for her welfare.

WELCOMING AN ADULT RESCUE DOG

Here are some tips for helping settle a new dog in to her home:

- Experiment with her sleeping arrangements. Typically, we suggest keeping the area smaller to begin with. If you have a large open plan house, consider a crate or a pen, as all that space can be overwhelming for a dog who has been locked in a kennel environment for 20 hours a day. We have no dramas with dogs sleeping in bedrooms, but we advise against the dog sleeping on a human's bed from the get-go. Jumping up for a cuddle is one thing, but consistently sleeping on human beds straight away can create problems down the track (guarding of the bed or anxiety if you wish to remove the dog from this arrangement for any reason).

- Gradually work out her optimum diet and feeding regime. The change of home can be very stressful – this can lead to runny stools and/or constipation. Settling her stomach will take time and experimentation; be patient and make any changes gradually. As a general rule, you should only introduce new food items every three days in small portions (10 to 25 per cent of her daily food intake). When it comes to training the new dog, we want her healthy and food motivated. Neither overfed nor starving dogs make great choices during training.

- Don't take them to the dog park for a while, or to any other off lead, uncontained environment. It doesn't matter how the dog behaved at the previous facility/environment; don't do it. Some dog parks are better than others, but broadly speaking they are chaos, and the majority of dogs at a busy dog park behave like teenage boys in a mosh pit. Your new companion is unlikely to be able to recall (come when called), remember who you are, or be confident enough to deal with the advances of a rambunctious Labrador.

Safety and Security

Puppies are generally very overwhelmed the day they leave their mum and litter. When you arrive home, keep your puppy's immediate world calm for the next couple of days. Make sure she has a hidey hole to retreat to (a crate serves this purpose well) and a small space to get used to at first (a puppy pen in the corner of the living room is an ideal small space for a pup). The same applies for an older rescue puppy or dog.

The first 48 hours are critical in letting a dog adjust to her new surroundings, monitoring her response to fresh stimuli and ensuring that she is safe and secure. It is in this time that you are at the greatest risk of a new arrival escaping, as she is not yet settled and will naturally explore or test the boundaries of her new home, and may even attempt to make her way back to her previous residence.

The backyard where our dogs hang out most of the time is a decent size: comfortable from the perspective of dogs and fairly typical of a rural 'house paddock'. It's by no means a fortress, but at a glance most people would assume it would safely contain dogs. Rafa, our Malinois, can easily clear a 2 m fence without needing anything to grab onto, yet our fence is only 1.2 m and he has never gone walkabout (and never will, we hope!). The fact of the matter is that he doesn't want to escape because he is happy and content here. Sally, our working Cocker Spaniel, is just 7 kg and very short. However, we know she has mild storm phobia and if she is left alone and a storm comes, she will jump any of our fences looking for someone to keep her company. Dash, one of our newest Springers, has the skinniest head in the world and is the most agile dog we have ever owned. She can fit through or scale virtually every boundary fence on our property if she wants.

These three dogs have unique temperaments and each responds differently to the same environment. We know them well, so are not surprised by their behaviour and can manage them as the situation requires, ensuring that they receive the appropriate stimulation and security. These same assumptions cannot be made about a new dog in a new environment.

Any dog running away from home is bad enough under normal circumstances, but the problems are compounded with a new dog. You are unlikely to have any rapport or trust with the dog just yet; she may not have a name tag with your number; she won't think to return 'home' and is likely to be in a highly stressed state. So during the first 48 hours it is important to manage every new dog or puppy very carefully, making sure that they are either always supervised or contained in something that is physically impossible to escape from. As we discussed in the previous chapter, setting up these safe spaces and having a collar with a phone number on her ready to go on day one will also help you to be prepared.

Food

At the end of the day, we are trainers and our focus is on the behaviour of an animal. Vets, nutritionists, dieticians and breeders will be able to provide a wealth of additional and important information when it comes to types of foods and ideal weights. What we can advise on are the best ways to offer your dog her food to ensure she doesn't become fussy, and enjoys meal time and food-based training sessions.

Depending on where your dog has come from, you may have been given some kind of food with your purchase. If the dog looks in peak physical condition, and has good bowel movements, you may wish to continue with the current feeding regime. However, if your dog doesn't look like the epitome of health or you have your concerns about the current food or its availability, it might be worth consulting a vet and switching over to a new diet.

How much and how often to feed?

For puppies, we suggest following the breeder's, vet's or shelter's suggestions on feeding.

In terms of how often, here are suggested frequencies:

- Dogs aged 8 to 12 weeks can be fed three times a day (note: some or a lot of this food may come via training or treats, so we often adjust or skip some meals if we are doing a lot of training and therefore giving the dog lots of treats).
- Dogs aged 12 to 16 weeks can be fed two to three times a day, depending on body condition and volume of food via training.
- Dogs aged 16 weeks to 12 months can be fed twice a day (again, some, if not most, of this food may be given via training).
- Dogs aged 12 months and older should be fed once a day, provided the dog is in good physical condition.

Puppy size and weight

Generally speaking, between 8 and 16 weeks, puppies should put on weight as follows:

- Small breeds should put on 100 to 500 g per week.
- Medium breeds should put on approximately 0.5 to 1 kg per week.
- Large breeds should put on 1 kg or more per week.

As time passes, you can adjust the amount and frequency of feeding based on how much your dog weighs. Obviously, there will be great individual variation, but this is a rough guide.

Should you leave food in a bowl for your dog to graze on throughout the day?

No! If your dog is older than 8 weeks of age, not a chance, not under any circumstances – not even if your dog is tiny, sick and underweight. This is the one topic you won't get us to budge on. Your dog doesn't need food to be left out all day and, to be frank, it's a behavioural hand grenade.

What are some of the potential concerns with leaving food out all day?

- Your dog becomes overweight.
- Your dog develops resource or food guarding habits.
- Your dog becomes a fussy eater.
- Your dog loses food drive.
- Your dog is harder to train.

Not all of the things listed above will happen if you allow your dog to graze throughout the day, but we can guarantee that at least one of those things will eventually occur. Instead, give her breakfast. If she is not interested or eats a portion of it and walks away, remove the food bowl from sight.

We know this sounds counterintuitive but if your dog is underweight, fussy or has low food drive, you need to present her with a small amount of food for a small window of time. Better yet, get her to do a short training session for a small amount of food or work out a food puzzle in a small amount of time.

Why does this help?

If your dog is underweight or growing and she gobbles up the small amount of food you present her with for five minutes, you can always . . . give her more! Whereas if you give her a large volume and leave her with it for half an hour, you'll be trashing her value of food.

We know from experience we can create value for food and manage a dog's weight and diet much better if we follow the basic rule of 'a small volume for a limited time'. Once your dog is mature, obedient, happy and healthy you don't need to worry about this: feed her what she needs, whenever it suits you. All of our mature dogs enjoy working more for toys, so if we aren't doing a stack of new training with them we will feed them once a day whenever it suits us – they never turn their noses up at it!

Swapping your dog's food over

If you intend to swap your dog's diet over, we suggest doing it gradually and while closely watching their bowel movements as you do it. Sometimes it's not always possible to do this gradually, particularly with rescue dogs, but if you can, we suggest implementing the new food source mixed in with the old food source (at about 10 to 25 per cent of the meal per day), provided they seem to be coping well with it. To enable this, a sufficient supply of their old diet along with the food you intend to transition to will be necessary.

Toilet Training

I know we've only just met . . . but let's discuss your puppy's toileting habits! That way, we can minimise accidents from happening in the wrong location.

Puppies are clean animals, if whelped correctly, and will naturally (most of the time) seek out absorbent surfaces on which to do their business.

There are many things you can do to help fast track a puppy to learn where the right place is to go. If you find your puppy is having too many accidents inside or in the wrong place, try to implement some of the points below.

1. Spend quality time outside with your puppy in the area where you want her to toilet (rather than making several short trips outside). By hanging out there with your puppy, you will help her feel relaxed and comfortable in this space. Allow time for her to play and sniff – this helps to stimulate her need to toilet.

2. Restrict access to free roaming around the whole house unsupervised.

3. Practise the cafe dog tie-up and crate training exercises (see Chapter 7), which promote bladder control. These exercises are best practised after the puppy has had some outdoor stimulation and has gone to the toilet.

4. Eliminate access to absorbent surfaces. Close doors to rooms with carpet and roll up rugs. Ensure family members regularly pick up their clothes and place them in the laundry basket – otherwise they may find a little surprise the next day when they go to put them on.

5. Praise your puppy for going to the toilet in the right place but *do not reprimand* her for making a mistake inside. This might only teach her that toileting in front of you got her in trouble, and next time she will choose a hidden spot like behind the couch or in the closet to relieve herself. Reprimanding her after the deed is done is pointless. She won't draw any conclusion from this.

6. Puppies generally won't toilet near where they eat, sleep or drink (again, if they were whelped correctly), so if there is a regular spot she continues to toilet in, try putting a water bowl there or feeding her at that spot. We regularly give our puppies scatter feeds (i.e. scattering their biscuits or food) all over the back deck to ensure they learn not to pee in that area just because it's convenient. As a result they will walk the extra 5 metres to the lawn and pee there instead.

7. If you are training your puppy to pee inside on a pee pad or newspaper, don't put pee pads all around your living room. This defeats the concept of 'training' her to seek out one location. Choose one spot and remove all other absorbent

materials in the room so as to encourage all motions to happen on the pee pad area.

Don't be disheartened if your dog makes a mistake inside. Unless you are a neat freak and have the time to follow her every move and analyse every sniff, it's going to happen. Shrug it off, clean it up well and revisit the points above in case there is something you could improve.

These top tips for the first 48 hours are not an exhaustive guide to the many considerations you should have for a new dog in your home. However, if you take these into account and apply them with your new dog, you will make a great start in helping her feel safe and secure in her new environment and building the strong, trusting bond we all hope to share with the dogs in our lives. The time it takes for your dog to be ready to move beyond these tighter initial restrictions is entirely dependent upon her nature, her previous experiences and how she responds to the stimuli she is exposed to with you. Take it slow, get a feel for your dog's personality and let her show you when she is ready to take the next step.

Chapter 6

Socialisation and Confidence Building

We believe every new puppy owner's goal or mantra should be:

To raise a confident, independent and happy dog.

Write that down and stick it on your fridge! It sounds like a school motto, we know, but raising an emotionally stable dog is *everything*. Yet it's often undervalued during puppyhood, even though that is the most important time to invest in a dog's emotional development.

You can train a dog in almost any behaviour, at any age. However, instilling confidence and independence are skills more easily mastered if introduced while the dog is young.

Say we walk into the pound tomorrow and find a 10-year-old dog with no prior training. Provided that he is emotionally stable and confident, we could teach him every behaviour under the sun and turn him into the perfect pet. But if that same dog is nervous, anxious or cautious, we would need to invest a huge amount of time and effort into slowly building his trust and confidence before we could even begin to teach him the same list of behaviours.

Developing confidence, independence and happiness at an early age sets up the brain's neural pathways to be capable of a lifetime of learning. So be mindful that emotions drive behaviour and fear inhibits learning. In other words:

A confident and happy dog = An easy-to-train dog.

Until your puppy reaches maturity (around 1.5 years for small dogs and 3 years for large dogs), he will go through many developmental periods where hormones will surge and behaviour will change. For the parents out there, it's much like 'The Wonder Weeks' in human babies (now there's an idea for any entrepreneurial types: a Wonder Weeks app for puppy parents!). Some phases will see your puppy become more vulnerable and fearful of his surroundings and look to his owners for reassurance and trust, while other developmental leaps may inject a boost of confidence and independence, resulting in uncharacteristic behaviour like barking or running off. Being prepared for these phases and knowing how to handle them will better equip you for how to help your puppy best develop emotionally.

The Critical Learning Phase

The critical learning phase (also known in some training circles as the 'critical socialisation period') for a dog is between 3 and 16 weeks of age. Many experts believe this to be the most impressionable period of a dog's entire life. For the first two weeks of your puppy's life, his eyes and ears are sealed shut; the world around him is interpreted entirely through touch and smell. Between 2 and 3 weeks of age, after your puppy's eyes and ears open for the first time, he can now begin to absorb everything going on around him using all his senses. Your puppy's brain at this age is 'under construction'. All the experiences he encounters are being rapidly filed away and will, to some degree, influence the behaviour of your dog as an adult. It's during this time that he is learning what things to be wary of, what things are fun, how to learn, who to trust and generally what life is about.

A breeder's influence

The breeder or carer of a puppy holds this responsibility for exposure in their hands from birth to 8 weeks or whenever the puppy is passed over to their 'forever home'. Responsible breeders will begin the puppy's slow and steady exposure to the world during this time. They will do things like play a sound loop near the whelping pen (the area in which a litter spends the first few weeks of life) to start desensitising puppies to a range of noises. They will offer puppies opportunities to explore environmental stimuli such as ball pits, mirrors, wobble boards, textured surfaces, and so on. In contrast (without throwing too much of a dampener on things), a factory-farmed puppy may never see the light of day or leave a small, concreted indoor pen until the day he is transferred to his new home, losing out on critical weeks of opportunity for sensory development. Factory-farmed puppies are more likely to be nervous, fearful or reactive to new stimuli, bright lights and loud or unexpected sounds.

Your influence during the critical phase

Once you bring your puppy home, you take over as his guide through this important phase. In a perfect world, once the puppy arrives at his new home and has had the first 48 hours to settle in, it will be time to start getting him out and about. But before we look at ways to do this, let's look at the socialisation seesaw concept. It will help with approaching all new experiences in this phase and beyond.

Good Experiences, Bad Experiences and No Experiences

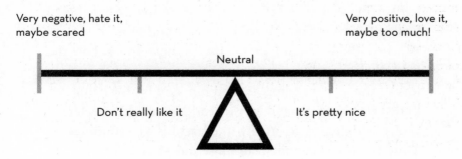

Let's briefly consider the impact of positive and negative experiences – as well as no exposure at all – on your developing puppy. We'll also talk about how to make an experience neutral.

An understanding of dog body language will be fundamental to decoding your puppy's way of communicating to you how he is coping with all the new sounds, sights and social experiences that will begin to come his way. You may wish to re-read Chapter 1 to brush up on this again.

Positive experiences

When exposing a puppy to new stimuli or surrounds, aim for positive or neutral associations. Positive experiences mean a dog is having fun, his body is loose and fluid and the overall experience is enjoyable. But just to make things a little confusing, sometimes an experience that elicits a strong, favourable reaction in a puppy can roll over into obsessive behaviour as an adult, particularly if it is repeated many times or for long periods of time. This is one of the reasons why it's important to make positive interactions or experiences short and sweet, so they can't conjure up a highly aroused state in the puppy.

How can you ensure your puppy has a good time when you venture out?

- Keep adventures, on-lead walks and social outings short. For an 8- to 10-week-old puppy, that may mean 10 minutes is enough. As soon as you see your puppy start to yawn, stop to scratch or shake or sit down a lot, that's usually a sign he has had enough. Exploring the world for a puppy is exhausting and once he is tired, he is no longer capable of positively absorbing the goings-on around him.
- When walking around, be mindful of how you handle the lead. If your puppy is experiencing a new location with lots of things happening around him and is also being pulled or jerked around by the lead, this could interfere with his ability to positively interpret his surroundings. Your aim is to keep the lead loose unless you need to prevent the puppy from getting to something. (More on lead use later.)

Negative experiences

A single scary event may have a dramatic impact on your dog's perception and behaviour around that stimulus, and if he has several negative experiences around a particular person or place, he will certainly remember that for life.

The impact of a single scary event

Jen's mum, Pam, regularly babysat our Australian Shepherd, Ari, when he was a puppy. One day when he was around 10 weeks of age, he was lying next to her while she was gardening, and a large hanging pot plant fell on his tail. From that moment onwards, he was never fully comfortable around Pam, no matter how much she tried to appease him.

Ryan has a retired shepherd, Hugo, who lives with Ryan's mum. One day when Hugo was a puppy he was running across black tiles and had to turn left at the last minute. As he was turning, he slipped on the tiles and hit the wall. Even now, 14 years later, Hugo will almost never turn left on black tiles. He is a super confident and happy old dog, but he will still do a 270-degree right turn, as opposed to a quick 90-degree left turn! (Perhaps Derek Zoolander had a similar incident when he was a child, preventing him from being able to take left-hand turns as well?!)

The impact of repeated scary events

A few years back we did a home consultation for Simone with her 9-month-old Kelpie, Sammi. Simone was concerned about Sammi's behaviour towards other dogs when on lead. Initially, Sammi was nervous and would shy away from other dogs, but had now started lunging and barking at them. After exploring Sammi's history, we discovered that Simone was told by the breeder that she could take Sammi for walks, but to prevent Sammi from contracting diseases Simone needed to immediately change direction and walk away from other approaching dogs, or pick Sammi up. This meant that from Sammi's perspective, for the entire critical learning phase, whenever she sighted a dog something unpleasant would occur: she'd suddenly be scooped off the ground, or dragged away on lead. The sudden scooping or dragging away were certainly unpleasant from Sammi's perspective and she started to associate other dogs with that happening.

A lack of experience

If your puppy has zero experience with a certain stimulus, this will naturally affect how he will react to this stimulus when he does encounter it down the track. We generally expect that anything a puppy hasn't experienced early on in life will result in some fear or at least apprehensive behaviour.

A common example is if a puppy has never experienced storms or fireworks in the first 16 weeks of life. It's likely, then, that when he does experience one for the first time as an adolescent or adult dog, these noisy and dramatic events are going to send him into a panic! If you aren't there to help your dog through that first storm, he may end up with storm phobia, which is very difficult to treat. Your goal should be to pleasantly and appropriately expose your dog in the first 16 weeks to any stimuli he is likely to encounter throughout his whole life.

Making experiences neutral

'Making something neutral' is an expression we use to explain how we want a dog to perceive a certain stimulus. If a stimulus is 'neutral', theoretically the dog is not going to be bothered by it and is more likely to be relaxed and well-behaved.

Take a look at the seesaw diagram on page 97. On one end of the seesaw, we have 'positive associations' and on the other end, 'negative associations'.

When an association is very negative, it is usually because the dog has had a few unpleasant events, or perhaps one very significant unpleasant event relating to the stimulus. An example might be a dog who was attacked more than once by other dogs and now fears and hates all dogs as a result (meaning that other dogs are the stimulus).

At the other end of the seesaw we have perceptions that are very positive. Perhaps a dog has been taken to a dog park every day to socialise and is now completely obsessed with other dogs – he cannot pay attention to anything else, harasses other dogs to the point of being boisterous and obnoxious and is impossible to walk on lead past dogs.

Most trainers would agree that both dogs in the above example need to view other dogs as more neutral.

For the fearful dog, this would involve more positive experiences in the presence of dogs. The boisterous dog doesn't need negative experiences, but he does need fewer interactions with dogs in general, and the ones he does have need to be more controlled. The dog park needs to be boycotted and his owner needs to become much more positive with him in order to achieve any engagement from him.

New experiences generally fall into two categories: socialisation experiences and environmental exposure. Let's look at these and how to approach them.

Socialisation

When you receive a new pup, there is a huge emphasis on getting your pup 'socialised'. But what does this actually mean? Most commonly people think this means just getting out there and meeting as many dogs as possible, and joining puppy school so your puppy gets a good dose of socialisation with other puppies. They figure this will ensure their pup grows up to love all dogs and be super friendly.

However, it's not quite as straightforward as that. For starters, socialisation should include all living creatures: other pets, farm animals, wildlife and people of all shapes and sizes presenting in a myriad of different ways (wearing hats or glasses, holding umbrellas, riding on scooters, in prams or in wheelchairs). And of course, social-isation involves interacting with other dogs too. The common factor is that all social experiences during the critical phase – whether they be with a pigeon or another puppy – should be short and sweet, and ideally result in a pleasant or neutral experience.

Dog-to-dog socialisation

You've probably picked up on a theme in this chapter: it's all about finding the right balance of enough exposure without overdoing it. Dog-to-dog socialisation is no different.

Do too much and your dog is likely to be obsessed with dogs. This could make him difficult to train, as he will value dog companionship more than you or your treats.

Don't do enough and your dog may be fearful of other dogs when out walking and become reactive towards other dogs later in life.

During the first 8 weeks of his life, a puppy receives most of his social requirements from other puppies in the litter. In fact, most mature dogs don't actually need or want to socialise with unknown dogs. Of course, a weekly meetup with a known doggie friend is appreciated and enjoyed, but the utopian idea of a dog park with pooches making instant friends of all shapes and sizes is fundamentally flawed!

When it comes to socialising your pup, it's important to find a happy medium:

- Allow your pup to meet calm, adult dogs for short and pleasant interactions.
- Avoid long, rumbling (tackling, rolling, barking, pinning) playtime with other pups or dogs for the purpose of 'tiring your puppy out'.
- Find a puppy school that promotes brief and controlled interactions between pups.
- Teach your puppy to ignore some dogs. Other dogs shouldn't be seen as the source of all fun and social experiences. You and your family should be.
- Only put emphasis on developing relationships with dogs your pup is likely to engage with in adulthood on a regular basis (i.e. dogs within your family or the extended family) and even then, keep interactions to less than 10 per cent of the day. For example, we will let our puppy have playtime with one of our other dogs but then follow it up with a tie-up exercise, so the dog also learns the valuable lesson of relaxing around other dogs too.

Our view on socialisation during puppy preschool is that timid puppies should not be forced to socialise off lead with rambunctious puppies, and rambunctious puppies should not be allowed to play rough with all dogs. Dogs should be happy in each other's presence, but it's probably best for them to start off by learning to ignore each other or have a pleasant experience with their owner while other dogs just happen to be in the room. Off-lead rough play isn't necessary to develop good social skills. The cafe dog exercise we discuss in Chapter 7 is a good one to practise so your dog can get used to being in the company of other dogs.

The rules and guidelines for dog-to-dog socialisation can and should be applied to all other animals. You don't want your dog to chase and rumble with other animals, but it's also important for him not to be afraid. The best thing you can do for your dog's relationships with and perspective towards other living creatures is to make him comfortable in their presence, with the end goal being the ability to ignore them. As we type this, our chickens are free-ranging around our adult dogs, and will often perch on or next to them. Notice we said 'adult dogs': although our puppies look comfortable around the chooks, we don't trust them to do this yet! Their interactions with the chickens are always on lead.

Kids and puppies

Given that so many people choose to get a puppy to join a growing family, socialising a young dog with children is a key topic.

Here are some general rules we instil in our kids for the purpose of keeping them safe and protecting the welfare of all dogs out there:

- Assume all dogs want space. Some dogs can feel quite nervous or threatened by a child's unpredictable and erratic behaviour.
- A child should always ask a parent's permission if they would like to pet or interact with a puppy or dog. The best way to engage a dog is to crouch down and call the dog over to you rather than approach him and lean over the top of him. This is especially important if he's an unfamiliar dog.
- Never use a scooter, run or scream in close proximity to dogs, especially if they are tied up in a public place. Even if it doesn't spook or scare the dog, it will tap in to his prey drive, possibly encouraging the dog to chase and nip. Best to dismount bikes and scooters and walk slowly past, giving him a wide berth.
- *Never* interact with a sleeping, eating or bone-chewing dog, or climb in to a restricted space like a crate with a dog . . . ever! The dog is very much in a zone when sleeping or eating and can either behave protectively towards his resources

(bed, food, bone) with the advancement of a child, or be sleeping and get a fright by a child creeping up to him or falling on top of him. These situations can result in an uncharacteristic snap or bite to the child.

The T-Rex phase

There is generally a 'grace period' when you bring your cute little puppy home at 8 weeks and your kids are ecstatic and in love and you can't pry them away. The puppy is cuddly, calm and adorable and it seems like all parties are getting along swimmingly.

We hate to be the bearer of bad news, but this will change: when your puppy hits somewhere around 10 weeks (depending on the breed), his confidence grows and he becomes a jumping, teething, biting Tyrannosaurus Rex! That beautiful relationship that seemed to be developing between child and puppy has now been replaced with shrieks, tears and nerves. Fortunately, this uncomfortable phase is only temporary and you can shorten it further with correct management.

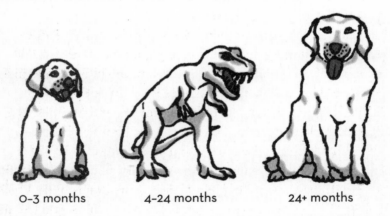

0–3 months   4–24 months   24+ months

What's the best way for young families to prepare for and navigate through this period?

1. Set up puppy-only spaces around your house and put your puppy in them for rest periods, ideally from day one. This will help acclimatise your pup to these areas, so when he does start biting and chasing children you have a safe space he is comfortable with and used to being in. This should mean you

don't have a whimpering puppy to deal with on top of the biting! Teach your kids to leave the puppy alone when he is in a crate or pen.

2. Watch all interactions closely. The second the biting begins, intervene! The more a puppy practises something, the more he will continue to do it. Kids are targeted more than adults with nipping and biting because they are more erratic in their behaviour. When a puppy jumps or nips, a child often reacts by running, screaming or jumping up and down squealing. Puppies think this is magic! The better option is to teach a child to be a statue if the puppy is becoming too much . . . but this is easier said than done! So watch and separate before things get heated.

3. Talk to your kids. Prepare them and explain why the puppy has become so jumpy and bitey. Teething puppies need to bite stuff to help their sore gums, and pups communicate and play a lot via their mouth. We just need to teach them alternative ways to do this. (See Chapter 8.)

4. Replace cuddles with training. We recommend that adults begin teaching the puppy new behaviours, but once the cue (such as 'sit' or 'come') is understood by the pup, get the kids involved. This will help to facilitate the right interactions during this time instead of perpetuating the wrong ones. Use the lead to help give kids confidence during interactions. Sometimes children are scared to give the puppy a treat for fear of being bitten, which means they jerk their hands around like crazy. Sudden moving hands means the dog is more likely to snap for the treat. If this sounds like your child, you can get them to say 'Good' and throw the treat on the ground or even deliver the treats via a wooden spoon!

5. Get the kids to help make up enrichment activities for the puppy and do these activities while the puppy is in the pen area. For example, give the kids a stopwatch. How long will it take the puppy to get the treat inside the enrichment item? Ten seconds, two minutes or 10 minutes? (There are plenty of DIY ideas out there . . . just google!) This works at giving kids

indirect ways to connect with the puppy when the teething is at its peak. Another great activity is giving each child a small bucket with some dog biscuits (or the equivalent) in it and asking them to hide the biscuits around a section of the yard (so long as they are old enough and trusted enough not to eat the biscuits themselves!). Once they have hidden all the food (like the Easter Bunny does for them), let the puppy out to find it all. Fun for kids and even more fun for the puppy!

Preparation, time and management are the main keys to getting through this phase without your child becoming fearful of your puppy or your puppy learning to view your children as the best tug toys ever.

Meeting other kids

Let's say you have a fairly shy 10-week-old Australian Shepherd and you need to 'socialise' him with children outside of the family to help build him confidence. Do you:

A) Take your puppy to the school gates at pick-up so the 200 overtired, screaming children can greet and pat your puppy as they leave school for the day?

or

B) Invite a few responsible friends of your children over, ask them to sit down in the backyard with a couple of treats and encourage the puppy over for a treat and a pat?

These two situations are likely to create a very different response from the dog as he matures. Use gradual, calm and controlled exposure to help your puppy get used to the presence and behaviour of children, starting with your own kids (if you have them) and introducing others over time. Therefore, option B would be best.

Environmental Exposure

Socialisation involves exposing dogs to living creatures, but there is so much more to life that we need to help them feel comfortable with, long term.

Environmental exposure (or conditioning) involves systematically exposing your dog to all the things in life you'd like and expect them to be comfortable with as an adult. There are some things most dogs take to without much thought, such as the radio on or the construction next door, but there are other components to our lives that dogs usually need well-thought-out exposure to. Bikes, skateboards, mowers, vacuum cleaners, leaf blowers and even mops are just some of the typical household items that dogs often obsess over or fear. So we really want to make these objects neutral or even pleasant.

A puppy barking at a broom or a skateboard might be cute at first, but if you allow that behaviour to continue it is likely to become entrenched in the dog as an adult. You should immediately start to think about popping your puppy on lead and doing a scatter feed, with the mopping action happening in the distance, to take the focus off the object itself and pair it with something pleasant. By having the puppy on lead you can prevent any chasing behaviour and by doing a scatter feed of kibble or treats near the object of interest, you can help the puppy ignore the broom or skateboard in a very positive way. If your puppy is unable to take treats in the presence of the broom or skateboard because he is too fixated on it, you are probably too close to the object and need to do more in-depth training. In Chapter 12, we discuss 'counter-conditioning' for fear or reactivity towards certain stimuli. If your dog is already obsessed with or scared of something like a broom or skateboard, you will definitely want to read this chapter, or maybe even skip forward to it.

Sound-proof puppies

Ryan once visited a lovely family who had adopted a 9-month-old Kelpie from a farm in rural NSW. For the whole of his 9-month life, the dog had never been inside. The new family owned a large home and wanted desperately for the dog to be an inside dog. However, on the first night home, when the family brought him in for cuddles on the couch someone decided to whip up dinner in the Thermomix. The poor dog lost his mind and from that moment on the kitchen, with all its foreign, noisy appliances – kettle, blender, toaster popping – was a place to be feared.

Needless to say, there are plenty of common sounds that dogs find overbearing due to their sensitive hearing and because some sounds may be out of context and confusing for the dog. Depending on where you live, you may want to put more effort into some sounds over others: thunder, fireworks, gun shots, motorbikes, sirens, planes and even heavy traffic can upset sensitive dogs.

How can you help your puppy to be fine with loud, unpredictable noises as an adult?

1. Pray for the heavens above to open and unleash a mix of weather conditions during your puppy's critical learning period. Thunder, lightning, wind, rain – the lot! If this happens, don't pick out your favourite movie on Netflix and cuddle up with your puppy under a doona. Instead, pair the thunderstorm with a fun activity or maybe a training session. And be mindful of your own response to the storm: if you get spooked by the thunder and jump a mile, your poor puppy is going to feed off that.
2. Download the Sound Proof Puppy Training app! We've found this app is a fantastic way of desensitising your puppy to over 27 different sounds, from hair clippers and vacuums to storms and fireworks. It also has the ability to record your own unique sounds and play them on loop. If you notice your dog has a problem with a specific sound, you can play it at low volume while the dog eats meals or plays games so he gradually becomes more comfortable with it.
3. Just as you will with all other social and environmental exposure, slowly build up your puppy's sound tolerance to things like busy roads. Start by going for walks in quieter parts of the neighbourhood and slowly gravitate towards the main roads.

Handling and grooming

When we say 'handling and grooming' we mean we want you to think of preparing your dog for a vet, vet nurse or groomer to handle them in a more technical or thorough manner than what you may normally do. Many dogs take offence to certain parts of their body being handled or being physically manipulated. So it is up to you to make sure your dog can handle being handled!

We encourage you to go above and beyond with this, and make it so much fun for your dog that he actually enjoys it. Because in all likelihood, when your dog needs to be handled by someone unfamiliar, it will either be at the vet because he is injured or unwell, or the groomer because he is matted and filthy. So your dog won't be in a good mood to start with! If your dog has injured himself, has been taken to a strange place and is being manhandled by a stranger, we have what we call a 'trigger stacking event' which may make even the friendliest of dogs snap out in aggression. Nobody wants that.

WHAT IS TRIGGER STACKING?

This is something humans are very familiar with, but it's easy to forget that it can and does happen to dogs. Trigger stacking is when you have a few difficult experiences in close succession that make you 'snap'. Ninety-nine days out of a hundred you could be the happiest, most laid-back person in the world, but let's say one day you wake up with a sore neck. It's not enough to make you complain, but it's there chipping away at you. Then you stub your toe walking down the hallway, which makes you spill your coffee all over the carpet. Now you're running late for work because you're trying to clean the coffee you so desperately wanted out of the carpet, and you've had to skip breakfast. Traffic is a bit worse while you're driving to work because you've left later than normal. You try to change lanes and go to check your blind spot, but you can't because of your sore neck. You try to merge anyway and suddenly hear a horn from behind you. The horn frightens you and you scream an expletive and throw up the middle finger to the car that beeped. Turns out he was a lovely elderly man who was just beeping the horn to let you know he was there. Your reaction was completely out of character, and now you feel terrible.

That is trigger stacking, and it happens in dogs too. They might be sore, hungry, frightened of storms or of people holding unusual equipment, and if you're unaware of your dog's ailments or fears and aren't familiar with how to interpret his body language, even the most laid-back dog can growl or bite when these unpleasant events happen in close succession.

So what can you do?

- Make regular visits to the vet and/or groomer if you are able to, just to say hi, weigh your puppy and get a treat from the nurse/receptionist (most practices are happy to accommodate these types of visits for free).
- At home, introduce medical and grooming equipment in light-hearted ways: let dogs sniff equipment, feel objects like clippers against their chest and score some treats.
- During training sessions for cues like 'sit' and 'drop', touch and manipulate different parts of your dog's body. Touch his paws, lift his tail, touch his mouth and after each unusual movement say 'Good' and give him a treat. If at any stage your dog starts showing, through his behaviour, that he is scared or threatened (as described in Chapter 1) dial the exercise way back. This needs to be fun.
- Incorporate some light grooming and body inspections to your cuddle and affection time. You might be rubbing your dog's belly one minute and briefly inspecting his ears or butt the next. Keep it light-hearted and watch him for signs of discomfort. If you do it well, your dog shouldn't really care or notice a difference between scratches for affection and grooming or inspections.
- If you find a 'weakness' or concern in your dog's handling and grooming exercises, follow the cooperative care training protocols described in Chapter 9.

If you have even a little bit of time, you may be amazed at what can be achieved with a few treats and gradually building up the dog's confidence. Whether it be getting into a car or introducing some grooming equipment, giving the dog a few minutes to explore the space, feel the freedom to move away and have a sense of time and opportunity you may have a much smoother experience and save yourself and the dog from severe stress or discomfort.

Handling in an emergency

Sometimes, for the safety of the dog, you will just need to handle him without his consent or enjoyment. It might be something like trying to get a new dog from the pound into your car or removing a thorn from a dog's foot. We would love you to be able to train your dog to participate in everything voluntarily, but sometimes life doesn't permit this.

If you do have to handle a dog in an emergency without any training beforehand, here are a few things you should do:

1. If the dog does need to be lifted or restrained, have this be done by someone who is most familiar to the dog.
2. Keep the dog's mouth away from other people's faces. Even the nicest of dogs will bite out of fear if they are in pain and being restrained.
3. Try to make sure the dog feels physically supported and stable. If he is being carried, try to have a nice even weight distribution across the chest and under/behind his rear legs. If he is being put onto a table or restrained on his side, make sure the surface isn't slippery.
4. Don't lift or restrain the dog by the collar, tail or limbs.

A Phased Approach

Now that you've got a good understanding of socialisation and environmental exposure, here's an example of some activities you can aim to do between 8 and 16 weeks as the puppy grows. Remember, these are just some examples – the more you can do with your puppy during this period, the better.

8.5 weeks: An on-lead trip to the letter box to say hi to Pat the neighbour while she's watering her garden and sight the neighbourhood kids riding past on their bikes.

9 weeks: A slow on-lead meander up the street to take in the friendly man with a long beard, his chickens, the distant cat and the woman going past on a mobility scooter.

9.5 weeks: A short drive to the beach to sit on a park bench, to absorb the sound of crashing waves and the smell of the salty ocean, hear the distant squeals of kids in the playground and feel the sensation of sand beneath puppy's feet.

10 weeks: A drive to a friend's property who has a socially competent Schnauzer, a couple of horses and some kangaroos in the back paddock.

12 weeks: A short on-lead stroll down to a quiet cafe to take in a slightly more bustling environment, a variety of people of different ages, ethnicities and sizes and a couple of dogs from a distance.

13–16 weeks: Mix it up and expose your pup to as many of those things that are important and relevant to your life, every day if you can. If you noticed your pup wasn't overly comfortable in one of the above locations you might want to repeat exposure more frequently, with more rewards and fun. Think: skate parks, play grounds, boats, work sites, cafes, motorbikes, post office, hardware stores, groomers, vets, beaches and more! Remember to keep exposures short and sweet!

You can see how lots of planned, short and pleasant outings over a period of 8 weeks will progressively help with establishing the foundation for a well-socialised, confident puppy by 16 weeks.

But what about the vaccination schedule?

A puppy's critical socialisation period coincides precisely with the puppy vaccination schedule. In Australia, a puppy won't be fully vaccinated until around 16 weeks.

Some vets and breeders may suggest keeping your puppy indoors until 16 weeks to ensure his safety due to the high prevalence of diseases in your area. If this is the case, you need to come up with appropriate solutions to socialisation and environmental exposure that don't put your puppy at risk. Keeping a puppy inside your house until he is 16 weeks is not an appropriate risk management strategy. If your puppy never leaves your house in his first 16 weeks, we can almost certainly guarantee that he won't cope when he goes exploring outside for the first time.

How can you get the balance right, ensuring your puppy stays disease free but ends up well-socialised and adjusted to life?

Start by doing as much research as you can to determine the prevalence of disease in your area. Reach out on community Facebook pages and ask your local vet about any recent cases. We have raised a handful of puppies across two locations that were at different ends of the disease spectrum. Finn, Ari, Taylor and Rafa were raised in a busy suburb where no cases had been logged in years. 'Busy' meant more stimuli outside our front door that we needed to expose them to. We made a calculated decision to get them out and about from 8 to 9 weeks old and this gave us time to slowly increase the social and environmental stimuli based on how each puppy was coping with each step. We still avoided high traffic, grassy areas until 16 weeks, and dog parks for much longer (as we've mentioned previously, for more reasons than just being unvaccinated).

Dash and Piper, meanwhile, were raised in a rural area where there were active cases of the deadly parvovirus. This meant we needed to get more creative with how we provided them with exposure, in order to keep them safe while effectively building their resilience during the critical period. We even drove to Sydney a few times to areas where there was a low disease risk to ensure they had a few pleasant experiences in a busy town compared to a 'sleepy seaside village'. Here are some ideas for socialisation activities with low exposure risk:

- Go for short drives to different locations: the beach, a park, a kids' playground, a farm and so on. Back the car up and have a picnic in the boot or practise training behaviours. Your pup can have a training session, or enjoy simply hanging out with you in the boot or in the back seat with the door open, in a variety of locations.

- Visit your local vet to weigh your puppy and receive a treat from the nurse or receptionist.
- Become extra social and invite a range of living creatures over to meet and play with your puppy: kids, adults, and vaccinated, socially competent adult dogs for short greetings.
- Visit your neighbours' or friends' properties (if they have no dogs or fully-vaccinated dogs).
- Tick off as much of the checklist below as you can without needing to go for walks in public places.
- Download the Sound Proof Puppy Training app from 8 weeks of age to start desensitising your puppy to unfamiliar noises.

Socialisation/Environmental Exposure Checklist

To help you start the process, we have put together this list of exposures that would be useful to most lifestyles and situations. You can work through it to expose your puppy to as much as you can before they reach 16 weeks of age. We've left a section at the bottom for you to add anything else that you believe your puppy will come across often as an adult and should be exposed to while he is young.

PUPPY SOCIALISATION PLAN					
Socialisation with people					
Adults					
Teenagers					
Children					
Babies					
Elderly people					
School kids					
Different ethnicities, sexes, heights					
Wearing sunglasses/hats/helmets					
Shy/nervous/loud/boisterous people					
Prams/toddlers					

Socialisation and Confidence Building

Socialisation with other animals					
Puppies					
Adult dogs					
Other animals					

Objects and transport					
Cars					
Bicycles/motorbikes					
Postie's bike					
Garbage truck					
Lawn mower					
Garbage bins					
Boats/kayaks/surf boards					
Rake/broom/vacuum					

Environments					
Other people's houses					
Parks/playing fields					
Skateboard parks					
Social gatherings					
Cafes					
Shopping centres					
Bushwalks					
Busy roads					
Rainy and stormy days					
Vet clinic					

Puppy handling					
Lead and collar					
Brush					
Paws/ear/tail/mouth					
Nail clippers					
Being picked up/put down					

Add your own here					

How to use the checklist

1. Start by adding any additional things to the bottom of this list that may be particularly relevant to your lifestyle such as tractors, horses, and so on. If you live in the country but are planning on visiting the city (or vice versa), consider ways to expose your puppy during the critical phase to this environment to ensure the move doesn't overwhelm him.

2. Start at a distance where your puppy is able to observe unusual stimuli such as bikes or kids playing basketball, and build on their comfort levels. Avoid picking your puppy up, but allow him the option to move away from something if it's uncomfortable or overwhelming, especially when he is on lead.

3. Learn to read your puppy's 'worried' or overwhelmed signs. Things to look out for include: ears pinned back, tail tucked close to the body, eyes open wide, barking a lot, licking lips or yawning more than usual. If you notice any of these signs, it may be an indication that you are moving too quickly.

4. Add at least four to five ticks to each box before your pup reaches 16 weeks of age.

5. When exposing your puppy to new stimuli, aim for short (two to 10 minutes), pleasant or neutral trips, sightings or interactions. For example, in order to expose a puppy to a kids' playground, we would sit 20 m away from the playground and play with him on the ground. If he seems happy enough we might then take him for a walk around the playground at a comfortable distance.

Please note: during this time, if you notice any aggression or anxiety forming in your puppy, contact a professional dog trainer for further guidance.

Socialisation and confidence building are about ensuring your dog is at peace with all his surroundings. A well-socialised dog should be able to happily ignore everything in his environment except for you, the owner! Knowing how to read and interpret your dog's feelings through his subtle body language will help you to find the right balance by not overdoing it or underdoing it. In turn, you will create a dog who is easy to train and live with for the rest of his life.

Chapter 7

Raising an Independent Dog

The most common behavioural problems in adult dogs (and therefore the most frequent cause for dogs being rehomed) are related to separation distress or anxiety. This can manifest in the following ways:

- excessive barking or howling when left alone
- destructive behaviour – destroying furniture, chewing through doors and walls
- stereotypic behaviour, such as repetitive pacing
- unusual toileting habits only when left alone, such as toileting on couches or beds
- self-injury from trying to escape the property – jumping off balconies or scaling exceptionally tall walls
- digging at boundary fences.

Rehabilitating a dog who is suffering from entrenched anxiety is usually a long process. In more severe cases, dogs may require medication alongside an in-depth training regime over a significant period of time. Anxiety is an emotional response, so quick fixes to stop certain behaviours like barking or digging aren't dealing with the root cause of the anxiety.

As a preventative measure, it's worth investing from the start in helping to grow your puppy's confidence and acceptance towards being left alone.

What Do We Mean by 'An Independent Dog'?

An independent dog is social and outgoing, but also has the ability to switch off and relax anytime, anywhere, if her physical and psychological needs have been met. The goal is to raise a dog who is content and comfortable with being left alone for periods of time and is also happy being looked after by friends and family. Sounds ideal, right?

Dogs are gregarious creatures and, for the most part, aren't naturally equipped to cope with long periods of time on their own. It doesn't help that most of us live such busy lives, and school and work schedules mean a dog is likely to be left alone for anywhere between six to nine hours a day, on average (while this may be the norm, it is still a fairly long time for a social creature to be by themselves). We need to manage this and build resilience into our dogs to ensure loneliness and separation anxiety don't start to develop.

How to develop independence in your puppy

What can you do, while your puppy is young, to help develop her independence and reduce the risk of distress when she's left alone?

- If you work full-time, take an appropriate amount of time off when you bring your new puppy home. (We suggest a minimum of two weeks.) If you are home full-time, ensure the puppy is still experiencing short bursts of time separate from you – you never know, your situation might change and your dog needs to be able to deal with this. Whatever your circumstances we suggest you aim for at least two weeks of flexibility for your puppy to bond with you, but also gradually get accustomed to being left alone for longer periods of time (keep in mind that if she is 8 weeks old when you bring her home she has probably never been alone). Two weeks off work might seem like a big commitment, but these two weeks could save your dog from a lifetime of anxiety-related issues.
- Crate train your puppy at night. It's the perfect middle ground between leaving your pup alone in the laundry and having her snuggle in bed with you. A crate by your bed for the first week helps your pup not feel abandoned or alone after leaving her littermates and mum. The crate becomes the comforting factor, rather than you and your bed, and eventually you can move

the crate into another area. See later in this chapter for more information on crate training.

- Set up a 'Puppy Space' in the main action room of your house. When you are not training, supervising or playing with your puppy, put her in this area. The puppy begins to develop very necessary independent skills by virtue of not being able to follow you everywhere but she will still feel as if she is part of the action.

- Practise the cafe dog exercise, which we'll cover later in this chapter.

- When you leave your puppy alone for the first few times, keep her in a smaller area rather than a large backyard, and aim for short stints to begin with, gradually varying the duration she is left alone.

- Don't make a big deal about leaving; be matter-of-fact. Combine walking out the door with giving your puppy breakfast or some other enrichment. When you return, as hard as it is, refrain from beelining for puppy cuddles the minute you walk through the front door. Instead, calmly say hello and then unpack bags or do whatever else you need to do. Once your pup has resettled with you being home, *then* you can go bananas with the greeting.

- Enrichment. One thing puppies love just as much as social interactions and companionship is food! Feed her at times when she is experiencing separate time and give her lots of food-based enrichment when outside, penned or crated to make time away from family worthwhile (see 'Behavioural Enrichment' on page 121).

- When your puppy is experiencing any form of separation time, keep a calm and relaxed disposition yourself, especially if she seems frustrated or distressed. Emotions are contagious and she can feed off your relaxed state.

Common Situations to Avoid in the First 6 to 12 Months

To help encourage independence, try to steer clear of the following:

- **Sleeping in bed with your puppy** – We are fine with well-adjusted adult dogs sleeping on your bed, but if they start off with this sleeping arrangement as young puppies, they will struggle to cope with sleeping anywhere else in your home, let alone a friend's house if you decide to go on holidays.

- **Letting your puppy follow you around the house all the time** – A sure-fire way to fast-track separation distress or anxiety is allowing your puppy to follow your every move while she is young. We go by the rule of thumb that if you are not training, playing with or supervising your puppy, she should be experiencing some form of independent time.

- **Letting another dog keep your puppy company when you are busy** – It's very easy to let an older dog babysit the new puppy, to prevent distress when left alone. But this means the puppy will not develop an independence of her own and will instead become reliant on that other dog to feel comfortable and safe.

- **Too much alone time too soon** – In order to help a puppy feel comfortable with being alone, it's important to *gradually* build her tolerance to being separated from you and the family. Throwing her in the deep end and just letting her 'get over it' or 'grow out of it' rarely helps build independence long term. Every dog's ability to handle alone time is individual and needs to be catered to accordingly. As we've mentioned before, you really can't expect a puppy to tolerate a whole day at home alone within two weeks of leaving her litter. So you might want to engage a friend or neighbour to do some puppy sitting or visits throughout the day.

- **Strict routines** – Humans by nature form routines. As we mentioned in Chapter 2, they can also be beneficial to a dog so long as there is a bit of flexibility. Things like meal times, walks and exercise, bed time and the time a puppy is let out in the morning should be variable. If you like strict routines, even just changing them by 10 minutes or so here and there is a good idea. Why? Life isn't going to remain in that routine forever – humans change living arrangements, jobs and lifestyles. A puppy who has learned a fixed routine in her first year of life struggles to adapt to a new one down the track. If you consistently follow through with an activity at the same time each day, your dog will absolutely be able to tell the time and expect that activity at that time. Then, if you suddenly try to change the timing it can result in some protest from your dog.

If you can resist all these things, you'll already be on the road to raising a dog who's comfortable in her own company.

WHEN LIFE THROWS YOU A CURVEBALL

We saw an increase in separation-related distress and anxiety from puppies and dogs who were acquired during the COVID lockdown period. Many families rarely left their houses during this time and if they did, it was probably to walk the dog, meaning these dogs never fully experienced time on their own. If you acquire a dog and spend most of the day at home, it's crucially important for her long-term emotional wellbeing that your dog doesn't spend all of the day by your side. Life has a way of throwing curveballs and changes at us. Much of the work of raising dogs involves projecting possible changes that might happen in the future and teaching them early on to cope with these changes. You may change to a job that requires you to work from an office, or perhaps you will need surgery at some point down the track resulting in a week or two in hospital. Follow the steps below to help provide your dog with a balance.

Now let's look at the two things we need to understand before beginning any form of independence training: behavioural enrichment and stress.

Behavioural Enrichment

What is 'behavioural enrichment' for dogs? It's all about offering dogs opportunities in their daily life to explore, problem-solve and experience novel stimuli as a way of improving their overall psychological and physiological wellbeing. It's like doing a crossword or sudoku puzzle each day to keep your brain sharp (or in our son's case, he has us trying to solve Rubik's cubes every spare minute!). Many animals are born neophilic, which means they enjoy new things, and that's certainly true of dogs. So enrichment for your puppy should never be overlooked – it's not an optional extra. Enrichment is easy to create and should be forever changing.

Enrichment has a host of benefits:

- It makes time alone more fun.
- It prevents undesirable behaviour.
- It's an outlet for a teething puppy.
- It's a means of encouraging independent play.
- It's an energy burner.
- It develops a puppy's problem-solving skills.

Toy versus food-based enrichment

Most puppies struggle to entertain themselves with a toy unless there is a human at the other end of that toy making it move and come to life. We therefore tend to focus more on food-based enrichment, especially when attempting to keep a puppy entertained while separated from the family in her Puppy Space. Keep in mind that dogs are omnivores, which means they can eat a variety of fruits and vegetables along with meat. This means the sky's the limit for what we can drop into our puppy's pen for her to explore, such as:

- ✓ frozen ice blocks with broth, veggies or kibble
- ✓ mince smeared inside commercial enrichment products like KONGs
- ✓ pig's ear, cow hoof or deer antler dog treats
- ✓ brisket bones or chicken necks inside old cereal boxes
- ✓ frozen carrot or apple pieces
- ✓ half a cup of kibble inside a plastic bottle (ensure the lid, o-ring and any stickers removed).

You can even set up a clam shell sandpit or digging pit with buried treasure in the back yard. The list goes on and on! And you'd be surprised how much entertainment can be made and how much energy can be expelled by an inquisitive pup over a single blueberry. All of these activities are designed to make the dog feel happy and will in turn make her a calmer dog.

A side note: don't underestimate the power of offering your puppy lots of things she *is* allowed to explore, in order to prevent her from exploring the ones she's *not*, such as your lawn, door mat, couch or Achilles tendon!

Good Stress versus Bad Stress

> *Resilience: The capacity to recover quickly from difficulties; toughness.*
> – Oxford English Dictionary

Good stress, also known as 'eustress', is fundamental in building a resilient adult dog. If a puppy is not exposed to or never experiences *mild* forms of stress, therefore never learning to overcome it, how will she ever be able to cope with more challenging situations or increased stress as an adult?

It's a little like children being allowed to win everything: if they never experience a loss during childhood via friendly and competitive games with other children or siblings, they are likely to struggle to process difficult outcomes, like failing driving tests or job interviews in their late teens and early adulthood.

On the other hand, *bad stress*, also known as 'distress', can lead to anxiety disorders and health problems. However, there is quite an obvious difference between a puppy who is frustrated with something as opposed to one who is highly distressed or anxious. Understanding those differences is important before tackling any independence training exercises.

An obvious example of this would be the first night you bring your puppy home and where you sleep them that night. Most puppies will feel scared and somewhat overwhelmed by the day's events. Being placed in a dark room like the laundry with no living creatures nearby can cause a puppy distress. Ongoing wailing, howling and crying is a sign that the puppy is not coping. Popping her in a cosy crate by your bed and staying with her until she settles will usually result in less crying. The puppy will not be alone and is far more likely to feel emotionally supported through this nerve-wracking transition.

Below are two scenarios involving barking dogs. One is a good opportunity to work them through some good stress; the other not so much.

Scenario 1: Your dog has just learnt she loves fetch so much that she's started barking when you pick up the ball. This might be just pure excitement, or the dog might think she needs to bark at you in order to make you throw the ball and continue the game. Either way, this a perfect learning opportunity to teach the dog she needs to do something other than bark before you throw the ball. You might get some extreme barking when you initially withhold the ball and the dog might bark louder than ever before. But if you persist – if you only throw the ball during moments of silence, perhaps while the dog performs 'sit' or 'down' – the dog will learn a very valuable lesson. **Stress type:** Eustress – this is an example of a dog working through a mild burst of frustrated stress to learn and achieve something new.

Scenario 2: You've just moved house and put the dog into the new backyard. The dog goes off sniffing and doesn't see when you go back inside. She suddenly starts barking like mad, running around the yard non-stop looking for an escape route. You might think initially, 'If I go and see what's wrong, I might be rewarding the barking'. But in this circumstance, the dog is likely emotional and unaware of her actions, barking out of instinct and fear. If you don't go out and let her know where you are, the barking is likely to continue. The dog will become more stressed and associate your new yard with the unpleasant event of your disappearance, making her even more prone to separation anxiety in the long term. So in this instance, do go out to your dog, but be relaxed about it. Don't get down on the ground and talk to her like a baby but instead simply join her and say, 'Hey, hey, you're fine, I was just inside.' Spend a bit more time with her out there; perhaps play some games and think about making this yard a more family-orientated, positive space before leaving the dog alone in there.

Stress type: Distress – this is an example of a situation where the dog isn't capable of learning something new or making an informed choice because she is suffering from a high level of stress.

If you can, do your best to look at the situation and ask yourself: is my dog making a conscious decision to perform a behaviour or is she driven by instinct and emotion? If she's being driven by instinct and emotion, your dog may need comforting or need to be removed from the situation she is in. If the dog is *choosing* to perform the behaviour, you may wish to implement a training session or better management strategies.

There are some signs you can look out for to indicate bad stress:

1. The dog is not capable of following any instructions she knows.
2. The dog doesn't seem to be enjoying herself.
3. The behaviour seems involuntary.
4. The behaviour gets worse if you ignore or allow it to continue to happen.
5. The dog is not capable of eating or taking a reward.

Another example would be pulling on lead. Here are two more scenarios:

Scenario 1: Jimmy the Poodle loves to pee so much that every time he sees a tree on the corner of a road, he pulls like a freight train to get to the tree to mark all over it. Allowing Jimmy to practise pulling in this setting might seem convenient, as he needs to urinate while on the walk. However, if you allow him to practise it often enough, he will most likely start to generalise that pulling on lead gets him whatever he wants, which means it is more likely to happen at other stages on your walk. This is not good for your back and shoulder, and not good for Jimmy's trachea, either. This is a perfect opportunity to teach Jimmy he is not allowed to get to the tree if he pulls, but if he is walking on a loose lead, you will take him directly to the tree to pee as much as he likes. The pulling may initially get stronger, and Jimmy may become frustrated as you pass the tree that he is not allowed to visit. But if you're consistent, and even include a few treats here and there for loose lead walking, or perhaps introduce a different piece of walking equipment, Jimmy will quickly realise that pulling is no longer successful after only a few days of mild stress. You've now saved hundreds of dollars on physio visits for yourself and Jimmy won't run the risk of permanent trachea damage.

Stress type: Eustress – this is a good opportunity for teaching Jimmy the right behaviour.

Scenario 2: Betty the Bulldog pulls like crazy every time you walk on a busy road with traffic. She doesn't seem to have a particular motivation for the pulling. You may think this is the time to stop, tell her 'No' and start working on a nice heeling pattern beside the busy road. But in fact Betty is terrified: she won't take treats or respond to simple instructions. She's probably trying to get away from the fast-moving, noisy traffic. She is likely to be incredibly stressed and is therefore not capable of learning in this state. What she really needs is a break from traffic and a well-thought-out counter-conditioning program (see Chapter 12) for these busy roads.

Stress type: Distress – Betty won't learn anything in this scenario. Allow her immediate distance from the busy road and make a game plan for the future to help her feel more comfortable walking in these locations.

Dogs are resilient creatures if we allow them opportunities to problem-solve and deal with slightly uncomfortable situations. So, much as we love and want to protect our pups, it's worth remembering that we're actually doing them a favour by exposing them to some good stress now and again. It will build a more resilient dog down the track.

The Crate Debate

We mentioned crating your puppy in Chapter 5. There is a mixed bag of opinions and misconceptions out there regarding the idea of crating your dog. A common view is that it is cruel and unfair – you are simply locking your dog in a cage! Instead of judging too fast, let's give it some more thought.

What is the purpose of a bassinet or cot for a toddler? The main reason is safety – to prevent a young child from crawling around the room in the night and getting into danger – but it also provides a secure, familiar and comfortable place to rest their head and switch off for the night. It's for much the same reason that we crate train puppies.

Here are 10 reasons why we advocate crate training your dog:

1. It provides a safe, secure and comfortable place for your puppy to sleep and prevents her from waking up and wandering around the house in the middle of the night . . . generally getting up to no good.
2. Puppies need to sleep 16 to 20 hours a day and can struggle to settle without a designated area with low stimulation.
3. It allows puppies to practise 'mindfulness'. Just like humans, puppies can find the world an overstimulating place. If we teach them that the crate is a place of relaxation and there is no 'job' to do in there they begin to switch off as soon as they enter. Once a dog learns how to relax in one environment (such as a crate) it is possible to transfer their crate into other locations – which can be a game-changer for anxious dogs.
4. If puppies have to go to the vets or groomers they will be crated while they are there. If they are crate trained from a young age, this can help to reduce stress during these times.
5. If you need to travel on a plane, your dog must be crated, and again she will find this less stressful if she is familiar with being in a crate.
6. A crate is the safest form of travel in a car.
7. If you move house, there will be next to no night-time settling-in period for the dog, because her 'bed' (the crate) remains the same.

8. If you go camping, your dog can be safely secured in her crate in the ute/tent.

9. Friends and family will find dog sitting much more enjoyable if the dog is crate trained. A lot of great dog sitters will only take your dog if she's crate trained.

10. Using a crate helps with toilet training a puppy.

Note: Mature or anxious dogs may need more time and encouragement to progress with some of the steps outlined below.

How to crate train your dog

During the day
Use the crate during the day for sleep opportunities between training, play and explorations. When you close the door on the crate, stay with your puppy and help her settle.

If your puppy seems at all apprehensive with the idea of going in the crate, you can leave the door open throughout the day with some treats and chew toys inside. For the first few days at least, when you do physically put the puppy in the crate for sleep or management, offer her a treat once the door is closed. We want to make sure it's deemed a positive place.

At night
Here are our steps for crate training at night:

1. The best place to start the crate training process is in your bedroom, by your bed. Slowly but surely, over the coming weeks, you can gradually move the crate to the place you want your puppy to sleep eventually.

2. Ensure your puppy has had a stretch, play and sniff outside and an opportunity to go to the toilet.

3. Gently place your puppy in the crate and close the door. At this point, do whatever you need to do to soothe and comfort your puppy without opening the door and letting her out. Talk to her, put your hand through the crate, lie next to her on the floor. Remember to keep your disposition calm and relaxed as puppies can feed off our emotions.

4. Through the night, if your puppy has been sleeping for a few hours and wakes up and cries out, give her the benefit of the doubt and take her out for a toilet opportunity. Once again, when you place her back in the crate, do whatever you need to do to settle her *except* taking her out again.

5. When you go to let your puppy out of the crate in the morning, try to keep things fairly boring. It's normal to want to dive in for cuddles as soon as you see her little face, or take her outside for a play, walk or breakfast. But just be aware that some smart little pups can learn quickly that as soon as they wake up in the morning, fun stuff happens! All of a sudden, she may start barking earlier and earlier to be let out. Our suggestion: Try to mix up the time you let your puppy out in the morning to avoid her little body clock alarm system tuning in at 5 am every day. Give her a brief pat and a calm 'Good morning' and take her out for a toilet opportunity. Try to hold off breakfast and play for at least 15 minutes after waking up.

A dog who is fully crate trained should:

• willingly go into her crate – you'll be amazed at how quickly this just happens when you give her a few meals in there
• be happy in the crate regardless of its location – think inside, outside, in the car and in different rooms
• not be reliant upon food or chew items to relax in the crate – she should get them sometimes, but not every time
• be capable of sleeping and settling in the crate quickly – but this will only be successful if you are also giving the dog an appropriate amount of physical and mental stimulation as well as crate training.

If you approach crate training correctly and consistently, you are giving yourself a wonderful transport and management tool. But more importantly, your dog is gaining the skills required to develop independence, therefore reducing the chance of developing separation anxiety. No dog is too old to learn how to enjoy a crate.

The Cafe Dog Exercise

Do you want to be able to walk your dog to the local cafe and enjoy a coffee with a friend while your dog comfortably relaxes beneath you?

When we visit our local cafe, we often observe the behaviour of dogs around us. Some are curled up fast asleep, oblivious to the fast-paced energy and stimuli that surround them. This is the dream. However, many of the dogs we observe display signs that they are uncomfortable or nervous in this situation. They are either on high alert, barking or growling at the passing human or canine traffic, or they shy away at the end of their lead from an incoming hand attempting to pat them. They are stuck, unable to remove themselves from this situation.

It's unrealistic to expect puppies to chill out while being restrained on lead in a place like a cafe if we haven't made them feel comfortable and given them confidence that being restrained on a lead is okay. They need to learn that we will advocate for them and keep them safe.

How can we do this? By starting to practise this exercise in the familiarity and comfort of your loungeroom. Similar to crate training, we need to break this exercise down into achievable steps. Along the way, your puppy may experience slight stress or frustration from being restrained by the lead *but* she will manage to overcome it within a short period of time.

Stage 1: Ensure your puppy has been suitably stimulated, exercised, and has gone to the toilet. Choose a safe and familiar spot in your loungeroom to tie her to, one where she can't move or destroy that special piece of furniture.

Tether your puppy on a short lead – we usually suggest a lead length equivalent to their body length (usually around 50 cm). You can place her bed underneath her and give her a chew toy or enrichment the first few times you practise this, to help her settle.

Stay with her, and then untie your puppy when she has visibly calmed down or, better yet, fallen asleep. Again, like crate training, if she appears stressed, you can talk to her or even give her some affection to help calm her down. Just don't untie her while she is pulling on the lead. When you do untie her, don't make a big deal about it – the whole exercise should be calm.

Once the exercise is finished, it's a good time to encourage her to go outside for a toilet opportunity and sniff around. When this stage of the exercise is done correctly, your pup should reliably settle after a couple of sessions a day for two to three days.

Stage 2: Once your puppy is settling more quickly and reliably with you right next to her, start to increase the distance you sit from her, and perhaps toy around with the duration, remembering to always untie her when she is in her most relaxed state.

Stage 3: Change the location of the tie-up. You can try the washing line, an outdoor table, the office, the front verandah. Always keep the length of the lead the same. When testing out a new location, again, remain very close for the first few times until she appears comfortable in this new setting and slowly build up distance and duration. In our opinion, no dog should be left unattended when tied up, particularly in a public space.

Within a few weeks of practising this exercise around the house, start to practise at a friend's house or on a quiet park bench. Every dog will progress at their own rate and this is an exercise that should never be rushed. But eventually, once you have practised this across various locations in your own home, and other less familiar but still low-distraction environments and your puppy is coping well, it may now be time to graduate to a real live cafe trip. Keep in mind that the first few times you visit the local cafe to dine in you should treat it as a training session. Focus more on your dog's behaviour rather than getting too distracted by conversation, good coffee or the friendly waitstaff!

> **NOTE**
> The cafe dog exercise is an important one to practise when socialising your puppy with other dogs. Allow your puppy opportunities to have short play sessions with socially competent adult dogs, but then practise a tie-up exercise in the presence of the dog to ensure she can equally settle around other dogs.

Puppy Pens, Baby Gates and Other Barriers

There is nothing 'pretty' about raising a puppy! As we mentioned in Chapter 4, you'll need to surrender to the fact that for the first few months of having a puppy, your home may need to become a fortress of bars and gates, pens and crates. But the long-term gain from the short-term interruption to the aesthetics of your home will be invaluable.

When we visit homes to set up their space for the arrival of a puppy, we will usually suggest putting a couple of baby gates and a puppy pen in the loungeroom area. Unlike in the tie-up and crate training exercises, with these spaces we are not attempting to teach our puppies to 'switch off'.

We are creating spaces within the house that:

- have been 'puppy proofed' and are deemed safe
- encourage further independence building.

Once again, they are a great way to prevent your puppy from following you upstairs and down hallways. The greatest benefit is that they stop a puppy from accessing the front door when visitors arrive. A puppy can very quickly learn the appeal of someone approaching the front door or the doorbell ringing, and will race over to be first in line to greet and jump on the 'new person'. It may seem innocent enough and most strangers are delighted to be met by the advances of an 8-week-old ball of fluff. But this behaviour becomes entrenched very quickly and you can end up with a much larger dog barking and charging every time someone comes over. It's best to prevent this from occurring in the first place by allowing visitors to come in and ignore your puppy while she settles her energy back down. In the long term, this will result in a far more pleasant experience for all.

THINGS TO REMEMBER WHEN BUILDING YOUR DOG'S INDEPENDENCE

- Always set your pup up for success by ensuring she is sufficiently exercised and has had an opportunity to go to the toilet before practising tie-up, crate training or puppy pen time.

132

- Stay close by and build on her success and ability to relax.
- If you are not playing, training or keeping a close eye on your puppy, utilise some form of independence-building exercise to help with management and development.
- Avoid 'bad stress' where possible.

Multi-Dog Households and Raising Littermates

Can you raise an independent dog in a home shared with other dogs? The short answer is yes, though there are challenges involved. We have always had multi-dog households, but we raise each dog as an individual with two main concepts in mind:

1. The dog must be fine if she needs to be left alone, if all the other dogs are away working, or when the other dogs (inevitably) die.
2. The dog must like and value us more than other dogs.

The biggest mistake we see people make in multi-dog households is leaving the new puppy with another dog 24/7. Very quickly, the puppy becomes completely attached and reliant on the other dog, and even normal tasks become impossible without the second dog present. When this happens, training is very difficult and the puppy will seem not to care about humans all that much. These issues only get worse with time and age, so you can see how tricky it is to raise littermates to be independent.

The two worst scenarios we've seen many times and in multiple dog households where dogs have become reliant upon each other (particularly with littermates) are:

- One dog dies and the other is completely distraught, howls, cries, barks, won't eat and even self-mutilates from stress. Overall, she lives a very sad existence thereafter and in extreme cases needs to be medicated.
- The dogs have a fight one day, perhaps over a bone or a toy (anecdotally, this seems to be more severe with two bitches).

They hold a grudge and cannot be trusted together – they are a danger to each other. Simultaneously, they can't bear life apart. A very conflicting and complicated situation to be in.

Both of these situations are incredibly sad and could have easily been avoided with intervention earlier in life.

Tips for raising a new dog in a multi-dog household:

1. Be prepared to raise them separately for the first few months – as discussed, you can do this with crates, pens and time-sharing the house and yard.
2. Keep interactions controlled and supervised – you want the new and the established dogs to understand that you will mediate and control interactions for everyone's safety and confidence.
3. Take the new dogs and old dogs for walks together – walks are a terrific way to build a bond between dogs calmly and respectfully.
4. In the first four to six weeks, aim to keep the contact between the new dogs and the established dogs under three hours per day – that will mean they should sleep separately, which will also allow the new dog to bond with the humans.
5. Remember, you want your new dog to enjoy the company of your established dogs, but they should not be more important than you – obedience training is very difficult if your dogs are more interested in each other then they are in you.

When a New Baby Arrives

Some dogs welcome visitors and children into their home happily and calmly, while others can find the experience over-arousing or stressful. If you're welcoming a baby into the home there will likely be many changes to your lifestyle and routines. This can be stressful for even the most relaxed dog, so a little bit of planning and training before bub arrives can make a substantial difference.

As parents ourselves, we know first-hand how beneficial it is to prepare in any way you can to reduce stress and workload once a new baby arrives. Investing energy into preparing your dog for the new arrival is worth considering. That doesn't mean spending more time with them, though. We recently spoke to a friend who is several months pregnant with her first baby and she told us she was upping the exercise and cuddles with her dog, to squeeze in as many solo hangs as she could before her free time became consumed by a newborn. As animal behaviourists, we actually suggest the exact opposite of this. Let's face it: you are going to have less time with your beloved dog when the baby arrives, but if you ramp everything up just beforehand – more couch cuddles, more beach runs and more walks – your dog will struggle even more with the sudden deficit of affection and attention when the baby arrives.

Here are some things you can begin doing, starting a couple of months out from the birth, to make the transition easier for your pooch:

1. If you haven't already done this, crate training or teaching your dog to settle in a space separate from the family is a must! It will prevent her from getting under your feet and in trouble when you are feeling stressed and tired.

2. All our dogs are conditioned from a young age to have 'days off' where they don't get much exercise or attention from us. On these days, we might give them a bone or multiple enrichment opportunities to keep them entertained and occupied along with a five-minute training session at most. For families that are about to be blessed with a time-consuming newborn, it's worthwhile introducing this system so that your dog isn't nudging or staring at you constantly, trying to will you into walking her! Over the months leading up to the due date, start varying routine and reduce exercise every now and then.

3. Increase enrichment. Don't feed your dog all her meals in a bowl or at set times, so they can have more food enrichment to stimulate them. Stock your freezer before the baby's due date with frozen stock blocks, stuffed KONGs, bones, etc., so you have plenty of different dog-friendly food on hand for them to explore.

4. Think about novel things you can do with your dog. Walk them on a different route, take them to a different park or train them in a new behaviour. Why? Novel activities are very rewarding and can be better value for time when it comes to making your dog feel relaxed and satisfied. Time is a precious resource when you have a bub, so don't get stuck in the mindset of doing the same one-hour walk every day.

Other baby-related things to think about

We also recommend giving some thought to the following when a baby is on the way:

- **Pram training:** Many dogs act out towards things with wheels, so take your dog and pram for a few training sessions prior to adding a newborn to the equation.
- **Crying:** Download the Sound Proof Puppy Training app and follow the instructions on how to desensitise your dog to the sound of crying. If baby cries, avoid pairing this sound with your dog getting in trouble (or stepped on).
- **Dog walkers:** Consider organising someone to exercise your dog in the short term to help you through the first few months.
- **Doorbell desensitisation:** Your sleep will be especially precious for the next few months, so if your dog tends to bark when someone approaches the door or rings the doorbell, now is the time to start training them out of this behaviour. It can be as simple as rewarding your dog with a treat every time you ring the doorbell (and do it multiple times per day) or teaching her to go to her bed when the doorbell rings (see Chapter 9). If time is scarce, prepare a big waterproof sign and erect it outside your house with a very obvious sign stating 'Please do not disturb. Sleeping baby + guard dog + door bell rung = tired and dangerous parents!'
- **Dog and baby photo:** DON'T RUSH IT. And *don't* trust your dog with your new baby. No matter how intuitive your dog might seem, we often see the consequences of this 'trust',

so take your time. However, when the time is right to introduce them and take a snap (if that's something you wish to do), the results can be adorable!

Knowing that your dog is happy and relaxed while you go off to work or out to dinner is a luxury many people with anxious dogs dream about. The key to making this a lifelong skill is to focus on appropriately and gradually building independence while your dog is still young. If your dog is mature and hasn't developed this skill yet, it's not a lost cause; you just need to allow a bit more time, and plan each step of training based upon the dog's current abilities and comfort levels. The joys of owning a confident and independent dog can't be underestimated.

Chapter 8

The Problem Puppy

Puppies are adorable but they sure can be destructive, teething, peeing, pooing machines. This 'naughty' behaviour is not due to bad intentions or their strong will to 'dominate' you, however. At a young age they're merely being guided by instincts, and as a result their inquisitive nature and lack of training can often get them into mischief.

Puppies naturally experiment with all types of behaviours. It's a way of learning and developing new skills that are likely to be useful later on in life. However, some of these skills would be more relevant if they were living a wilder existence like their ancestors, fending for themselves. Unfortunately for modern-day dog owners, skills such as barking, digging and biting aren't all that useful or appreciated – especially in a landscaped, suburban home with young kids and close neighbours!

In this chapter we'll tackle the most common 'problem' behaviours you're likely to come up against:

- biting
- chewing
- digging
- jumping
- barking
- growling
- toilet accidents
- coprophagia (eating poo)
- resource guarding
- frantic zooming
- travel sickness.

Generally, from 8 to 10 weeks of age, puppies can 'do no wrong'. They tend to be docile, cuddly, and 'easier' to have around. They are still young, settling in and teething hasn't fully hit yet. It's during this time that you want to focus all your 'training' attention on making places like pens and crates enjoyable for your puppy to be in. By doing so, when the more confident, teething Tyrannosaurus Rex puppy comes to life, and he is suddenly no fun to be around, you'll have laid the groundwork so that you can place him in his pen with something proactive to do – preventing him from developing habits you *don't* want him to! – and he won't scream the house down.

How do you get through this puppy period while keeping your sanity (and limbs!) intact and preventing these undesirable behaviours from becoming long-term habits? Let's take them one at a time.

Health First

As we mentioned in Chapter 2, it's always important to make sure the foundations are okay – so don't forget to check that your puppy's new behaviour is not due to poor health!

Obesity

In Australia, most poorly-behaved adult dogs are overweight. This is either because they are getting too much food, the wrong kind of food, not enough exercise, or all of the above.

There are a couple of things you can do to work out your dog's optimal weight:

1. Weigh him regularly at your local vet or pet shop, and compare to breed standards, which in Australia can be found on the Australian National Kennel Council website.
2. Feel the ribs and waist. Dogs shouldn't look like beer kegs with legs. They are supposed to have a waist – even Bulldogs. You want to be able to feel the ribs, but they shouldn't be overly exposed. One of our old agility instructors used to say: if your dog's ribs feel like your palm, they are overweight; if they feel like your knuckles, they are too thin; if they feels like the back of your hand, they are just right. If you don't have access to scales, or your dog is very fluffy, it's not a bad trick in our eyes.

Dog Size-O-Meter

Size-O-Meter Score:

Characteristics:

1 Very Thin
More than 20% below ideal body weight

- Ribs, spine and hip bones are very easily seen (in short haired pets)
- Obvious loss of muscle bulk
- No fat can be felt under the skin

2 Thin
Between 10-20% below ideal body weight

- Ribs, spine and hip bones easily seen
- Obvious waist and abdominal tuck
- Very little fat can be felt under the skin

3 Ideal
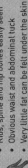

- Ribs, spine and hip bones easily felt
- Visible waist with an abdominal tuck
- A small amount of fat can be felt

4 Overweight
Between 10-15% above ideal body weight

- Ribs, spine and hip bones are hard to feel
- Waist barely visible with a broad back
- Layer of fat on belly and at base of tail

5 Obese
More than 15% above ideal body weight

- Ribs, spine and hip bones extremely difficult to feel under a thick layer of fat
- No waist can be seen and belly may droop significantly
- Heavy fat pads on lower back and at the base of the tail

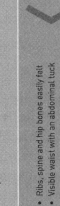

- Your pet is a healthy weight
- Seek advice about your pet's weight
- Seek advice as your pet could be at risk

Please note

There are some cases where the natural shape of a dog may mean this simple system doesn't translate as easily. For example, Whippets and Greyhounds tend to have lean physiques while a Staffie will have a broader shape. A Bichon Frisé will have a nice fluffy coat for you to contend with. If you need help using this chart, please take it to your vet or pet care professional for advice

www.pfma.org.uk
pfma
pet food manufacturers' association

Derived from BCSC validated by: Laflamme DP. Development and validation of a body condition score system for cats. A clinical tool Feline Practice. 1997, 25:13-17 Laflamme DP, Hume E, Harrison J. Evaluation of zoonotic measures as an assessment of body composition of dogs and cats. Compendium 2001;23(Suppt 9A).88

Illustration from Pet Food Manufacturers' Association Dog Size-O-Meter. For more information, please visit www.pfma.org.uk

If your dog is overweight, it might be worth visiting your vet and improving your dog's diet and exercise.

The Bitey Puppy

Unfortunately for humans, dealing with puppy teeth can be the most frustrating part of raising a young dog. Getting nipped is painful, constant and can really interfere with your ability to bond with him (especially if he's already got you exhausted and sleep-deprived!).

So why do puppies mouth and bite *everything*? Understanding what's driving a puppy to sink those needle-sharp teeth into whatever they come across is the first step to working out how you can best manage it. There are a couple of reasons behind this behaviour.

1. Teething

At around 5 to 6 weeks of age, puppies should have all their 'milk teeth'. This is the razor-sharp, first set of teeth. Around 12 to 16 weeks of age, movement inside the mouth starts again as each of these milk teeth fall out to make room for adult teeth, which are generally all through by 6 months. Just as with teething toddlers, this can cause a puppy discomfort and pain while his new teeth come through. During this teething period, puppies have an increased desire to mouth and chew on certain things to help relieve that soreness. You may notice a decrease in your dog's willingness to play 'tug' games or fetch balls, which is due to the movement of his teeth.

What can you do to help?
Lots of food-based enrichment! A frozen slice of apple or carrot, home-made frozen (beef or chicken) stock ice blocks, commercial food-based puzzles, enrichment items and pigs' ears will help to soothe your puppy's mouth and keep him busy. Pop him in the puppy pen or a contained area such as a crate and give him something to chew on while in this space. This will prevent him redirecting his attention to your clothes and furniture.

2. Communication, exploration and play

Dogs are social animals who play, bond and communicate a lot of the time through their mouths. Just look at the way dogs play with other dogs! They also use their mouths to explore and interpret the environment around them. With this in mind, you need to teach your puppy that biting humans isn't how we want him to play and communicate with *us*.

How do we begin to do this?

Management
Whenever you aren't actively training, supervising or playing with your puppy, put him in a contained area with some enrichment as mentioned above. This gives your puppy plenty of opportunities to bite and mouth appropriate objects and not chase you down the hallway practising biting at your pants!

This might sound obvious, but it's worth closely considering the clothes you and your family choose to wear during the couple of months in which your puppy is teething. Greeting a puppy first thing in the morning in a fluffy, floor-length dressing gown is a recipe for disaster! Skirts, scarves and Byron Bay hippy pants are out; steel-capped boots, thick jeans and an old fitted shirt (or equivalent) are in. Remember, it's not forever – and will reduce the risk of any of your favourite things getting ruined.

Training
Teach your puppy that 'sit' is the absolute best thing in the world. Sitting gains your attention, affection and treats! You can then utilise this trained behaviour for teaching your puppy impulse control when playing games with them. (For more on teaching 'sit', refer to Chapter 9.)

Appropriate outlets
Encourage your puppy to play with you via the game of 'tug of war' with a toy. This allows a puppy opportunities to bond with you through play and you can heavily reinforce the following: biting a

toy brings the game to life; biting the skin makes all fun stop. If this game is taught well, a puppy quickly learns that retrieving a toy and bringing it to you is the quickest and easiest way to have fun with a human. Use the following cues or commands:

- 'Yes' – bite the toy.
- 'Leave' or 'Give' – spit the toy out.
- 'Ouch' – the dog has connected with skin and the game will stop for at least 10 seconds. (See Chapter 11 for the 'tug of war' instructions on how to train this.)

If at any stage your puppy becomes too overbearing or he is no longer going for the toy, put him in the puppy pen with something to do.

BITING

There are particular breeds that are more prone to biting than others. The working group of dogs, especially Cattle Dogs, needs to be closely monitored and managed – especially around young kids. They are bred to react to moving things and nip them. This is their 'special skill' and it's what makes them ideal farm herding dogs. The gun dog group also tend to have a more mouthy teething phase than other groups.

The Chewing Puppy

Puppies chew for those same reasons related to teething discussed above – it's almost a rite of passage for every puppy raised in winter to run off with a boot or a slipper to gnaw on and for summer puppies to masticate a thong at some point. Shoes are magnets for teething puppies! Obviously, our advice is not to leave shoes (and other important articles) lying around when there's a young pup in the house, but we ourselves have been in this position and admittedly have lost a few shoes over the years because, well, life just happens!

Hot tip for anyone who has experienced the loss of footwear: if one of your shoes falls victim, don't give it up and allow your pup to hang onto it as a new source of enrichment. In doing that you may just be encouraging a lifelong shoe thief. You want to be consistent in teaching your puppy from the beginning that all shoes are off limits.

If the puppy gets hold of something he shouldn't, avoid chasing him. This can very quickly teach a puppy to experiment with picking up random objects as it results in a great game of chase that he enjoys and considers a form of play. Similarly, trying to reef an object out of his mouth that he shouldn't have could just be encouraging a fabulous game of tug of war. By the same token, saying 'No' and pointing a finger draws attention to the behaviour and can make the puppy think that you're playing with him (as puppies will growl at each other during play). You want it to seem like it's no big deal and redirect his attention. Here are three strategies to help you when your pup picks up something he shouldn't have:

1. Attempt to get his attention while he is parading the item in question, then excitedly bolt in the opposite direction, *fast* – like someone has just announced there is a million bucks at the end of the corridor. This action will hopefully send your puppy into hot pursuit after you to work out what all the fuss is about, and he'll drop your treasured possession in the process.
2. Grab a nearby puppy toy and bring it to life, animatedly pretending that you are having the ultimate fun time with whatever it is. The idea is that your pup will make the decision to drop the boring, lifeless toy in their mouth and come over to investigate the epic one you have. Then, while they are fully engaged with the dog toy, slink on over to the important item and remove it from sight.
3. If you are not in the mood to be theatrical, wait for your puppy to settle somewhere with the prized possession, then calmly walk over, take it off him and divert his attention to something else. At this point revisit your management strategies (puppy pens, baby gates or an alternative contained set-up) in an attempt to prevent history repeating itself.

Dog beds can be seen as a world of fun and source of enrichment for a teething little pup (Labrador puppies are especially skilled in the area of dog bed deconstruction). Anyone who has experienced a dog continuing to destroy his bed will know just how frustrating it is to come home to. They are expensive and it's amazing how one little bed, when opened up, can become a catastrophic mess that will engulf your living room. If you notice your puppy has taken to chewing his bed, it's well worth investing early on in a 'non-destructible' bed. It might not look or feel as cosy, but it'll do the job, and you can integrate a fluffy one later on. Our recommendation would be Rover Pet Products' TuffMat.

The Digging Puppy

There are a few different reasons why puppies dig. Determining the cause for the digging is the first step to stopping the behaviour.

1. **Overfeeding:** Are you feeding him too much or does he have lots of bones lying around the back yard? This can promote a behaviour known as 'caching' – where your dog will dig holes so he can bury excess food supplies or a bone he has and wants to stash for later.
   Solution: Revisit your dog's diet and look at reducing his daily food intake (including bones).

2. **Digging to escape:** This is more likely to happen close to the boundary of your property or gates. It tends to occur because the dog isn't comfortable being contained in the backyard space, or because he is bored or suffering from separation distress.
   Solution: Talk to a professional about helping your dog learn to relax at home and build his independence. Refer back to Chapter 7.

3. **Digging to cool down:** Some dogs (and many other animals) will dig a depression in the soil and lie in it in an attempt to cool their body temperature down. It's a very different type of hole to the ones above.
   Solution: Ensure your dog has sufficient shelter from the sun – maybe invest in a clam shell with water for your dog to bathe in on hot days.

4. **Digging for grubs:** In summer, grass gets grubs! Grubs smell great to an inquisitive pup. This type of digging is generally characterised by lots of sniffing and lots of small bursts of fast digging.
   Solution: Deal with the grubs and the digging should stop. Most pesticides will require you to keep your dog off the grass for a few days, so check the material safety data sheet (also known as the 'MSDS') on the back of the container to see how long you need to keep the dog out of the area.

5. **Young pups like to dig** . . . just because they can! The most likely cause for digging in an inquisitive young pup is for fun.
   Solution: Management and redirection are key in preventing the behaviour from sticking for life. Give him a 'digging space' such as a clam shell sandpit and bury enrichment in it for him to dig up. As well as this, remove access to the lawn or garden while puppies are young and unsupervised.

The Jumping Puppy

Why do puppies jump? It's fairly simple: they want to get closer to your face. This means that (without meaning to) people train young jumping dogs to repeat this behaviour, by bringing their faces down, closer to the dog and offering up goos, gahs and cuddles – which encourages the pup to jump again. A bit of jumping might be cute when your Malamute pup is 8 weeks old but however affectionate it may be now, this behaviour won't be so enjoyable when he is a 40 kg adult! Like most things in life, this is definitely one of those times where prevention is better than cure.

From the minute you bring your puppy home, offer praise and affection when all four of his paws are firmly planted on the ground. Train him that if he wants to be invited through the front door, to get dinner or to cross the road, he must *sit*. Because if he's sitting, he's not jumping!

This also means that if he does jump out of excitement, arousal or instinct, and doesn't immediately get what he wants, he will generally resort to what has worked for him before – which is sitting.

If your puppy jumps and then sits, and you immediately praise the sit, you may be inadvertently teaching him the sequence of 'jump, sit' to gain praise. If this starts to occur, implement the 10 second rule – don't praise the sit if it happens within 10 seconds of your puppy jumping up.

Here are some common situations when a puppy is more likely to practise jumping and a few tips on how you can be one step ahead of the game.

Meeting people out and about

Jumping up to say hello to friends, family, strangers and visitors is by far the most common time this behaviour is reinforced and can be the most difficult situation to manage, because it involves you being very regimented and sometimes asking the on-comers to stop coming on. We suggest taking treats with you every time you go out and having them at the ready in a good, accessible treat pouch. As people approach, instead of letting your puppy pull towards them and jump, ask your puppy to sit, give your pup a treat and then say 'Free' as a cue to greet the person. Ideally, you should also ask the person to crouch down to say hello. The puppy will start to naturally learn, through repetition and consistency, that sitting gets the attention from the new person.

Greeting people coming through the front door

With a bit of management in place, this is easy to prevent. If you can semi-permanently put up a baby gate to prevent your puppy from ever gaining access to the front door, that's the best solution. Otherwise when you hear a knock at the front door, pop the puppy in his puppy pen to allow the visitors to enter and settle in. Then ask your guests if they wouldn't mind doing some training with your dog. Give them a treat to hold and when you let the puppy out, ask them to say 'sit', treat and then pat.

During food preparation in the kitchen

Having a dog who 'counter surfs' or jumps up on kitchen benchtops is not only frustrating for you but also dangerous if you are cooking hot food or using a knife. To avoid this scenario, take the opportunity while you are cooking meals to practise puppy pen, crate or the cafe dog exercise (see Chapter 7).

The Barking Puppy

The most common complaint councils receive regarding dogs is related to barking. We've seen many clients who have been at the receiving end of an anonymous letter from a neighbour, or a council ranger visit. They are usually very stressed and looking for quick fixes. Much to their disappointment, trying to train an adult dog out of entrenched barking habits takes time and usually a holistic approach. It's definitely worth identifying why a puppy has started barking and work at preventing it from further occurring rather than taking the 'he will grow out of it' approach.

The three main reasons a puppy barks are separation distress, attention-seeking and fear-based barking. Determining the driving force behind the bark will inform how you deal with it.

Separation barking

Separation barking usually occurs as an emotional response when a puppy is experiencing time separated from social interactions with the family or other dogs. It can be high-pitched or fast and unceasing.

A puppy who's barking because he is scared or anxious can't control it. Reprimanding him may appear to temporarily fix the problem by ceasing the barking, but it won't change how that puppy is feeling below the surface, and in fact will usually increase the amount of barking down the track.

What to do

- If your puppy is in a crate, tie-up exercise or puppy pen and you are able to walk closer to him but without letting him have full access to you, walk back to a distance where he no longer looks distressed and reassure him with a calm, confident voice. If possible, stay at this distance a while longer until he is visibly much calmer or (even better) asleep.

- Give your puppy more things to do, such as enrichment or food puzzles, when he is experiencing separation time, to make alone time more fun. (See Chapter 7 for more on this topic.)
- Practise incorporating short bursts of separation time while the family remains in close proximity, letting your pup regain access to you when he is relaxed.

Attention barking

Some barking is a conscious decision in the puppy's brain, when he is seeking out a response. An 'attention bark' is usually short and sharp and directed straight towards the object, animal or person the puppy wants attention from. This type of barking can be reinforced *very easily* – especially in suburbia, where dog owners commonly wish to do right by their neighbours and stop the noise in its tracks. Be mindful: if your puppy is barking at the back door for your attention and you let them in because you are worried about disturbing the neighbours, you will only increase this behaviour tomorrow.

What to do

- If your puppy looks at you and barks, turn in the opposite direction and ignore him for 10 seconds (after the last bark) before giving him any attention. If he continues barking, put him in a location separate from you. This will show him that barking at someone or something for attention only drives him further away from that object or person that he is seeking, so it is a self-defeating behaviour.
- If your puppy is barking at the back door to come in, wait for a 10 second gap between the barking before opening the door. If there isn't a gap, you can clap your hands or use some sort of noise or word to break the behaviour to help initiate the break. Just aim for 10 seconds of silence before opening the door.
- Drop a letter in all your neighbours' letterboxes saying something along the lines of:

Dear Neighbour,
We have recently brought home a new puppy and have every
intention to raise him to be the perfect adult dog. Please bear
with us while we work with our puppy trainers and navigate
the puppy stage to the best of our ability. 'Short-term pain for
long-term gain', as the saying goes. We would also be very
grateful if you could let us know if you hear any barking. This
will put us in a better position to help our puppy long term.
Yours sincerely . . .

Fear-based adolescent barking

Most dogs do their first 'real' barks between 3 and 9 months of
age. If your dog falls into this age bracket and has begun reacting
unusually towards something or someone, 99 per cent of the time it's
stemming from a fearful or nervous emotional state. This is likely due
to a developmental leap known as the 'secondary fear phase'. Barking
or growling is his way of communicating that he is not comfortable.
Rarely (if ever) is it because he is just being 'naughty', dominant or
'aggressive'. He is having a reaction to a stimulus that, for whatever
reason, has made him feel emotional: a plastic bag floating down the
street, his reflection in a glass door, or maybe something as normal as
Pat the neighbour saying hi. For some reason, today Pat was scary.

We can liken it to a child's reaction to Santa Claus. Children under
18 months of age are less likely to care about this strange character.
As they mature into toddlers, however, they become instinctively more
cautious about their surroundings, and the big man in red can be met
with trepidation, resulting in a meltdown. Let's flip this to a young
dog. Puppies between 4 and 12 weeks of age are generally accepting
of all stimuli, so long as they are not overwhelmed. But over the following months they start to determine what is 'normal'. If they see
something or someone that looks different, for whatever reason, they
may respond with reactive behaviour. This is the dog's equivalent of a
toddler seeing Santa.

Your next actions can ultimately determine your dog's behaviour
towards that stimulus for the rest of his life. To be blunt, the last thing

he needs is a person yanking on the end of the lead saying 'Bad dog, stop barking'. This can make him more reactive and confirm in the dog's mind that this person or stimulus is bad.

What to do

When your dog has his first meltdown, give him space from the scary stimulus and use an upbeat (not sooky or harsh) tone to help redirect him and demonstrate verbally to him that it's all good. Once your dog is at a distance where he can regulate his emotions, you may want to give him a few treats when he looks back at the thing that triggered his reaction. Next time you head out on a walk, remember this reaction and give your dog a treat or initiate a game with him in the distant presence of that stimulus, to start a bit of a counter-conditioning process (see Chapter 12 for more detail on counter-conditioning).

The Growly Pup

Growling during puppyhood is a form of communication that can stem from two very different emotional states: happy and playful, or highly stressed and uncomfortable. Despite popular belief, a puppy isn't growling to 'dominate' you.

The happy growl is generally paired with roughhousing, playtime or witching hour. The body is loose and fluid in motion or the puppy is racing around like a headless chook, occasionally growling as he stops to survey the room or pounce on a toy. There is absolutely nothing wrong with this growl. Your puppy is happy, having fun and enjoying life!

In contrast, a puppy who growls because he is feeling stressed or uncomfortable has usually been communicating less obvious cues of his discomfort prior to the growl, but these may have been ignored. Body language like scratching, lip licking, yawning and body shaking could be a mild indication that your puppy is not liking the situation. If these signals are ignored and he continues to be subjected to an uncomfortable stimulus, this is when he will growl.

What not to do

Don't punish a growling puppy. This puppy is feeling scared and isn't coping with something in the environment around him. Use it as information to understand what the puppy doesn't like.

A common scenario when a puppy might growl is when a young child picks them up. There is generally no warning sign he is about to be scooped off the ground, and the child is unlikely to be able to support him properly and may even drop him once or twice. The puppy will start to see this child approach them and offer up a yawn or body scratch. The child ignores the language from the puppy saying 'Please stop', and continues to pick them up. This happens a few more times until the puppy really can't handle it and growls. Because the growl is 'scary' to a child, they will generally listen and put the puppy down. The 'problem' with this is that the growl has now become successful for the pup, and the puppy learns to growl whenever he feels uncomfortable.

What happens if we punish the growl? The puppy might learn, for now, not to growl because the growl resulted in an even bigger, scary event. But nothing has changed the puppy's emotional state that caused the growl in the first place. He is still feeling scared and is now feeling even more nervous of the child's advances. The puppy might tolerate being picked up a few more times by the child until he's at breaking point, and what comes after a growl? A bite! With no warning.

If you find yourself in this situation, you need to get to the root of the behaviour. Educate the child on better ways to interact with the puppy that give the puppy a choice and don't make him feel threatened or scared. Jump back to the section in Chapter 6 on 'Kids and puppies' for a reminder.

What to do

If your puppy is growling out of context:

1. Survey the environment to try to establish what has caused the growl.
2. Allow your puppy space or the opportunity to back away from the scary stimulus.

3. Add the stimulus to the socialisation checklist (see Chapter 6). Make a conscious effort to build up your puppy's tolerance to this person, place or object in slow steps.
4. Consult with a dog trainer.

If a puppy is growling over a resource (i.e. he has a toy, bone or food, or he is in a car, crate or on his bed and growls when someone approaches), skip to the 'Resource guarding' section later in this chapter.

Toilet Accidents

Submissive urination

Many puppies will urinate upon greeting other dogs or people as part of an act of submission, which is usually due to a lack of confidence and maturity. The worst thing you can do is get cranky at the puppy or make a big deal about it as this will make the puppy feel worse, less confident and in turn more prone to the submissive urination!

What to do

Don't create a fuss, just keep greetings very low-key and casual. In fact, where possible, ask people to ignore the puppy and let the puppy explore them at their own rate without a direct greeting. When it comes to other dogs causing your puppy to urinate upon greeting, don't place your puppy in a situation where he is going to be bailed up by other dogs off lead (or on lead for that matter) and don't allow your puppy to rush up to other dogs. Often the young pup will rush up and greet an older dog, at the last minute realising he is terrified, and then either roll on his back or pee himself. Either way, that whole scenario is an undesirable circumstance and can be an early warning sign to reactivity later in life.

In terms of correctly socialising your submissive puppy with other dogs the focus shouldn't be on dogs playing with each other. We suggest shy puppies go for walks with confident and calm adult dogs who are likely to ignore them. The pup has a lovely walk in the presence of an adult dog who doesn't put any pressure on the experience. These sorts of controlled training sessions are instrumental in building confidence.

Eating Poo (Coprophagia)

If we had to guess, we'd say every dog has done this at some stage. Although they have super smelling powers, dogs actually have relatively underdeveloped taste buds compared to ours.

When a dog is young, eating poo a couple of times out of pure curiosity is expected, but repeating it regularly is often a sign of something lacking in your dog's diet or excessive hunger, in which case it might be time for a visit to your vet.

What to do

If you do notice your dog eating poo, calmly call your dog towards you. Don't chase him, yell, scream or make a big deal about it. In our experience, if you make a big deal about it the dog is more likely to repeat the behaviour.

Needless to say, if your yard is free of dog poo this behaviour is unlikely to become a problem. However, when you do pick up poo around your yard, do it calmly. If you rush to pick up poo as soon your dog does one, he is likely to observe your excitement and perceive the poo as a valuable resource! We have witnessed dogs race their owner to the poo in order to quickly scoff it down before the bag or scooper gets there.

There are a lot of fables about spraying poo with vinegar or rubbing chilli on it. Just think: if your dog is literally eating poo, adding vinegar or chilli is unlikely to deter them. It might even add more flavouring!

Resource Guarding

Resource guarding, in a nutshell, is a dog's way of protecting or 'guarding' resources he perceives to be important and necessary to his life. Dogs can naturally develop resource guarding towards food, their favourite person, toys, crates, their sleeping area and cars. A dog who displays resource guarding will present some of the following behaviours: fixed stare, lowered head, bared teeth, growling and even snapping or biting. It's instinctive in most animals. We can confidently say that if anybody attempted to kidnap our children or ransack our bank account, we would bare our teeth, growl and bite them too!

What we can teach a puppy from a young age is that he doesn't need to be concerned about protecting valuable possessions from us. We will never put him in a position where he won't have food, shelter or toys.

What to do
Try this exercise to prevent resource guarding (ADULTS ONLY – kids should not try this exercise):

Step 1: Give your puppy his dinner and walk away.

Step 2: While he is busy enjoying his feast, walk back over calmly. When your puppy has clocked you being nearby, drop something more delicious into or near his bowl and walk away again. It doesn't matter what emotional response you are met with – a stare, a glare, a growl or no reaction. Drop the food and walk away.

Step 3: Repeat tomorrow night. And the next. Ideally with different (adult) family members so he learns to generalise the concept to all human beings.

The idea is that if your puppy is feeling the least bit threatened or concerned the first night, by the fifth night of this same exercise, he is now familiar with the fact that when a human approaches him while he's eating . . . something better happens!

Please note: if your puppy does produce a growl or bares his teeth (possibly appearing to smile), we urge you to contact a dog trainer to help you with this process.

Breed-specific training note: This exercise is a MUST for Cocker Spaniel, Springer Spaniel and Golden Retriever puppy owners. These three breeds hold the top spots for exhibiting resource guarding tendencies as adults.

What not to do

- Get the whole family to pat the dog while he is eating.
- Take his food bowl away midway through eating.
- Growl at your dog if he shows any signs of resource guarding.

These things will only create more anxiety in your puppy long term.

Frantic Zooming

A panicked phone call from a concerned owner of a new puppy explaining that their sweet little bundle of joy has suddenly turned into a reckless and aggressive demon is something we deal with on a regular basis. Nine times out of ten, we are able to reassure the client that they are simply experiencing . . . witching hour!

Puppy zoomies, also known as FRAPs (frenetic random activity periods), are fairly common in all puppies and very normal. Much like witching hour with babies and children, they're more likely to occur around 7 to 9 pm at night, when puppies are overtired and usually overstimulated.

It's suggested that these so-called FRAPs are an animal's way of releasing pent-up energy and excitement. These sudden bursts of crazy energy can result in your puppy doing speed laps around your lounge-room, his tail tucked and showing the whites of his eyes, barking and banging uncontrollably into things as his back legs seem to be moving faster than his front ones!

There is nothing wrong with allowing a puppy to relish his evening zoomage, and stopping a puppy mid-zoom can be difficult.

There are two ways in which we aim to handle this period. Generally we won't do the same thing every day, depending on whether we have time to train the dog or not:

1. **Use it to your advantage.** Take the dog outside around this time, bring a bunch of toys with you and let the dog take out his excitement on the toys. This is a time we will particularly practise tug of war and fetch training – pairing energy exertion with mental focus!
2. **Set up for better management.** Have the puppy pen, some tie-up points or a crate ready to go. Allow the puppy to hang out with the family but as soon as you sense all hell is about to break loose, utilise one of your management strategies that will prevent the exorcist puppy from destroying the house.

Here's a tongue twister to say ten times over:

Preparing and planning prevents puppy pandemonium!

Witching hour is a completely different experience in every household. Some people may never experience it with their puppy (though it's uncommon not to), and others may experience it for weeks or months. Preparing yourself for it each night and ensuring your puppy has space to zoom, things to do or focus on, or that you have the time to invest in training him during this period will help you handle this energetic couple of minutes or hours! The main thing to remember is your sweet little angel will return again shortly (and, hopefully, sleep all night because of their early evening zoomingtons).

Travel Sickness

Car sickness is a fairly common issue in puppies; some puppies are just predisposed to it. It can be difficult to overcome, as for some it's an emotional response to a nerve-wracking situation – similar to children feeling like they want to vomit before a public speaking event if they have had a previous bad experience.

For most puppies, the first time they experience a car ride is the most disruptive and scary day of their short life: the day they leave their mum and litter mates. It's possible that the second day they experience a car trip is to visit the vet for their vaccinations. It's no wonder puppies can start to form stressful associations with car trips.

What to do
Note: Avoid driving with them in the car for a week while you practise this.

1. Park the car in a safe space with the engine off and feed your puppy dinner in the car or do some training on the back seat. We want to begin to form a positive association with the car, rather than 'car = long drive'.
2. Open up all the doors and let your puppy explore the car.
3. Repeat Step 1, but with the engine on. Then graduate to a short drive around the block and gradually build on your puppy having happy but short experiences in the car.

A Few More Tips

Patience and time are two things that will make a huge difference in surviving the first few months of having a puppy at home. A good puppy school will expand on all of these points and offer ongoing advice and support. It's no coincidence we often hear people say 'It's just like raising kids!' To some degree, it is.

KEY POINTS TO REMEMBER TO SAFELY AND EFFECTIVELY GET THROUGH THE PUPPY PHASE

- Keep calm! What an annoying phrase to hear when you are at your wits' end with the chaos and sleep deprivation of the puppy phase, but puppies will feed off the different energies around them.
- Getting cranky and reprimanding your pup rarely prevents poor behaviour from occurring unless you follow through with some form of consequence. Worth noting, the act of pointing your finger and saying 'NO' to a confident pup might be interpreted in his eyes as you wanting to play or engage with them. From their perspective, you're waving your limbs around and bringing eye contact and your face closer to them. Instead, we suggest averting eye contact and crossing your arms (see page 150). If the bad behaviour persists, refer to the next point.
- Management, management, management! Prevent your puppy from being able to practise undesirable behaviour in the first place by utilising management strategies and giving your puppy something productive to do.
- If you are faced with a problem behaviour, think about what you want your puppy to do instead and teach him how to do it. Don't want jumping? Teach your puppy to sit for attention. Don't want biting your clothes? Teach your puppy that biting onto clothes results in puppy pen time, but biting toys results in play with people!

Chapter 9

How to Train Your Dog

It will come as no surprise that training your puppy while she is young will help ensure you have a well-behaved adult dog. Training also establishes good communication pathways. Puppies aren't born understanding English, and for the most part people don't know how to speak dog! So if we can surmount the language barrier and learn to understand and interpret their language as well as teach them ours, we can take the communication process as far as we like – the sky's the limit.

It's amazing how much a dog can naturally pick up on. Just saying the word 'walk' may naturally result in the dog waiting for you at the front door with excitement, while 'bathtime' might send your dog hiding in the backyard. Throughout this chapter we will teach you how to intentionally condition your dog to understand that different words mean specific things.

What's more, teaching your dog new behaviours or tricks for the next decade will result in a happier and more fulfilled life for your dog. Dogs love to learn and problem-solve, plus they enjoy company, food and play. The beauty of training your dog is that it combines all of these great passions into a lovely little package.

In training, we prioritise the fundamentals first – those behaviours that have the potential to save your dog's life and maintain sanity within the household. These are the essentials like 'sit' and 'come'. However, once you've established the basics . . . *don't stop!* Teach her spin, shake, roll over, jump into your arms, collect the mail and find your phone or your daughter's teddy. Whether the behaviour you are teaching her is useful or whether it's just a snazzy trick to show your friends, the experience of learning is an activity that provides important mental stimulation for your problem-solving, sociable four-legged friend.

It's worth noting that when we say the word 'behaviour' we usually refer to teaching your dog an action that is functional and/or natural, to achieve an obedient dog or a commonsense outcome. 'Come' and 'stay' are examples of 'behaviours'. A 'trick' on the other hand is usually something optional that is taught for mental enrichment or fun for the dog and owner, like 'shake' or 'spin'. Animal training jargon can differ quite dramatically between trainers and countries, but this is the most important distinction to understand.

TRAINING TALES

A classic case of the power of training is Banjo the Kelpie, who was rescued by Jen's sister, Sammy. Sammy had not owned Kelpies before, but was fully aware of the physical requirements of owning that breed before she took the plunge. She'd wake before the sun rose every morning to take Banjo for an hour's run in the bush, then in the afternoon would do either a trip to the dog beach or park, or a solid game of fetch with a ball chucker. Banjo was in good physical condition but struggled to wind down after activities and was beginning to act out: barking, rounding up other dogs at the park, chasing other animals and refusing to respond to known cues like 'come' and 'stay'. We explained to Sammy that while she was doing a great job meeting the physical needs of a Kelpie, she wasn't doing much to 'work' and satisfy that very intelligent Kelpie brain. We set Sammy a new training plan. Every second day, instead of going to the dog park, she had to teach Banjo a new skill. With our guidance, in just a few months Banjo knew: drop, crawl, flip to heel, spin, speak on cue, shake, kiss, and how to find vegemite in a jar hidden in the backyard. In Sammy's own words, she 'couldn't believe how enjoyable it was to teach Banjo new things once we got going'. We paired this with some crating exercises to help Banjo learn to relax. He was a new dog and Sammy has a newfound love and understanding of training!

The Three Stages of Training

To successfully teach a dog a new skill or behaviour, you need to move through three stages:

Teaching Phase: Introduce the skill or behaviour. In this step, you want to reward your dog *every single time* she successfully does the right behaviour. Continuous rewarding (reinforcement) in the teaching phase will help the dog repeat the right behaviour faster.

Proofing Phase: Proofing the behaviour means taking this newly trained skill and practising it across a variety of locations, among different levels of distractions. *And* still giving your dog a treat every time!

Maintenance Phase: You have reached the maintenance phase once your dog truly understands what is being asked and is capable of offering up the behaviour in a variety of distracting locations after only being asked once. Now you can start to vary the reinforcement options. This means swapping the treat for praise, play with a toy or sometimes even no reward at all. We suggest starting with the '1 in 10' rule: one time out of every ten, offer alternative reinforcement or no reward. Slowly but surely, you can mix that up even more to reduce the number of treats given. By changing up the reinforcement and occasionally not rewarding your dog for the behaviour, you will make it more resistant to extinction (i.e. prevent it from breaking down).

CHOOSING TREATS

A couple of things you need to think about before you get started:

1. **Is your puppy motivated by food?** If you hold a tasty treat in between your fingers and wave it under your puppy's nose, is she sniffing, licking and mouthing your hand in an attempt to get to it? There is no point in attempting to train your puppy

if she doesn't value the reinforcement on offer. The best time for training sessions is before meals, because the motivation for food is at its strongest.

2. **Do you know what your puppy's favourite food is?** Yes, she may respond well to dog biscuits, but she may respond ten times better to barbecue chicken! Generally, we suggest wet, meaty options for training (because they smell good and can be eaten quickly, which means the dog can eat and stay engaged), but we have come across the odd puppy that prefers something unusual, like carrot or blueberries. We often change up the treats on offer to keep our dogs guessing and interested. But avoid using something that the dog has to stop and chew or may be prone to dropping.

   People often tell us they don't want to give their dog a treat every time she does the right behaviour because they worry she will become dependent on needing a reward for the rest of her life. And our response is: 'Nor do we!' It's impractical and unnecessary to be carrying treats on you everywhere you go, for the rest of your dog's life. As you'll see from the maintenance phase above, food treats can be phased out later. But at the beginning, when you are teaching your puppy or dog something new, there is a good reason to consistently give her a treat.

Training Lingo

As with the words 'behaviour' and 'trick', the language used when it comes to training animals can be confusing and different depending on who you talk to. So to make sure we're all speaking the same language, here are a couple of important words that we'll be using in this chapter.

Cues and commands – the difference

These words can sometimes be used in the same context. The difference is that a 'cue' is a signal associated with a trained behaviour, whereas a 'command' is a direct, non-negotiable order.

An example of a cue might be 'Fetch'. Once you've trained your dog this word, it should mean: *If you bring me the ball, I might give you a treat and throw it again.* On the other hand, an example of a command is saying 'Outside' to a dog who is inside the house. If the dog doesn't voluntarily go outside, you will likely follow through to make it happen.

Pre-Training Essentials

Here are some cues and communication methods that you'll use regularly during training to help communicate more effectively with your dog:

The 'bridge'

Also known as the 'reward marker'. This is a word or sound that you use to 'mark' the precise moment your puppy does the right thing during training and inform her that a reward is on its way. We use the word 'Good' for food rewards and 'Yes' for toy rewards. You don't have to do this, but we find it useful if different rewards create different responses from your dogs. We usually use food for intricate behaviours and for keeping dogs calm, whereas we use toys for established behaviours or times we want the dogs in a high level of excitement. As soon as we say 'Yes' the dog will usually run out in front of us anticipating a ball to be thrown.

Great trainers have brilliant timing when it comes to the bridge, and will often use a clicker. Back in our days of training seals at the zoo, we used a whistle.

Practise the bridge a couple of times with a friend and a tennis ball and film it on your phone. Get your friend to drop a tennis ball from a height. Try saying 'Good' at the exact moment the ball hits the ground. Record how often you can do this. It's not as easy as it seems and will train you to be more precise with your timing to better the communication with your dog!

Exercise: teach your dog the 'bridge'
Step 1. Have a delicious treat ready to go in your hand. Say 'Good', short and sharp and clear, so your puppy hears it. Straight away present a treat to her nose.

Step 2. Repeat this several times. It doesn't matter what your puppy is doing, so long as she receives a treat within a couple of seconds of hearing the word. This is called 'classical conditioning'. We are creating a conditioned response to the sound of the word 'Good'. For more information on classical conditioning, see Chapter 12.

Step 3. Now that you have repeated this process a handful of times, say the word 'Good' and wait to see whether your puppy responds by looking at you, anticipating the presence of the treat. If she does, you've successfully taught her the bridge! If there isn't a response, continue working on Step 2 a few more times.

Luring

Luring is the process of presenting a treat to your dog's nose without actually giving it to them and getting them to follow your hand.

Exercise: practise the luring technique

Place a treat in front of your puppy's nose (in between your thumb and forefinger or in a fist for more mouthy puppies) and, while keeping the treat connected to her nose, try to encourage your puppy to walk in a figure 8 purely by 'luring' her with the treat. Once she completes this, say 'Good' and give her the treat.

The 'release' cue

The release cue is a word that communicates to your puppy that the behaviour is over and she can now do as she pleases. This cue is particularly useful in helping to gain duration of a behaviour (i.e. sit for 30 seconds instead of five seconds). Otherwise, what's the point in training her to sit if she only sits for half a second before wandering off? That's not much use in real life situations!

We use the words 'Free' or 'Okay' for this cue. When saying the release cue, use a happy voice and clap your hands or use encouraging body language to help her out of the position she was in.

A Few Final Tips Before You Get Started

Here are some other pointers for successful training sessions:

1. Start all initial training on lead and in a low-distraction, familiar environment.

2. Have your treat pouch on you, and full of high-value treats.
3. Make training sessions short and fun. The ideal time for a puppy (or even an adult dog) who is learning something for the first time is 30 seconds to three minutes. This keeps it interesting! Aim to finish your training session on a high, or at least quit while you're ahead and the dog is enjoying herself. If your dog tells you she's had enough (starts looking around, sniffing the ground or is not interested in your rewards) before *you've* had enough, your sessions are probably too long for the dog at this stage of learning.
4. 'If I've told you once, I've told you a thousand times' – don't repeat yourself! If you repeat a cue without your dog responding to it, she essentially learns to ignore you and perceive your cues and commands as optional. This is a common mistake to make. It can potentially be a recipe for disaster when training dogs to come when called. Saying 'Come' in a variety of tones while your dog effectively flips you the bird and goes chasing kangaroos teaches your dog it's fine to ignore you in that situation.

So what's the solution to a dog who ignores you?

• Set your dog up for success. Don't say things when you know your dog can't or won't pay attention. For example if your dog is looking at a pelican for the first time, you are unlikely to have her undivided attention, so wait until you are a little further away from the majestic bird before asking your dog to perform a behaviour.
• Reward your dog consistently. Generally, dogs who ignore their owners haven't been rewarded enough when they get it right.
• Be prepared to follow through on the request to your dog. If you say 'outside' and the dog jumps up on the couch, put a lead on the dog and take her outside – and still reward her when she gets there.

Okay, time to get into some training!

Sit

This is the very first behaviour every new puppy owner should train their dog to do. It's a simple skill and can be applied to more facets of the puppy's life than you might think.

When raising a puppy, it's very easy to reinforce undesirable behaviour without realising. Most people see food as the only training reward for their puppy, but the puppy actually views many more things beyond just treats as 'rewards' – such as toys and play, praise, access in and outside, meal times or enrichment, social experiences, attention from visitors, and coming out of a crate or getting out of the car. We call these things 'life rewards'.

Any behaviour your puppy exhibits prior to one of these things happening will naturally be reinforced. This means if your puppy is barking, jumping or scratching at the back door and you open the door to let her in, she has just learnt to do that behaviour in order to get inside. Or if your puppy pulls on her lead, jumps up on someone and immediately receives pats, bingo! This combination of action and reaction tells her jumping on people is how she should now communicate if she wants pats.

But there is one very easy way to resolve or prevent those annoying habits from happening: teach your dog to sit.

- ✓ Sit before play
- ✓ Sit before greeting people
- ✓ Sit to go in and out of doors
- ✓ Sit to cross the road
- ✓ Sit before cuddles and attention
- ✓ Sit before dinner
- ✓ Sit for kids' attention
- ✓ Sit to come up on the couch
- ✓ Sit to clip the lead on and off.

This way, sitting becomes your puppy's default position and everything she perceives to be fun in life happens *after or while* all four paws are firmly planted on the ground. It's a simple and easy behaviour worth perfecting and applying to all aspects of life!

TRAINING TALES

When we are training our dogs for specialised conservation field work such as koala detection, it's extremely important that they don't chase wildlife when they are off lead in the bush searching for koalas. How do we teach this? By training our dogs to sit when an animal moves in front of them. Because when a dog sits, she cannot chase!

Exercise: teach your puppy the 'sit' cue

Step 1. Lure the 'sit' position: Present the treat to your puppy's nose (between your thumb and forefinger or in a fist for mouthy pups) and slowly draw your hand up over her head so her nose is moving towards the sky. As she tilts their head back to follow the treat, her bottom should naturally hit the ground to give her balance. The moment her bottom hits the ground, mark the behaviour with 'Good' and give her the treat. Then say 'Free' and encourage her to leave the sit position by clapping or patting the ground. Repeat a couple of times.

Breed-specific training note: Poodles and 'oodles' are notoriously bouncy little puppies and love to paw your treat hand during training this exercise. Try to only bridge and reward when all four paws are on the ground. Otherwise you might end up training 'beg' instead of 'sit'.

Step 2. Introduce duration: You likely don't want a puppy that just sits for a second and then runs off. So from the beginning, we can teach the puppy there are many incentives to remain in the sit for a little bit longer. We teach duration by giving not just one treat, but sometimes two, three or many more before we say 'Free'. In the beginning, you may need to give these treats in quick succession while your puppy is still focused and sitting, but you can gradually start to space these treats out by a few seconds. Before you know it you'll have a puppy that's sitting for longer and longer.

Step 3. Eye contact: A hugely beneficial feature of the sit behaviour is to teach your puppy to sit *and* look up at you. This can be accomplished by the way that you hold your treats and how you move your treat hand. Once you successfully lure your puppy into the sit position and giving two or three treats, change to holding all three treats in your hand from the beginning. As you give one to your puppy, bring your hand back up towards your face (we want a straight line between your eyes, the treat and the puppy's eyes; this will help shape the eye contact). Your puppy will be following your 'treat hand' with her eyes and pretty quickly will be looking straight up at you. You can even use the moment she is looking up at your face to mark with 'Good' and bring your hand back down to her mouth to deliver the treat.

WHY IS EYE CONTACT BETWEEN YOU AND YOUR DOG A GOOD THING?

While intently staring at a stranger is usually a sign of an agitated dog, when a dog looks into the eyes of her owners it leads to a myriad of brilliant things.

Eye contact will:

- boost oxytocin levels in your dog and even more in you
- create and reaffirm your bond with your dog
- help your dog 'reset' if she is struggling with training
- boost your dog's confidence in herself and her ability to communicate with you.

Step 4. Introduce the 'sit' cue: When your puppy can consistently sit every time you lure her to, it's time to incorporate the word 'sit'. Before now this word wouldn't have actually meant anything to your puppy, so it's best to wait until she can be lured into the right position easily before introducing it. It's important to *first* say 'Sit' and *then* offer the luring action. After a few repetitions you should be able to say 'Sit' and she will anticipate what's next and no longer need your hand movement. Don't forget to say 'Good', reward with some treats and say 'Free' at the end.

Step 5. Increase distraction: By this point, hopefully you can now say 'Sit' and your dog will sit and wait for your 'Good' and reward. They will remain in the sit while you give them a few treats and wait for that important word 'Free' to tell them they can get up and move around again. Now you're ready to start asking for the 'sit' behaviour in different locations at different times.

Drop

'Drop' (or 'down', as it's also called) is one of those behaviours that doesn't immediately appear useful (and it can be tricky to master), but it's a nice follow-on from 'sit' and a lovely calming position for a dog to learn. It also sets up the dog for more important and complex behaviours to come. The skills your pup learns during the 'drop' exercise will help her become better at following hand signals and generalise the concept of being still and calm. We often take one of our dogs to puppy school with us and ask them to 'drop' or lie on their side, allowing all the puppies in the class to experience the presence of a calm and confident adult dog.

Breed-specific training note: If you own a Dachshund, and you manage to teach her 'drop', you're a brilliant trainer! In all our years teaching puppy school, we've successfully managed to get only a handful of Dachshund puppies into the 'drop' position on cue (they are already so close to the ground that the luring process in a high distraction environment is incredibly difficult). So if you are struggling, don't worry – move on to 'Come' and revisit this behaviour later.

Exercise: teach your puppy the 'drop' cue

Step 1. Lure into 'sit', then the 'drop' position. We say *lure* rather than *ask* your puppy to sit, to prevent your puppy from confusing the two behaviours. If you ask your puppy to sit, give her a treat before attempting to teach her 'drop'. Otherwise your puppy will begin to drop every time you say sit. Present the treat to your puppy's nose (while she is still in a sit) and ever so slightly meet her pressure on your hand (i.e. don't allow her to push your hand forward) and lure the treat down the front of her body, close to her chest and to the floor. Very slowly experiment with moving your hand slightly forward or slightly back towards her. She should reshuffle and fall into the drop position for a better opportunity at trying to get the treat from your hand. The second her belly and elbows hit the ground, say 'Good', pump her full of treats and then say the release cue (once again, before she leaves the position). Repeat a couple of times until your puppy starts to understand and drop with a little more intent.

Cheat note: Practising this exercise on tiles or floorboards that are slippery can naturally help a puppy slide into position when you start lowering your hand.

Step 2. Introduce duration: Similar to the way we gain duration with sit, once you've bridged the puppy for being in the drop position, offer her a few more treats for holding this position before saying 'Free'. Repeat this step a handful of times, attempting to vary the length of time she holds the position by drawing out the time offered between each treat.

Step 3. Introduce the 'drop' cue: Lure your puppy into the sit position and bring the treat up towards your face to gain her eye contact. Say 'Drop' clearly and then lure the puppy down into the 'drop' position again. Bridge, reward and release. Repeat this step a handful of times.

Step 4. Removing the lure: Once your puppy can successfully be lured into the 'drop' position and hold it for a couple of seconds, we want to fade out the lure. This time, put the treats in your other hand so your 'luring' hand is now free, *but* still hold your hand the same way you did when there was a treat in your hand. We are going to trick your puppy into thinking it's there. Once she is in the drop position, open your hand up and allow the puppy to see there is nothing there. At the same time, say 'Good' and bring in the other hand with the treat. If your puppy is successful with this, slowly start to open your luring hand up with each new repetition.

Come When Called

A bomb-proof recall (the ability to come when called) has the capacity to save your dog's life one day *or* the life of another animal. There have been several occasions where our dogs have been prevented from serious injury because of their recall. But it's the most common behaviour that breaks down during adolescence. You need to teach your puppy from day dot that *every time she hears that word* it's as exciting as *Christmas* and *Disneyland*. Otherwise, when she gains her independence and becomes more confident with the world, she will weigh up what's more fun: coming back to you or . . .

- the muddy puddle?
- the rabbit across the road?
- the dogs at the park?

Achieving a bomb-proof recall takes time, patience and loads of little and successful step-by-step exercises over a period of time (usually months), but it is absolutely worth it. Once you've achieved it you'll be able to call your dog through a busy dog park where balls are flying, dogs are running, juicy bones are being flung in front of her nose and she will ignore it *all* to get to you!

With this particular behaviour, the more methodical you are in the early stages of this training, the more capable you will be at building a strong emotional response to the word 'Come'. This means your puppy's brain doesn't have a chance to consider whether coming to you is the better option, because her body is already running back to you.

THINGS TO REMEMBER WHILE TRAINING THE RECALL:

- Keep training sessions short and enjoyable.
- Practise each step several times, across various locations.
- Make sure your dog experiences great things every time she arrives back to where you are, and remember to say 'Free' and encourage her back to the fun activity she left.
- Don't say 'Come' if you are angry at your dog or you can't back it up with reinforcement. (Use her name instead as an informal cue to get her attention outside training this exercise.)
- Set each session up for success and ensure your dog makes it to you every time, even if it means you have to go back and lure her with food if she gets momentarily distracted.

Breed-specific training note: Attention, Husky and Beagle owners! Drop everything you are doing and focus all your energy on recall. These breeds are genetically driven to 'press on' and work away from humans – they are the most common breeds we are asked to work on recall with. If they're at puppy school, reinforce puppy school training with ongoing recall training classes at home. Be really consistent with the above points and during their adolescence use a lead or long line to prevent them from practising running off.

Exercise: teach your puppy the 'come' cue

Step 1. Associate the word 'come' with you: Have your puppy on lead and say her name. Then, very clearly and in an upbeat voice, say 'Come', present the treat to your puppy's nose and walk backwards a couple of metres, luring your puppy with the treat in your hand. Once you stop moving, draw the treat slowly upwards to your face to help the puppy into a sit position. Bridge (say 'Good'), reward and then say 'Free'. Repeat a few times.

Why practise such a robotic step first when your puppy is already capable of coming to you when you call her from a distance? The spot where recall breaks down when the dog is older, down the track, is the final 2 metres. Many dogs will respond to the word when they hear it, but once they get close and determine your body language is suggesting you might leave the park or they will be clipped on lead, they will bail before you have time to catch them. This step is helping to formalise the last 2 metres of the exercise. 'Come' means they must race over – *all* the way – and sit in front of you waiting for further instructions.

The lead should remain loose during this exercise. It's there purely as a method of preventing your puppy from running off

Step 2. Building drive: The next few steps require two people. Ask a friend or family member to hold your puppy back while you wave a treat under her nose, tease her and run down the hall or across the loungeroom. Say her name to get her attention and when she is looking in your direction, say 'Come' and throw your hands out to the side in an excitable manner (at this point the helper needs to let go of your dog!). When she gets close, use that treat again to draw her closer and into a sit. Bridge, reward and 'Freeeeeeeee'. The act of teasing – running away with a treat while she is being held back – does huge things towards creating a strong desire to want to come to you. Do this a couple of times and then attempt to call her without teasing and running.

Step 3. Increasing difficulty: Repeat Step 2 in slightly more distracting environments. Don't forget to aim for success. Is your dog interested in the treats you have? Is she full of energy to burn? Have you added a lead or long line to prevent her from wandering off?

Step 4. Increase distraction: Slowly start to work on recalling your puppy away from bigger distractions. This might mean setting up a recall training session when your puppy is in the middle of playing tug with someone. To help the puppy succeed, when you say 'Come', get the person playing with the puppy to become boring and stop engaging in the game. When your puppy arrives back to you, bridge and reward. And the *best* thing you can do at this point is say 'Free' and encourage her back to the person with the toy. Because if your puppy experiences leaving something enjoyable to score a delicious treat from you *and* then gets to go back and resume whatever fun thing they were doing, why wouldn't they respond to that word every time? It's a win-win for them.

Step 5 . . . and onwards: So, what do Steps 5 to 100 look like? Small, successful training sessions, increasing distraction and difficulty from the previous step and setting up formal training sessions to prevent failure from occurring.

Here are a few ideas to try along the way. Call your dog:

- while she is off sniffing something in the backyard
- away from her dinner
- away from a doggie friend in a backyard
- away from a bone
- while she is swimming
- mid-way through chasing a ball in your backyard.

If you are training on your own, use a long line or lead. That way you can prevent your dog from running off, or use the lead for guiding the dog back towards you if she ignores the cue. Setting your dog up for errorless learning is the key.

You'll know you've truly taught the 'come' cue when you can successfully call your dog mid-rumbling play with other dogs at the park, or in the bush surrounded by the temptation of wildlife. These are the ultimate tests!

Stay

'Stay' is a more formal cue you can use to let your dog know she will need to hold a position (like a sit or drop) for longer than usual and possibly in the presence of a distraction (like opening a door). You might be communicating to your puppy: 'I'm going to disappear from sight momentarily, but I will return, so just sit tight!' This being said, it's important to always return to the original position you were in when you cued your dog to stay, in order to 'free' her. Don't fall into the trap of combining 'come' and 'stay' training by asking your dog to 'Stay', walking away and then saying 'Come'.

Exercise: teach your puppy the 'stay' cue

Step 1. Introduce the 'stay' cue: Put the lead in your left hand and the treats also in your left hand. This frees your right hand up to do the open palm hand signal for stay. Ask your puppy to sit. Then say 'Stay', along with an open-palm hand signal (like a stop sign). Say 'Good' and give her a treat followed by the release cue. Repeat a few times.

Step 2. Work on duration: Repeat Step 1, slowly increasing the time between asking your dog to 'stay' and bridging and releasing her from position.

Step 3. Add in a mild distraction: Now that your puppy can hold the position for a couple of seconds before you 'free' her, you want to introduce a very mild distraction. We love to do a little leg shake out to the side. So, keeping the lead and some treats in your left hand, say 'Stay', present the visual cue of the open palm, but before you give her a treat this time, quickly wiggle your leg out to the side, say 'Good', reward her for holding the 'sit' position (by holding the 'sit' position, she is learning the 'stay' concept) and say 'Free'. If she leaves the position while you are doing this, lure her back into the sit position and practise step one a couple more times. Otherwise repeat this step a few times before moving to the next.

Step 4. Start increasing distance: Ask your puppy to 'Stay' and take a quick step back. Then step forward, bridge, reward and 'Free'.

We've found that 'stay' is one of the easiest behaviours to train, but also one of the first to break down, as people try to push their dog's abilities on this too quickly. For 'stay' in particular, it's especially important to focus on increasing difficulty in such small increments that your dog still succeeds every time, rather than 'test' her capabilities too soon and have her fail every third or fourth time.

Spin

We teach our puppies to 'spin' because it's fun and easy to do, but it's also a great little behaviour to get them to clean their feet on the doormat before coming inside.

Exercise: teach your puppy the 'spin' cue

Step 1. Lure the 'spin' motion: Present the treat in front of your puppy's nose and start to move it in a clockwise circle, leading your dog's head around to her right. If she is focused intently on the treat and still following your hand as you lure her head around, you can move in a full circle and lure the whole spin. Once she gets all the way around, you can bridge and reward with the treat in your hand. If she only follows your hand part of the way around, that's okay – it gives you a starting point. In this case, lure her a quarter of the way around and then bridge and reward. Then lure a little more than a quarter, and next time a little more, until she is going halfway around. Once she is halfway around it shouldn't be long before you can lure her a little more than halfway, and once you bridge she will likely turn the rest of the way around to take the shortest route to the treat. Once you have successfully lured her in a complete circle, you can move on to Step 2.

Step 2. Remove the lure. Pretend to place a piece of food in your hand and make the same hand motion as you have been doing to lure your puppy in a circle. Once she completes the spin, bridge and reward with a treat from your treat pouch. Once she has the experience of receiving a treat right away, despite there not actually being a treat in your hand, you've successfully removed the lure.

Step 3. Reduce the cue. Now that your dog understands that it is not essential for the hand to have food in it, you can start to reduce the size of your hand movement and create a formal cue. Say the word 'Spin', then move your hand around in the same motion you have been doing but just about 2 cm higher than you normally would. When your dog spins around, say 'Good' and reward as per usual. Repeat this step five to ten times per training session, aiming to move your hand 2 cm higher each time. This way, the cue will appear similar to your dog, but with each repetition you aim to make the circle incrementally higher and smaller. So you start with your hand at the dog's nose and work up until your hand is at your waist. You should be able to have the dog responding to the word 'spin' and a visual spin of your index finger within three to four training sessions.

Touch

The 'touch' behaviour is when your dog moves towards you and touches her nose to your flat palm when you present your hand out. Your hand is the 'target' she needs to touch with her nose. It's a seemingly simple behaviour that can open up the door to lots of other behaviours – it's a great way to ask your dog to move to different places and different positions. This comes in handy when, for example, you want your dog to step onto the scale at the vet or simply to put her head in a steady position while you do a health check of her eyes and ears. (More on behaviours for health checks later in this chapter.)

In the zoo animal training world this behaviour is called a 'target'. Training this one behaviour revolutionised the way zoo keepers could move, medicate and health check their animals. Instead of forcing the animal into a place or position, you can train a fun game of 'touch the target'. The target might be a ball on the end of a pole, your hand, or anything in between.

It's an easy game to start. Touch the target, get a treat . . . touch the target, get a treat, and again. Once the animal learns that touching the target means a reward it's not a far leap to ask them to *move* to where the target is in order to touch it. Voila! You have a crocodile that will step onto a scale to be weighed, an elephant that will line up next to a fence to be hosed down for a bath and a lion that will hold its position during a hand injection.

How can you utilise the 'touch' exercise to benefit your puppy? You can use it:

- if your puppy needs eye or ear drops
- to closely investigate an injury
- to help with communicating directional cues like 'inside', 'outside', 'in the car', or 'off the couch'
- to improve general obedience and focus.

Exercise: teach your puppy the 'touch' cue

Step 1. Lure the nose to the hand with smell. Have some tasty treats ready (the smelly, wet treats are best). Rub the smell of the treats on the palm of your hand. Close your fist and then bring your hand down next to your dog's head about two inches away, open your palm and say 'Touch'. Most likely your dog will turn her head to sniff or lick your hand. The moment she touches her nose to your hand mark it with 'Good' and give her a treat. Repeat this step four to six times. Once she can consistently touch your hand with her nose when your hand is right next to her head, you can move on to the next step. If for some reason your dog won't make contact with your hand, bridge her when she looks at it or sniffs closer to it. Some dogs are sensitive (meaning they are not overly confident with everything in their environment) and just need a little more time on this step.

Step 2. Introduce head movement needed to touch the hand. Place your hand at least 5 to 10 cm away from her head and say 'Touch'.

Sometimes you might have to wait a moment so she realises that she needs to move her head to touch her nose to your hand. This step will need to be rehearsed two to ten times over a few training sessions before the dog understands it, and some of the more sensitive dogs may need more repetitions.

Step 3. Introduce distance. Now try placing your hand down at least 30 cm away from your dog (at nose level and out in front) and say 'Touch'. If she's worked out the game, she'll have no trouble taking a few steps and touching her nose to your hand.

Step 4. Extend the distance. Start to move your hand away to different distances. Hold your hand a short distance away, and sometimes further away. Hold your hand to the left of your dog and to the right.

Step 5. Ask for the behaviour in new settings. Try out the behaviour outside, inside, at a friend's house and even during a walk.

Shake

The 'shake a paw' behaviour has to be one of the most popular and quintessential 'tricks' that any dog owner should train their dog to do at least once in their lifetime! It can also be a nice ice-breaker behaviour to help your dog feel confident and comfortable in a new setting by asking for something easy that she knows how to do. The 'shake' cue can become a useful cooperative care behaviour down the track, if you think your dog has a splinter in her foot or you need to check her nails.

Side note: Hold off training 'shake' until your puppy is a bit older and has learnt that 'sit' is the preferred behaviour for affection or attention. It's common for puppy owners to train 'shake' early on and then ask us how they can stop their puppy from scratching at them all the time. A behaviour that was initially fun and easy to train can quickly turn into an annoying habit. A way to avoid this is to only give your puppy a reward if you have asked for the behaviour. If she offers it up off-cue, ignore her.

Exercise: teach your puppy the 'shake' cue

Step 1. Capture the 'pawing' at your hand. Hold a nice, tasty, smelly treat in your fist and present the fist to your dog at her chest level. She may at first sniff and nudge your hand with her nose and mouth, but most puppies will then try to paw at your hand to get at the treat. That moment she lifts her paw up and hits your hand, you can bridge and reward by opening up your hand and giving her the treat. Note: you may not always get the paw to hit your hand on the first repetition, so you may need to bridge and reward your dog for even lifting the paw off the ground or introduce your other hand (the one without the treat) down lower to meet the paw and bridge the moment your hand touches the paw. (Don't worry, it's not rocket science and it's not serious, so experiment and have fun with this.)

Step 2. Remove the lure. Pretend to have the treat in your hand and bring your fist out in front of your dog. When she paws at it, bridge with 'Good' and reward with the other hand.

Step 3. Change the cue. Say 'Shake' and have your fist slightly open when you bring your hand down to your dog. When she paws at it, bridge and reward. Open up your hand slightly more each time and reward the pawing behaviour. Eventually, you should be able to offer your open hand for her to 'shake' with her paw.

Step 4. Ask for the behaviour in new settings with new situations. Have your friends and family ask for the shake too.

Roll Over

'Roll over' is a fun party trick, but many dogs quite enjoy it as well, and it's not a bad energy burner when your dog has a bit of extra spring in her step. It's easiest if your dog already knows 'drop'. If you haven't yet trained her in 'drop', consider going back first and then attempting 'roll over'.

Breed-specific training note: Some dogs and even certain breeds can pick this up really quickly and may not need as many steps, while other dogs may find it more difficult. For example, Great Danes may need many slow, careful approximations and it may even be worth considering skipping this behaviour – their long legs and large body don't make it the most practical activity! However, an excited Jack Russell might offer the 'roll over' in the first attempt to lure. It's always important to consider which behaviours might suit your dog's breed the most.

Exercise: teach your dog the 'roll over' cue

Step 1. Lure into a drop on one side. Start with your dog in the 'drop' position. Using the lure technique, hold the treat right in front of your dog's nose and slowly move it towards your dog's left or right shoulder. The idea is to have your dog start to turn her head back towards one shoulder. As she does this she will usually fall onto the other shoulder or kick out her hips to the side and may even turn her whole body to be lying on her side. Bridge that moment with 'Good' and reward. Any of these movements should be considered a success- ful step towards a roll!

Step 2. Lure into a drop on one side with at least two to three paws in the air. Start with your dog in the 'drop' position. Using the lure technique, hold the treat right in front of your dog's nose and slowly move it towards your dog's left or right shoulder (whichever was successful in step 1). This time, instead of stopping at the moment she rolls onto her side, try to bring the lure a little further until at least two to three paws are up in the air. Bridge that moment with 'Good' and reward.

Step 3. Lure into a roll. Start with your dog in the 'drop' position. Using the lure technique, hold the treat right in front of your dog's nose and move it towards your dog's left or right shoulder (again, whichever has been most successful). This time, continue the motion as she rolls onto her shoulder, then her back, and all the way onto her other shoulder. At this stage, for some dogs it may be helpful to lure more quickly as the fast motion of your hand can give them the momentum they need to do the full roll. Bridge the moment she is heading back onto her opposite shoulder with 'Good' and reward.

Once she is consistently doing the full roll when lured, you can move onto the next step.

Step 4. Remove the lure and reduce the cue. Just as in the 'drop' behaviour, it's time to remove the lure (the food in your hand) from the 'roll over' behaviour. If you're not quite sure how to do this, refer back to the 'drop' section. Once she is consistently rolling over with just your hand motion as a cue, you can also start to reduce the size of this hand motion. Initially, your hand will be right in front of her nose and her head will follow it for the whole roll. Start to make this hand motion a few centimetres from her nose and just make a circle with your hand. Next make this hand motion even further from her nose and again just a circle. By reducing this hand motion gradually, you can work your way towards a final cue of just motioning in a circle with one finger, and the dog will roll over. Remember to take these steps slowly. If your dog stops doing the behaviour when cued, you may need to temporarily go back to a closer, more exaggerated cue.

Step 5. Ask for the behaviour in new settings. Try out the roll over in new places with new distractions.

Go to Bed

This is also known as 'go to your mat' or 'go to your place'. It is a very handy behaviour for around the house where you might want your dog inside but not begging for food or racing towards the front door when visitors arrive. This is a very easy behaviour to train provided you keep your goals realistic and your instructions clear. If your dog already understands 'sit', 'drop' and 'stay', you'll breeze through this exercise. The nuts and bolts of it are that the dog must understand that when you say 'Bed' that's where she needs to go and she must stay on the bed until she hears the word 'Free'.

Exercise: teach your dog to go to bed
Step 1. Build a positive association towards the bed. Have the dog bed in a familiar location. Lure your dog onto the bed and give her a few rewards in a sit or a drop position. Insist the dog stays in that

location until you say 'Free'. It may only be a few seconds to begin with. If she breaks position from the bed lure her straight back onto it. Repeat this step a few times over a few training sessions until the dog looks very comfortable and happy with jumping onto the bed to practise sit or drop.

Step 2. Stay on the bed. If your dog already understands the 'stay' or 'sit and free' exercise this should be a breeze – we're going to run through the same steps you did with stay, but with one difference: we don't say 'Stay'. We want it to be implied when the dog is asked to go on the bed that no matter what we do, she has to stay in that area until she hears 'Free'. So lure the dog onto the bed. Usually most dogs will offer up a sit or a drop, but it doesn't matter so long as they are on the bed. Start by doing the leg wiggle as in the 'stay' exercise. Reward your dog for not leaving the bed when you move your leg. Very quickly your dog should realise this is just like the 'stay' exercise. You can then progress to stepping away, and then back towards your dog to bridge and reward. Make sure the dog doesn't leave the bed until you say 'Free'.

Step 3. Introducing a cue. If your dog understands the bed is a fun place for training you can introduce the cue 'Bed' before you lure your dog over. We often say 'Bed' and point towards it, then walk over there – 99.9 per cent of dogs will just follow us to the bed. If your dog needs any help just use your treat as a lure onto the bed. If you reliably repeat this step before each training session, within a few days your dog will certainly run towards the bed when you say the word or point at it.

Step 4. Slowing down rewards. This exercise becomes a terrific management tool around the house, and it is really easy to reduce the frequency of the rewards provided your distractions aren't too high, the bed is comfortable for your dog and you are nearby. We usually put the bed near a couch and put on one of our favourite TV shows. We invite our dogs inside, say 'Bed' and then sit down next to them. We might give them one treat at the beginning of the exercise but usually end up patting them and giving them some physical contact as the reward for staying on their bed. If they break position from the bed we usually pop a lead on them to make sure they don't succeed in roaming far away. By fading away food rewards and making this exercise more associated with affection and quiet time we end up making 'bed' a calmer and more relaxed behaviour. If you think your dog is getting agitated or is over it, say 'Free' and release the dog to an alternative area of the house, but preferably not somewhere like a human bed or a couch – it's pretty hard to make the dog bed a reinforcing place if you allow her immediate access to something even better!

Find the Keys

If reading this whole book doesn't inspire you to train your dog to go find something with her nose, we've failed! A dog who doesn't use her nose to sniff things out is like a bird that doesn't use its wings, and almost all dogs like going on a little hunt. The best part is you can benefit from this behaviour as well. Baby brain is a real thing and when Jen was pregnant with the twins, this handy little trick was called upon more than Jen would want to admit!

On cold, rainy days when motivation to entertain kids and exercise dogs is at an all-time low, you can sit on the couch with your dog and get the kids to hide the keys somewhere in the house. Tell them to come back into the room and say the magic words: *Find the keys*'! Then for the next five to 10 minutes you can take a load off, knowing all dependants are busy being entertained or exerting energy of some kind.

It doesn't have to be a set of keys, it could be any item: wallet, gold coin, a magic rock . . . or even a unique odour such as Vegemite, lemon zest or Lynx Africa deodorant!

Whatever you're teaching your dog to find, make sure it is unlikely to be damaged by your dog and doesn't pose a risk to her. If you have a dog with a history of eating or chewing obscure objects, then perhaps don't get her to find something valuable or ingestible. Odour in a jar is a better option for your pooch.

TRAINING TALES

We did a consult a few years back for a client who was struggling with their 'naughty' little Beagle, Samson. The dog was under-stimulated and possibly 'overqualified' to be *just* the family pet. We began going through appropriate genetic outlets; scent detection being, of course, the number one priority for a Beagle. It came up in conversation that the family's business was a pest eradication company. From that moment onwards, Samson became the new employee, trained up to detect termites! A match made in heaven.

Exercise: teach your dog 'find the keys'

Step 1. Create a positive association with the keys. Start in a room or quiet space with limited distractions. The idea is to reward your dog for any interest in the keys. This could mean just looking at the keys, walking towards the keys or even sniffing the keys. First, place the keys on the ground within about 1 m of your dog and then watch your dog for her first response that is oriented towards the keys. Remember to bridge with 'Good' and reward (instead of rewarding her from your hand you can drop treats closer to the keys to speed things up). After each time you reward her, wait a moment to see if she orients towards the keys again. Initially, she only needs to look at the keys for you to reward her. Once you've rewarded a few times try to wait for a slightly bigger response. For example, if she is only looking at the keys, you might reward this three times, and then on the fourth time, wait a few more seconds to see if she takes a step towards the keys. Keep the session short and fun. Once she is moving towards the keys, sniffing them or getting her nose close to them, you are ready to move onto Step 2.

Note: If your dog doesn't look like she is 'sniffing', don't worry. With enough repetitions of this game, your dog won't be able to help herself – her nose is operating constantly and the association of the smell of your keys will start to become established either way.

Step 2. Introduce the cue 'Find'. Hold your dog by her collar and then drop the keys on the ground at least 2 m away (or you can have a second person place the keys on the ground). Then say 'Find' and release your dog. When she goes to the keys, bridge and reward her nice and close to the keys.

Step 3. Increase distance. Hold your dog by her collar. Have a second person place the keys down 5 to 6 m away. Say 'Find' and release your dog. When she goes to the keys, bridge and reward.

Step 4. Out of sight. Hold your dog just outside the room. Have someone place the keys down in the middle of the room. Say 'Find' and release your dog into the room with the keys. When she goes to the keys, bridge and reward.

Step 5. Hide the keys in an easy location. Hide the keys in a spot that is going to be quickly accessible by your dog and even where they are still visible. For example, try just around the other side of the couch, under a table or one corner of the room. Say 'Find' and release your dog into the room. When she goes to the keys, bridge and reward.

Step 6. Hide the keys in a more difficult location. Try hiding the keys in a basket, behind a flower pot, or behind a pillow on the couch. Try to only make it slightly more challenging so that your dog is expertly sniffing out the keys every time. If she is finding it difficult, go back to Step 5 for a few more sessions.

Step 7. Ask for the behaviour in new settings. Try it out in the backyard, or even at a friend's house.

Cooperative Care for Minor Medical Procedures

In the zoo and aquarium industry, the bulk of animal training conducted revolves around what we call 'cooperative care' or 'husbandry training'. This ranges from simple things such as getting a kangaroo to stand still while we look in her pouch, to much more complex requests such as asking a leopard seal to lie still and present her belly on the side for an ultrasound.

This type of training is essential for animals that are too powerful, flighty or stressed to be restrained and is also life-saving for animals that are high risk for anaesthetic procedures.

The zoo industry has really shaped the way that modern dog training has evolved. Twenty years ago, nobody would have dreamt of training a dog to hold still for X-rays to be taken, present her teeth for cleaning or eyes for inspecting. It didn't seem worth the bother when you could just physically restrain the animal or knock her out. However, we now know that the training isn't really that tricky, and the dog will experience little to no stress, with the added bonus of avoiding a general anaesthetic.

For dog owners, cooperative care comes into play when you need to carry out mild medical procedures such as putting in ear drops, cleaning teeth or trimming nails. Regardless of the procedure, we would advise you to start the same way:

1. Designate a training space where your dog needs to step *onto* something. This can be a table, chair or even just a dog bed – something comfortable and easy for the dog to get on and off. This will be the basis for your dog giving 'consent' to your medical training. If the dog jumps off the training space, do not continue with the medical training. If the dog stays there willingly, she is probably having a good time!

2. Using just your hands, desensitise your dog to the touch of the area you need to treat. We want you to say 'Good' when your hand is touching the specific location and then reward your dog. If your dog likes to wriggle and move, you can throw the treat off the training area to give the dog some freedom with her treat: a double reward! If your dog isn't comfortable with you touching the specific body part you want to work on, then either work on something nearby or on the opposing body side. For example, your dog might have a sore left ear you need to treat, so start by training the concept on the right ear.

3. Expose your dog to the medical equipment by allowing her to look at and sniff it first. Don't try to hide the dropper or the clippers from your dog's line of sight; make it a positive item.

Show it to her and if she looks at it or sniffs it, say 'Good' and reward. If you have used something before and your dog knows what it is (and hates it), consider changing it for a period of time. You may be able to transfer liquids into new syringes or even wrap them in something different so your dog doesn't have an immediate negative association.

4. Once your dog is comfortable with the equipment, pretend to examine or treat a part of her body that you know she is comfortable with, such as her chest. Pretend to give it drops, or clip or brush it! We know this shouldn't be a big deal, but treat it like it is! Reward your dog heavily. Try to say 'Good' while your dog is still and looking confident. Remember if the dog leaves the training station, that is her way of saying 'I am not comfortable'. If you want this to be a long-lasting behaviour you need the dog to be comfortable, so don't try to restrain her or nag her to come back. You'll just be taking money out of the bank.

5. If your dog is happy with the above steps and you can handle the body part of concern easily with your hands, then it's time to give the treatment a crack. Keep it short, keep it easy and make your dog feel very special.

This process can take anywhere from a single two-minute training session to a few weeks or even a month if the dog is in any pain. If you suspect the dog is in significant pain or discomfort, please consult with your vet throughout the process. For some procedures, a general anaesthetic may be a more ethical way of dealing with the situation if it will take too long to train the dog to cooperate. But don't underestimate what your dog is capable of, particularly if you enjoy training her.

Continuing the Training Journey

The behaviours we've covered in this chapter are really just the tip of the iceberg. The training possibilities for your dog are truly endless. Any animal can be trained to do any behaviour that they are physically capable of doing, so long as the motivation is there and the communication is clear.

Here's some inspiration for other behaviours. Unfortunately, we don't have space in this book to cover them all, but you could look them up online:

- play dead
- weave between your legs
- shame (put paws over eyes)
- hold something in their mouth
- speak (bark on cue)
- crawl
- chin rest.

How many can you tick off before your dog turns 2 years old?

If you yourself learn the fundamentals of training and enjoy it, and your dog learns how to learn from an early age, you'll have the time of your life bonding and training together for the next decade. It'll not only be key in raising a well-trained dog, but it also becomes a fantastic alternative to exercising her on stormy days, or on days when you are busy and only have a spare 10 minutes. And it will keep her brain sharp until she's old and grey.

Chapter 10

Walking on Lead

There is nothing more pleasant than going for a walk with your dog and allowing him to peruse the diversity of smells along the nature strip, off lead, at his own pace while you enjoy the walk too. Seems innocent enough, right?

In fact, this seemingly harmless act is one of the biggest gripes within the dog-owning community – and these days we have a much greater understanding of why.

In a nutshell, here are a few reasons why we believe it's worth the effort and investment to train your dog to walk well on lead:

1. It's the law – in most countries, unless an area is signposted as an off-lead area, your dog needs to be on lead. Depending on where you are and what your dog does while off lead you can be fined several thousand dollars.
2. You will reduce anxiety in the stranger you cross paths with who is nervously walking their reactive dog on lead.
3. You will reduce the frustration from the stranger you pass who is trying their darndest to train their own dog to walk well on lead. A dog is more likely to react to an off-lead dog than an on-lead dog.
4. Somewhere in your neighbourhood, there may be someone who suffers terribly from cynophobia (fear of dogs) and struggles to leave the house some days for fear of encountering an off-lead dog. You will allow them the freedom to walk to the corner shop or the bus stop without having their phobia triggered.

5. You will be putting your dog's safety first. He may be well-trained 99 per cent of the time, but just like us, dogs have off days. One day, something out of the ordinary will tempt him to break away from his normal obedience. 'Come' won't save his life like a lead will.

Without a doubt, pet dog trainers around the world make more money out of teaching dogs to walk nicely on lead than any other dog-related problem. For some people and some dogs, it is a complicated process.

If you've skipped forward to this chapter because it's the most relevant to you, there is some other content you need to digest first. In order to make walking on lead successful, here's what your dog should already be able to do and understand.

- Your dog should be confident and appropriately socialised to the environments you wish to walk your dog in (see Chapter 6).
- Your dog must understand a bridge/marker (see Chapter 9).
- Your dog must be food-motivated (see Chapter 5).
- Your dog should be comfortable with the cafe dog/tie-up exercise (see Chapter 7).
- Your dog should also have alternate forms of exercise beyond walks (see Chapter 11).

If your dog is reactive or aggressive while on lead, see the additional content in Chapter 12 that you can integrate into your loose lead walking practice.

As always, genetics matter! More confident and athletic dogs will always want to walk in front of their owner, while smaller and more subdued breeds will be happier to stay by your side. Cattle Dogs and Sheepdogs may be triggered into herding mode at the sight of traffic, and scent hounds and Spaniels will start intensely tracking as soon as they smell any evidence of animals on the ground.

It is important to be realistic about how long it should take to teach your dog how to walk well on lead reliably. Most dogs can learn the basic skills in one day in a low-distraction environment, but that doesn't mean they can do it everywhere instantly!

Choosing the place to practise is key, too. If you've just rescued a dog and moved him to a busy city, but before this he's been chained up in a country yard his whole life, you must be considerate and thoughtful about where you practise your on-lead walking. Trying to learn new skills in a high-distraction environment will usually cause confusion and anxiety in your dog.

In this chapter we will do our best to answer every common question and run you through the best training techniques to set you and your dog up for success. There may need to be some flexibility in your training and plans, and at some stage you might want to go to a dog club, class or have a private lesson. But if you follow the steps in this chapter, you will absolutely be on the road to success.

Note: The training drills in this chapter are aimed at dogs older than 16 weeks of age. For dogs under 16 weeks, you should prioritise confidence building and freedom to explore before on-lead obedience. You can absolutely start some of these exercises with your puppy, but don't prioritise them above things like independence, confidence building and play.

1. Equipment Check

We suggest you get everything on this list and have it ready for every training session.

A) **A well-fitted collar or harness.** The most important thing is that the dog cannot escape from the walking equipment. It needs to be snug: you shouldn't be able to slip your dog's ear or leg out of the device without unclipping it first.

Be mindful that the broader the surface area of the connection device is on the dog, the easier it is for him to pull. So, if your dog is already leaning down low and dragging you down the street, a broad, soft harness that attaches at the rear isn't going to help your cause! Just do a quick google on the kind of devices sled dogs use to make pulling easier for them so you know what *not* to use.

What about 'no pull harnesses' and other 'no pull' devices? From our experience, don't expect them to work without actively teaching your dog where you want him to be.

There are literally hundreds of different pieces of equipment out there and some are better than others. We have seen a simple change of equipment be the defining moment for an owner being able to comfortably walk their dog, as it gives the owner the physical ability and confidence to walk him even if he suddenly pulls or becomes reactive.

Regardless of the piece of equipment attached to your dog, the only thing we never want to see is constant physical pressure on the dog throughout the walk. If your dog is connected to any kind of no-pull device or collar *but* still pulls for most of the walk, chances are the device is going to result in some kind of physical damage to the dog.

If you are not sure what kind of equipment to use on your specific dog, consult with a trainer.

B) **A lead or leash.** In some countries or in other dog-training circles, one may be considered more correct than the other, or one may be more strongly associated with training while the other is associated with restraint, but for the average pet owner, this shouldn't matter. We usually say 'lead'.

We generally suggest you get a lead that is strong, robust and suitable for your dog. We've seen plenty of lead clips snap over the years! For loose lead walking, the ideal lead length is between 1.2 and 2 m long. The idea is that when the dog is walking in the 'sweet spot' nicely by your side, the lead should be the shape of a 'J' without touching the ground. So, your height, the dog's height and how close to you the dog naturally wants to walk may all slightly affect this.

A 6 ft 8 inch person walking a Beagle may opt for a 2 m lead, whereas a 5 ft tall person walking a Great Dane may find a 1.2 m lead more than enough!

HOW DOES YOUR DOG REACT TO THE LEAD?

For many dogs the stimulus of the lead is associated with either extreme excitement or perhaps fear and anxiety. If this is the case you *must* work on the tie-up exercise described in Chapter 7. You need to neutralise the stimulus of the lead for your dog.

If the sight of the lead creates an overly emotional response from your dog, he needs to spend more time on lead doing absolutely nothing. You could tie your dog up to your table while you eat dinner, put your dog on lead while you watch a movie, put the lead on and just pat your dog. Just make it more 'neutral'.

C) **Treat pouch and treats.** If you want to achieve great on-lead walking, you need to take treats with you on the walk. All our dogs (minus the puppies) walk very well on lead and we legitimately don't 'need' treats on the walk, but we still take them. Whenever another dog rushes at a fence and barks at us, or lunges on their lead to have a go at our dogs, we praise our dogs and give them a treat. This does a few things very quickly. It reinforces our dogs for not reacting, but it also makes them very happy, which usually helps the other dog who is unhappy. A barking, lunging dog is generally helped, not hindered, by having the dog it is focused on completely ignore it and continue walking with happy, loose body language.

We were so consistent with this with Ari, Finn and Hugo (who we used as 'helper dogs' for aggressive and fearful dog consultations) that whenever a dog barked at them, their tail would activate into a nice happy wag and their emotions would immediately soften as they knew a bit of praise and treat was on the way.

High-value treats are usually best while training. You can test out what your dog likes, but we usually suggest you use treats that are delicious, soft, and easy to eat while still walking. This will make your process seamless; you don't want to use something too big or crunchy that will result in your dog needing to stop and eat.

D) **Other essential items.** You'll need poo bags, a water bottle, sturdy footwear (not thongs or flip flops so you are less likely to fall if your dog pulls). Possibly a spare lead or slip lead if you live in an area where you constantly find stray, lost or out-of-control dogs.

2. Where to Practise and Train

Look at the location you want to practise walking and think, could my dog relax in this place? If the answer is a firm no, then don't try teaching your dog new skills there. This is especially crucial for dogs who are out of control, fearful or triggered into aggression or chaotic behaviour based upon things that are in their environment.

We often use the analogy of a human learning to swim. You don't throw them off the side of a boat in huge swell and say, 'Righto mate, we're going to work on freestyle!' You start in a shallow pool where the person can touch the bottom and get used to the sensation of being in water before working your way up incrementally.

For some of you, the place to start your training may be your living room, backyard, driveway, garage, a quiet park, an industrial area on the weekends or a shopping centre carpark at night.

If your goal is to walk your dog through a busy city but right now you struggle to walk around your yard, then you've got to gradually work your way through a variety of different environments and build up to the city walk. But the idea is, you need a quiet, reliable place for you and your dog to master your skills before you go to new locations.

Finding the Right Position

If you are happy with how your dog responds to the lead and you have your training space and equipment sorted, then it's time to consider how you want your dog to walk. If he regularly goes crazy when the lead goes on but you still want to train him, just allow a few minutes for your dog to visibly calm down a bit on lead before you start.

Loose lead walking should be sustainable and relaxing for you and your dog, so when you start training the dog on what position you want him to be in, make sure it's realistic. Unless you're training for an obedience trial, aim for a slightly more relaxed position when just walking.

Our basic criteria or position for a walk are:

- The dog is on your left (99.9 per cent of dog trainers teach clients to walk their dog on the left and pass other dogs on the left, which is a polite and easy way for fearful or aggressive dogs to know they will be at a safer distance when they cross paths with other dogs).
- His front feet are approximately parallel to your feet.
- The dog is facing forward.
- He is close enough to take a treat from you easily.
- He is not crowding you, tripping you over or jumping on you for treats.
- There is *no tension* on the lead.

If the dog is doing all the above, we call this walking in the 'sweet spot'.

The sweet spot

In order to achieve this, you need to think about how you hold the lead, and which hand will be delivering the treats (and therefore where the treat pouch should be sitting).

For very strong dogs prone to pulling we generally hold the loop of the lead in our right hand as the 'anchor' and then use our left hand in a bicycle grip over the other half of the lead to guide our dog. As the left hand is doing the most work, in this circumstance we would suggest that you put the treat pouch on your right hip and reward the dog with your right hand.

If you are confident holding onto the lead with one hand, you may prefer to hold the lead across your body with your right hand, have the treat pouch on your left hip and reward the dog with your left hand.

However you decide to position your pouch or hold your lead, the aim of the game is the same: you want to be able to 'bridge' (say 'Good') and reward your dog easily when he is in the sweet spot.

It's important that if your dog goes to pull, he doesn't have a long length of lead available before he feels the tension. Some dogs can build up a lot of momentum with too much freedom and when they hit the end of the lead, this can be hard on their bodies and yours. We still want you to provide your dog with enough lead to feel free when he is in the sweet spot, but not so much lead that he can get a big run-up.

1. Putting your dog in the sweet spot

For your first real training session on loose lead walking, you should be in your ideal training space with all of your equipment and your dog nice and motivated for some treats (i.e. a bit hungry – don't try to start training straight after a meal).

The most basic way you can start training the 'sweet spot' position is having the dog on lead and standing with a wall, fence or other barrier to your left with, enough room for our dog to fit between you and the wall. Then follow the steps below. For all these steps, the idea is that you don't move your feet at all: the dog is learning to find the position.

1. Ask your dog to sit in front of you, say 'Good' and reward.
2. Lure him (with another treat) from the sit in front of you over to your left-hand side. For this initial exercise, you may find it easiest to lure with your left hand. He needs to move just far enough past you that he can do a 180° turn so he ends up facing forward (the same way you're facing). As soon as he is beside you and facing forward, say 'Good' and reward as

many times as you can in that position. At this stage, we don't mind if the dog is sitting or standing – if he is by your side, keep pumping the treats into him.

3. When you think he's had enough treats or might be about to lose interest, say 'Free' and release your dog.

4. Have a cuddle/pat and a moment to chill.

Vertical view of luring into the sweet spot

Some people may find this whole process much easier if they are able to move forward immediately, with the dog on their left between them and the wall. If you feel like the above is clunky or you just can't seem to get the dog in the sweet spot without moving forward, then experiment with getting the dog into the sweet spot while moving forward and perhaps revisit the stationary exercise later.

2. Move it!

Now you have a basic idea of where you want your dog and how to help him into position. Even if it looks pretty messy to begin with, the best thing you can do is start *moving forward* while keeping the dog in the sweet spot.

Utilise your wall/barrier to help you move in a straight line (which makes it easier for the dog) and to reduce the number of distractions. Try to do short repetitions of 2 to 10 m in a straight line against the wall.

All we want you to focus on is teaching the dog that if he's in the sweet spot while you're moving forward, you will say 'Good' and pump treats into him. When you hit the end of the wall say 'Free', play with your dog and, in the most seamless way possible, try to move back to the beginning without worrying about your dog's position too much.

If your dog regularly pulls ahead or lags behind, try increasing the frequency of rewards when he is in the sweet spot. For example, lure him into the right position. As soon as you start moving he should be in the exact right position as you take your first step, so start rewarding right away, keeping the rewards frequent to start with.

If your training space is a large square room, then you are in luck! You can just keep working your way around the space.

As soon as you start to have success and you feel like you and your dog are getting in sync with each other, you're ready to add in a cue/command for walk. We suggest people say 'Walk' or 'Heel'.

You say 'Walk' or 'Heel' as you step off for that first step. This will be the basis for any commencement of exercise until you either stop or say 'Free'. Each time you restart the walk, say 'Walk' or 'Heel'. Eventually, your dog will get that when he hears that word, he must be on your left, following your movements, until he hears the word 'Free'.

How Many Repetitions Should You Do – and How Much Practice is Enough?

For most training activities, you want to keep repetitions relatively low and sessions very short too. However, this may change depending on how your dog walks.

You'll be able to use your intuition to guide you, but below is the spectrum of how many repetitions and how much time you should put into training your dog each day.

At the lower end of the spectrum, say you have a dog younger than 6 months who is relatively sensitive. We'd recommend one to three repetitions of loose lead walking per day for two to 10 minutes each time. That's it. You want it to be short, sweet and leave the dog wanting more. Never walk a young or sensitive dog for too long.

If you have a dog older than 18 months who is boisterous, in your face, pulls a lot and seems to have boundless energy, do more! The number of repetitions should still be only one to three per day but the length of sessions should be between five and 30 minutes depending on your level of success. The greater success your dog starts to show, the longer your sessions can be. Putting in more effort and doing more drills may even make the process a little bit boring for your dog, which will help settle him down.

If you're managing your dog's diet well, providing other outlets and exercise and walking him in suitable (not overly stimulating environments), you should see a steady improvement over three to four weeks. If you've been practising in the right locations and your dog is food-motivated, that's all it should take to see a *huge* change. If you're not seeing change in the way your dog walks, you need to engage with a dog trainer or perhaps with a vet to make sure the dog is physically fine.

Turning Right

Turning right is a fundamental skill every dog needs to learn. We also find that right-hand turns are the easiest way to start training a nice loose lead walk pattern with a confident dog who pulls a lot. As soon as our client and their dog have a basic understanding of moving forward together, we usually start on right-hand turns – which might even be on our very first session.

How does it look?

Start with about-face turns

First of all, walk in a straight line with the dog in the sweet spot. As soon as the dog gets slightly out in front of you, or he has walked successfully for around 5 m, we want your feet to perform a smooth 180-degree right-hand turn. Think 'turning on a dime' as opposed to a big, sweeping turn.

Inevitably, the dog will end up behind you. Some may even hit the end of the lead if they aren't paying attention. Then, when he realises he is out of position, you have an opportunity to call his name. Have a treat waiting for him in the sweet spot and continue walking in the opposite direction to where you started the exercise.

As you would with straight-line walking, you should always be looking for opportunities to say 'Good' and reward the dog throughout the session when he is in the sweet spot.

You then have a choice to repeat the process again a few more times (without getting dizzy) or to release the dog with the 'Free' command.

Most dogs start to get the idea of this game after half a dozen turns, especially if you have them in a low-distraction environment.

If he isn't getting it, or you are getting frustrated, always go back a step in the training process. In this case, that may be a matter of working on straight lines against the wall. You can also mix up loose lead walking with some play, basic obedience or trick training. If you're hating it, the dog is too, so please make it fun and successful for both of you.

If you start to see the penny drop on the 180-degree turns, then you can work on 90-degree turns, using the same method of turning. Try to be quite specific and sharp in the turns you make so it is predictable for the dog.

Whether your dog is young and bold, or is old and has never been trained, you *should* be able to master this in one location in a week if you're doing enough repetitions and keeping him motivated.

Responding to Pressure

The idea of this exercise is to teach your dog to feel the difference between a tight lead (pressure) and a loose lead. Once he's learnt that rewards are given when the lead is loose, he can learn to respond to a tight lead (the pressure) by readjusting his own position and making the lead loose again. This concept works quite well in conjunction with your right-hand turn training. If on the about-face turns the dog hits the end of the lead, he might already be experiencing this concept, but for some of our more sensitive dogs, we may need to teach this skill separately.

This is an easy concept that you don't need to over-analyse, but you do need to be gentle and be ready to say 'Good' very precisely, when your dog responds to the pressure.

Regardless of what kind of equipment you are using, we want this to be gentle: no sharp lead 'pops' or cracks. No lifting the dog off the ground, no upward or excessive pressure. We definitely don't want to see signs of choking. Whenever we do this exercise, regardless of the dog breed or size, we aim to do it with *two fingers*.

How does it look?

Stand still with your dog on lead near you. Don't worry about what position he is in. When the dog is relaxed or, ideally, even looking off to the side or away from you, apply some gentle pressure to the lead until the line of the lead is straight and directed towards your hip (or at least the centre of your body). Once the lead is straight, do not apply any more force.

Watch the lead. As soon as it is no longer straight (i.e. the dog has moved towards you) say 'Good' and present the reward at your left leg, at the dog's nose height.

What we want to teach is a virtually automatic response that as soon as the dog feels pressure on the lead, it's not necessarily a bad thing: it's a signal for a potential reward, *if* he responds to the pressure.

This is a bit of a boring exercise from the dog's perspective, to be honest, so mix it up with some other obedience or trick training! You may choose to spend an entire two-minute session on responding to pressure followed by some 'sit', 'drop' and 'shake'. We wouldn't do more than one session per day of this exercise, and we expect that if you are combining it with other nice loose lead walking sessions you'll see the dog respond very well to the pressure. Your dog will potentially anticipate any pressure happily within a week of starting this step and be more in sync with you and the lead.

Turning Left

Unless you are very coordinated or have done a bit of pressure response training, this is commonly a tricky step.

The biomechanics of turning left with a dog on your left-hand side mean you could end up tripping over your dog or stepping on his toes if you turn too sharply, particularly if he is just learning. So unlike the right-hand turn, we need to start with 90-degree turns and can allow a bit of an arc in our turn.

In competition obedience, about-face left-hand turns are an opportunity for a very well-trained dog to show off. To achieve this turn, the dog simultaneously jumps his front feet left, and rear legs right, to match his handler. That is what it takes to do an immediate left-hand turn! So go easy on your new dog when working on this one.

How does it look?

Walk in a straight but smooth line in the middle of your training area. When your dog is in the sweet spot (and not out in front), look for a moment to do a nice, smooth, *single step* diagonally to the left. There are two exercises you can try.

Treat exercise

If you can manage it, hold a treat in your left hand. As you start the step, move the treat out and away from your body to lure the dog away. As you complete the 90-degree turn say 'Good', reward the dog and continue forward. If this feels even slightly successful, give it a few more goes in quick succession.

However, for many of you this may feel awkward or you may not be able to coordinate the treat in your left hand with the turn. If this is the case you can utilise the pressure exercise.

Pressure exercise

Put a slight amount of back pressure on the lead as you take the left step. If your dog has some understanding of responding to lead pressure, this will give him a moment to at least slow down or respond to the pressure enough so he doesn't get stepped on.

Don't overdo this exercise if you're struggling or stepping on toes. Please be careful. We've seen a couple of dogs regress significantly in their loose lead walking training if their owners step on their feet during the left-turn practice.

Figure 8s, Stops, Pace Variation and Putting it Together in Your Safe Training Space

The above work may take you a couple of weeks, depending on how motivated your dog is and his experience with training. But within three weeks you should start to introduce all of the exercises together and test your new skills.

Some variation exercises we like working on around this stage are: figure 8s (i.e. smooth left-hand and right-hand turns), 'stop' and 'sit' with the dog in the sweet spot (good to practise for crossing roads) and varying our pace (fast, slow and normal walking).

If your training is going well and you and your dog are enjoying it, this should be the point where it becomes really fun. When we instruct obedience and loose lead walking classes this is where we start to give our clients challenges, or run them through mock obedience trials. You can ask a friend or family member to do this for you and your dog. It will prepare you for the challenges of the real world. An exercise may look like this, with anywhere from one- to 10-second gaps in between new cues:

1. Are you ready? (*Use this as a cue to begin.*)
2. Go forward
3. Left 90-degree turn
4. Slow down
5. About-face right turn
6. Go fast
7. Stop and sit
8. Figure 8
9. 'Free' your dog.

When to Reduce the Treats

Without doubt, the place most people fail is when they start reducing treats. We recommend that when an exercise looks sharp 90 per cent of the time, you can start slowing down the treats. But if it still looks sloppy, your rate of rewards needs to be fast enough to keep the dog engaged.

It's common for an owner to become predictable with the number and frequency of treats given. This results in a dog who thinks, 'Treats only come every 10 seconds or so regardless of my behaviour, so I'll pull, then slow down for a treat, then pull and slow down for a treat.'

What needs to be done here is more work on variable reward placement. Keep the dog guessing at how many treats you're going to give him and when they might arrive. You might say 'Good' and treat three times in two seconds, or you may make the dog loose lead walk for an entire minute before you say 'Good' and reward once. The idea is the dog needs to understand and enjoy the exercise, but the rate at which the treats come is highly variable.

If you've done your homework, your dog enjoys loose lead walking, understands how to respond to pressure, and you've got appropriate equipment, then fading away treats is easy. Just don't be in a hurry to do it. If things are beautiful 90 per cent of the time, slow down the treats, then if they stay beautiful, slow them down even more. But when you take the exercises to new environments, you should anticipate needing to boost the treat level up again to ensure success.

Walking in Distracting Environments

Once you've really nailed loose lead walking in quiet, familiar spots, you can try taking the skill to places that are likely to test your dog's focus. This *must* be done sensibly and gradually, however. Don't practise in your loungeroom and an empty football oval for three weeks and then transition straight to a busy beach promenade!

We cannot stress this enough: if you're following our advice for training your dog to walk loose on lead but having low success, you are probably in an unsuitable environment. Some dogs start loose lead walking well as young pups, and then at 10 months will suddenly start lunging at every dog and every dropped bit of food in sight. In particular, an adolescent dog's ability to cope with distracting environments will change based upon his maturity.

Take your time, master your skills in low-distraction environments, ensure your dog has a solid sit, understands left and right turns with ease and *then* start testing yourself out. If you find that there are specific triggers your dog cannot deal with you may want to read our segment on lead reactivity in Chapter 12 and consider engaging a professional trainer to help you with these distractions.

Pulling

Pulling can happen unexpectedly and there may be many things that are out of your control, but your goal is to make sure that when your dog pulls, he does not deem the pulling as successful.

For example: your 8-month-old male Labrador is walking well and taking treats nicely until he spots a Beagle. He loses interest in the treats and pulls towards the other dog. The other owner says, 'Isn't he adorable? My Beagle is friendly, if they want to have a little play?'

This is a crossroad in your training.
You have two choices:

1. Well, he does like dogs, and he didn't pull too hard; it would be nice if he had a little play – 'Yes please, he would love to play with your Beagle!'

or

2. My training was going well up until this point. Perhaps I shouldn't allow him to play with the distraction (the Beagle) that has ruined our nice work – 'No thanks, he is learning to walk on a loose lead.'

If you're following this book, hopefully you'll know option 2 is the only option.

So how do you deal with the pulling when it happens? If your dog pulls out in front, you can either stop or change direction. If your dog pulls off to the side or behind you, give him a bit of encouragement and keep moving forward, with the goal of rewarding your dog when he is back in the sweet spot. In teaching your dog, you need to consistently reinforce that pulling will not result in him getting what he wants.

You may have succumbed to option 1 before, but be strong and say no. It's the best thing you can do for your dog.

Sniffing and Peeing on Walks

Dogs will generally like to sniff and pee on dry, absorbent surfaces and on corners or intersections of trails and streets. If you watch your dog on walks, you should be able to predict the kind of locations he likes to sniff. Then, if this is possible, anticipate these locations. When the dog is walking well on lead, we encourage you to say 'Free' and allow your dog some time to pee or sniff in that area, provided it is safe to do so. We usually say 'Free' and then gesture with our hands towards the beautiful corner tree or surface we know the dogs will enjoy checking out.

When we give our dogs specific times and locations to sniff and pee, we generally want them to just walk by our side and keep our pace for the rest of the journey. Having said that, we aren't complete drill sergeants. We allow a bit of flexibility throughout the walks, with some rules. These are:

- They may sniff so long as the lead is loose.
- They may stop to sniff so long as they respond if they feel tension on the lead or hear the 'Walk' command. (Note: Young Spaniels or Beagles may not be capable of doing the above without pulling, so we generally encourage them to keep their heads up while walking – via treats and walking them in an appropriate location – and make sure they get plenty of allocated sniffing time and exercises.)
- They can mark or pee on the walk so long as the lead is loose.
- If they attempt to mark or pee on a walk while we're still moving, then they need to turn off the tap and keep up with our pace. If need be, we put pressure on the lead. Peeing may not be allowed or appropriate in this location and we will then look for another suitable spot to stop and let them go.

Walking Multiple Dogs on Lead

Don't try to teach two or more dogs at once how to walk on lead. We almost always teach each dog how to do it on his own and then when he has mastered it, we add in another dog and expect that things may go backwards a little at the start. The competition seems to cause them to pull out in front a little more, so we generally revert to quiet locations for the first few times walking together.

If we have a shy or perhaps a little bit of a reactive dog we may walk him with a mature and relaxed adult dog who can give him some confidence and ideas about how fun and relaxing walking can be. The adult dog must be very stable, though. If you find this successful, use it as a stepping stone, not the end goal. You don't want your dog to rely on a canine companion to enjoy a walk.

Regression and Setbacks

Everyone experiences setbacks, particularly if the dog is young, aggressive, fearful or reactive. It's important not to be disappointed or angry with your dog. He doesn't know pulling or lunging on lead upsets you. He is probably really struggling emotionally with the situation. What he needs is for you to take a few steps back in the training process and make your walks more predictable – and fun – and include better rewards so he becomes consistently successful.

If your dog experiences a huge fright, gets into a fight with another dog or somehow responds with aggression, be mindful that these experiences are likely to create a spike in cortisol levels for around 48 hours, possibly more. We usually suggest, after a big setback, *not* to get back on the horse straight away. Instead, let your dog's cortisol levels settle down for a couple of days and do some low arousal exercises like scent-based games, training around the house or walks in very low-distraction environments.

For most dogs, walking on lead is a skill set that is essential to living in any kind of urban environment. Even for dogs who live in rural areas and rarely go for on-lead walks, this skill is still important for vet visits or going on holidays. Alongside a good recall, having a dog who walks politely by your side is one of the most rewarding behaviours you can train. When you achieve it, you should be very proud of yourself and your dog – it is a very significant milestone! Remember, if you get stuck, at some stage in the process you can always reach out to a dog trainer. Even if you only establish some of the content in this chapter, you'll be well and truly on the road to success.

Chapter 11

Exercise, Play and Outlets

Every dog's happiness is greatly affected by how many physical activities she is involved in each day. There is an old saying: 'A tired dog is a good dog'. Now, of course, the concept of being overtired and grumpy does exist in dogs too, but generally speaking, a dog who is appropriately mentally and physically stimulated is a much easier dog to live with. Remember that upper layer of the pyramid in Chapter 2? Ensuring your dog has enough outlets is the final puzzle piece for a happy dog.

Exercise is Not Just 'Walkies!'

We find the average dog owner (particularly those with poorly-behaved dogs) only offers their dog two ways to burn off steam: on-lead walks and trips to the dog park. But that is just the tip of the iceberg! There are so many more fun and effective ways to allow dogs to expend excess energy. With other types of play and physical outlets alongside the daily walk, you are far more likely to give your dog the stimulation she needs and, in turn, prevent behavioural issues from arising.

This chapter is called 'Exercise, play and outlets' and while it might sound like they are completely separate topics, they are all very much interconnected. 'Exercise' is any activity that involves physical effort. 'Play' covers activities that make the dog feel good, without needing to have a specific outcome. 'Outlets' are activities that fulfil the dog's genetic tendencies, desires or passions.

If you're doing any of these three things well, you'll be regularly moving between all of them at once. You can exercise your dog through a form of play that gives her an outlet paired to suit her genetics.

The concepts we'll explore in this chapter aren't just about getting your dog exhausted, but also about teaching her to use her mind while exercising and learn some new skills in the process.

A Few Words on Exercise

Exercise is a fundamental requirement for all dogs, but the amount and style of exercise will be dramatically affected by age, size and breed types. For example, it is unwise to do vigorous exercise with teenage giant breed dogs such as Mastiffs and Danes as this can harm their growing joints. On the other hand, a Springer Spaniel or a Jack Russell puppy will need a lot of exercise and stimulation in order to make sure they don't tear your house apart! If you own a non-sporting or toy variety of dog, you may find that a gentle walk on lead once or twice a day with a bit of sniffing is all they need, whereas a herding variety of dog or scent hound won't even be warmed up after a half-hour walk around town.

When trying to figure out the optimal amount of exercise for your dog, you should first consider what is suitable for your dog's joints and physical development. As a general rule, we don't like to do activities that involve out-of-control sliding, jumping or running downstairs with any young dog. Consult with your vet or breeder when developing an exercise regime for a new dog.

A base level exercise regime for any dog regardless of breed or age should involve walks, games with toys, and activities that encourage her to use her nose and instincts.

Play

Why is play so important?

To put it simply, your dog *needs* you to play with them. Play is one of the most common and important bonding and learning exercises for all social mammals, and dogs are highly social creatures. Through playing, puppies learn and rehearse virtually every skill that is important to have later on in life. Some behaviours learned during play are obvious and funny, like watching puppies stalk, pounce and attack each other. Others are a bit embarrassing, such as humping! But one thing is for certain, it's all normal and it's crucial.

Once your puppy leaves her litter or when a new dog joins your family, the best thing you can do early on is work out how she likes to play. Knowing this about her will establish and strengthen your bond and playing properly with your dog will also teach her how to think when excited. You're not only bonding but you're making your dog healthier and building skills that make her easier to train.

What does play look like?

Let's for a moment think of your puppy as a wolf: a calculated and efficient hunter. It might be difficult to look at your pug and consider her an apex predator, but for the sake of a different perspective, humour us!

Wolves need to hunt in order to survive. Since it's the most important skill set they need to develop when young, most puppy play revolves around hunting (and often humping, which is also vital for survival). We can break hunting down into what is often called the 'canine predatory sequence'. Think of it as a basic description of the processes a wolf might go through in order to have a successful hunt.

Wolves need to do some, if not all, of the following things with their prey: smell, track, spot, stalk, chase, catch, kill, dissect and finally eat it.

Most 'jobs' that dogs have been specifically bred for involve a component of this sequence. With this sequence in mind you can see that humans have selectively bred dogs who display some of these traits so we can use them for work, whether it be using scent dogs to track missing people, or herding dogs to round up livestock.

OUR DOGS

Our Spaniels are trained in scent detection, as they are experts at smelling prey.

Our Malinois is trained for bite demonstrations, as these dogs are the best at catching prey.

Our Australian Shepherd is used for herding stock, as these dogs are brilliant stalkers and chasers.

So the games we encourage you to play with your dog will in some way capitalise on these predatory instincts. Depending on their genetics, some dogs will thrive on certain components more than others, and the joy they feel will be greater if the activities cater to their natural strengths.

The beauty is that play doesn't need to be complicated, and virtually every dog will enjoy every exercise even if it's only for a few minutes a day. It might be as simple as hiding some food for your dog to sniff out and find instead of just giving it to them in a bowl, getting them to chase a toy on a string, or allowing them to rip apart a cardboard box to get to a treat inside (see 'Behavioural enrichment' in Chapter 7). All these games relate back to an instinct to hunt and survive.

So yes, play will make your dog feel wonderful and provide an alternative form of exercise, which is great – but possibly the best advantage of play is that if it's done well, your dog can learn how to think and behave even when she is excited. This is a wonderful skill to learn and has so many other applications throughout life! It's also something that is very difficult to achieve if all training and learning is done just with food and a lead.

When your dog is playing games like tug, finding food and chasing toys she is feeling similar heightened emotions to the times when we find dogs most difficult to control. Think about the challenges of walking dogs on lead when they spot or smell wildlife or trying without luck to get them to respond to your calls while they're playing off lead with other dogs.

By teaching your dog how to play and then implementing 'rules' into the games, you will be giving your dog the skills and ability to think while excited, which means you are more likely to get a recall while she is rumbling with other dogs or be able to get her attention while she is sniffing possum poo.

There is a fine line with these rules during play, though: too many and the dog loses interest; no rules and you essentially encourage out-of-control behaviour. This is where the science of dog training becomes a bit more of an art.

We often use the analogy of teaching a young child soccer. You might start by just getting them excited about playing with the ball:

it doesn't matter if they kick it, hit it with their hands or just run around like crazy, you start with the premise that this ball equals fun. Once the child starts to build that association you can then introduce the simple rule that they aren't allowed to touch it with their hands.

This makes the game slightly more complicated, but also more fun and engaging. We humans (and dogs) thrive on appropriate challenges, so this new rule makes the game more exciting. Perhaps if your child really enjoys kicking a ball you might then sign them up to a junior or little league for football. The coaches are generally going to be laid-back; the kids probably won't have set positions for the first couple of seasons; the pitch is short and the halves are even shorter. But as the years progress, the fields get longer, goal posts get bigger, rules are more complex and the game is vastly different from how it was in your backyard years ago.

Of course, there are dozens of factors that will influence how this process may unfold for each child. For example, it looks like our son will be on the short side. Both his parents are bad runners and never excelled in any land-based sports. He currently prefers to surf or ride his dirt bike rather than play large team sports. He loves to kick a ball with his friends, but considering all the above, it is unlikely he will play football for Australia. However, we have some friends who have a girl around the same age as our son. Her father and his brothers all played football for Australia, she is extremely outgoing and confident in social settings, and loves any team sport. So the likelihood of her playing elite football is significantly higher than it is for our son.

Applying that logic back to our dogs, their genetics and their household will greatly impact what kind of games they will excel at and what 'level' we should push them towards. As a reminder, you might like to flick back to Chapter 3, where we discuss genetics and the kind of tasks dogs are suited to.

Outlets

Let's break down some doggie games, activities, sports and forms of exercise. There's something here for every pup!

1. *Flirt pole fun*

Hunting instincts activated: spot, stalk, chase, catch and kill

For the uninitiated, a flirt pole isn't something that you do a sensual dance with! It's a flexible stick or pole with about 120 cm of thin rope attached to it that has a toy or rag hanging from the end. Flirt poles are very popular kitten toys, but a lot of people don't realise they can be brilliant for dogs, too.

Without doubt the flirt pole is the easiest way to 'shape' or create interest in toys. It allows more reserved dogs to get a little crazy without needing much advice from their owners, and it allows the crazy dogs to really go nuts! The beauty of the toy is it doesn't matter what your end goal is; at the beginning, it just gives the dog an excuse to have a bit of fun. The biomechanics of how a flirt pole works makes it very easy for anyone to activate, and they appeal to the predatory instincts of any dog. You can distance yourself from the toy while still having a huge amount of control over it and bring it to life to promote stalking, chasing and play.

Where to start

With a young or new dog, our flirt pole training sessions (games) may only last about 30 seconds. We usually drag the toy along the ground in mostly straight lines or perform the 'silly salmon' on the ground (flap it around like a fish) to entice some interest from the dog. If the dog stalks, chases, snaps or follows the toy on the end of the rope we consider that a good start. We keep our expectations very low and let the dog show us what kind of game she wants. Some will instantly bite it and play tug; others may just want to stalk, chase or pounce at it without making contact. Watching how your dog plays with the flirt pole may give you ideas about what other games they might thrive at.

Take it further

If your dog takes to the flirt pole well and clearly already likes it, you can introduce rules to make the play a little more complex. One such rule is that she can only chase it when you say 'Yes'. This is a concept often referred to as impulse control: an important skill for a dog to develop which allows them to think in highly exciting or arousing situations.

We start by having the flirt pole concealed or in our pocket and ask the dog for a simple behaviour like a sit. Then we say 'Yes', present the pole and bring it to life. Allow the chase to unfold for 10, 20, 30 seconds before letting the dog 'win' and nail it. If you repeat this process two to three times per day and have a 20 to 30 second chase, the dog will work out within two to five days that the word 'Yes' predicts the game. This is a powerful tool. You are creating the bridge that can be used to mark the precise moment the dog is doing something you like and is the signal that gives her permission to launch into play.

What you might progress on to next is to ask your dog to sit (which she should have nailed by now as it's associated with the game) and, without saying a word, slowly remove the flirt pole from your pocket or bring it out into reach. Be prepared to take it away again if your dog breaks the sit, but if she holds the sit position until you have the flirt pole all the way out then say 'Yes', bring the toy even more to life and let the dog have her game.

We like to build up to having the dog hold 'sit' or 'down' while we spin the flirt pole all around in crazy positions, right over the top of them, and only say 'Yes' when the dog is perfectly still, ignoring everything we do with the flirt pole. The energy expelled and focus this requires from the dog is second to none. In fact, the dog's ability to hold position and wait for the 'Yes' cue may very well be more exhausting than the actual act of chasing the toy! Combine the two together and you have one very satisfied pup on your hands.

2. Fetch

Hunting instincts activated: chase and catch

'Fetch' is surely one of the oldest games in the book, so it shouldn't need too much explanation, but there are in fact some right and wrong ways to play it. Some research suggests the mindless back and forth chasing of a ball can whip dogs into a frenzy that makes them difficult to settle, and there is a concern that constant fetching can create joint problems. This is only true if the game is done excessively without any rules or thought for the dog's safety or behaviour during the game. An example you may be familiar with is someone who walks with a ball chucker and continuously launches the ball into oblivion while their dog barks and jumps at them demanding a throw. There are not many healthy exercise habits happening in this picture.

That said, we advocate for this game because there are easy ways to avoid those problems and it's an incredible shame for dogs to miss out on one of their most enjoyable experiences for fear of overexcitement or injury. Anecdotally, dogs who can play a nice game of fetch generally don't end up in pounds. This is likely due to the fact that they have learnt some impulse control, which makes them easier to train elsewhere in life. Plus they have a really fun outlet that allows them to feel good and burn off steam – which makes them easier to live with.

The way in which you ultimately play fetch with each dog may need to differ. Some dogs like really long throws via a ball launcher, while others might just like to catch a small throw or scramble over a bouncy ball. You need to experiment and consider what is healthy and suitable for your dog. If you have a dog who is obsessive over fetch you may want to introduce a 'finish' command. We might say 'Finish' or 'No more', pop the ball in our pocket or in a cupboard, and generally don't engage in the activity for the rest of the day. If you repeat this process reliably, and don't give into the dog's sooky eyes or attempts to get you to throw a stick or anything else, she picks up the 'finish' command and will learn not to seek out the game unless you initiate it.

Where to start

The key to fetch is that it *must* have rules. The first one is to only use a few specific toys that are suitable for the game – not sticks, other dogs' balls, the kids' Pokémon and not bones! (If you begin teaching your dog 'fetch' with any object that can easily be obtained outside of the game, like a stick, you will end up with a dog who is constantly dropping sticks at your feet. It becomes obsessive and unhealthy.) It's important to use something that is safe for the dog and it's helpful to use something novel that you can remove from sight when you decide the game is over. If you have a dog who's obsessive or possessive, or even one on the other end of the spectrum who's just not that interested, then selecting a few special toys that only come out for fetch and get put away after the game will really help prevent any potential issues.

The second rule, as with the flirt pole, is to create the condition that the word 'Yes' means you will now throw the ball. This allows you to pinpoint the moment your dog is attentive – not barking, not jumping and perhaps doing something like a sit – before you say 'Yes' and commence play. We are instantly creating a brilliant form of communication and reminding the dog that barking, jumping and being obnoxious will not produce the ball, but rather, showing some control and holding a sit will start the game.

Rule three? Bring it back! It may sound obvious, but we want the dog to bring the ball back and either drop it directly in our hand or at least within 2 m of us. There are a few ways to achieve this and it will take some tinkering and experimentation. When working on any of the early stages of fetch we always suggest working in very quiet places with minimal distractions and having multiple toys and food rewards on hand. Then, we want to either say 'Yes' and throw a second toy when the dog brings the first toy closer, or offer a trade-off for a treat. Some dogs just like to parade the toy, others like to chew and destroy it, and some like to drop it 50 m away. Whatever the issue, it can normally be solved by incentivising the dog with better rewards and/or using a long line (an oversized dog lead you can use to either prevent the dog from running too far away or even to gently guide her back towards you). Remember, this is meant to be a game – and fun for your dog – so keep it light-hearted and don't get cross. While your dog is still learning, stick to short lessons of just 30 seconds to one minute.

Keep practising and persevering, and once your dog is offering a sit, waiting for 'Yes', chasing a nice toy and bringing it back, the fetch world is your oyster!

3. Tug of war
Hunting instincts activated: catch and kill
Tug is a great way to have close-contact mutual play. When you and your dog go back and forth in a respectful game with a toy, growling and roughhousing, you are building and establishing a much greater

bond than you would via an activity like feeding your dog a meal from a bowl.

This game sometimes gets a bad rap, and in certain parts of the world there are still government restrictions on what toys are permitted and how to play tug for fear of making dogs aggressive.

Provided your dog understands some basic rules and you aren't using a toy that looks like a living creature (or a human limb!) you'll be developing a tremendous game that makes your dog feel wonderful and connected to you. Dogs need activities that allow them to get excited and let loose in order to be calm at other times, and tug is one of the best ways to let loose!

Where to start

As with fetch, choose a couple of toys that are suitable for your dog and that fit your hands. They shouldn't be too long and need to provide a nice texture for your dog to bite and grip onto. Again, these toys only come out for tug and then they get put away after the game.

We like to have pretty sensible rules for tug. In line with our football coaching theory, with a new dog we don't really care what the game looks like as long as the dog shows some interest in biting and tugging on toys! However, once she really starts to rip in, growl and ragdoll the toy in an attempt to 'win', we suggest you start rolling out the rules.

The first rule: Only bite when you say 'Yes'. As with fetch and the flirt pole, this is essential. It means you can ask the dog to sit, then hold the toy out and say 'Yes', and your dog won't be mugging you or snapping for the toy. When you say 'Yes', be mindful not to shove the toy in the dog's face; rather, present it off to the side or slightly away from the dog. The toy is meant to resemble some kind of fake prey and prey doesn't ever jump into a dog's mouth! Furthermore, dogs are averse to things that move directly at their face, so it's a quick way to trash the game. So say 'Yes' and bring the toy to life off to the side or as you move away from the dog.

The second rule: Let go when you say 'Leave' or 'Give'. It's pretty self-explanatory, but often hard to master. When we teach this topic in classes, we could spend an entire day looking at different ways to get a dog to let go of something, but the nuts and bolts of it are pretty straightforward. As the owner, you need to keep a counterintuitive mindset, which is that 'Leave' or 'Give' doesn't mean 'I want your toy', it means 'I am offering you an opportunity for another toy or reward'. You may want to consider making the first toy you're holding onto very boring, show minimal resistance and offer the new toy or treat in a very excited manner. You may even want the dog on lead so you can let go of the toy without the dog running away.

Letting the dog win is totally fine. With young or sensitive dogs we often dramatise our actions of the dog overpowering us, let the toy slip and pretend we are really beaten. Having the dog think winning is a possibility makes the game more reinforcing for her! If you've trained her to 'Leave' well, you will never create a problem of possession.

4. Scent-based games

Hunting instincts activated: smell, track, catch, eat

In the world of pet dog ownership, games involving the dog's nose are probably the most underutilised pastime. If we had to choose the two best games from this list, we would probably go for the flirt pole and scent-based games. Games based on toys and chasing make your dog feel like a hero, for sure, but a dog's nose is truly her superpower – and when she realises you want her to use it for fun, it's a game-changer. No matter how old or young, active or laid-back, big or small a dog is, she will benefit from some form of nose-engaging game. Dogs who get involved with games using their nose are often described as more content, relaxed and less anxious almost immediately.

For new dogs we would say one to two minutes of using their nose is equivalent to about a 10-minute run. Of course, as your dog becomes more conditioned to the games her fitness for the particular activity will improve, but as a general rule there is no greater exercise for burning off steam in a low impact, low arousal way than scent-based games.

Where to start

Our favourite way to introduce this exercise is to fill our training pouch up with treats or kibble, have it on one side of our body, and hold the dog in place on the opposite side. We take one treat out, let the dog have a sniff of it and, while still holding the dog, throw the treat out into some short grass. We then say 'Find' and let the dog go.

Take it further
That is the entry-level game, but you can quickly progress with things such as longer grass, cardboard boxes and making the dog wait for longer before you say 'Find'.

You will very quickly condition the dog to understand that the word 'Find' means 'I've hidden something for you to find'. After a couple of days, or maybe weeks, you might be able to lock your dog inside, hide a few treats in the backyard, then open the back door and say 'Find' – and the dog will know the game is *on*!

If your dog likes toys, you can replicate this process with toys or even with people. You can have a person hiding with the dog's favourite treats or toys. The game is limitless!

This is the basis for how we train detection dogs for a variety of purposes – the only difference being that instead of finding the treat or toy immediately, the dog needs to find a unique smell or target which will make us produce her favourite toy or treat.

5. Dog sports

Hunting instincts activated: all of them!
Sports for dogs, you say? Yes, sports! Depending on where you are in the world, there are literally thousands of dog clubs devoted to activities that are designed to let your dog display the genetic traits they've been selectively bred for over hundreds of years. We have been involved in a variety of dog sports even prior to becoming professional trainers. Below we list just some of the available sports and the kinds of dog breeds or personalities that will excel at them. They will vary from country to country, but we urge you to at least check them out at some stage in your life. Even if you don't want to compete in any sport, the community atmosphere at these places is very much alive and can be a good source of fun and nourishment for the human soul!

Obedience

The word doesn't sound like a whole lot of fun, but some of our fondest memories with our dogs have been at obedience classes and trials. Almost every dog can, and will, learn to enjoy obedience, particularly if the exercises are taught with rewards. The dog and owner become in sync and the dog knows and loves the fact that you are 100 per cent focused on her, even if it's just for a short period of time. She knows it's just about you and her, and that is very special for a dog.

Agility and flyball

As the names suggest, agility and flyball are sports that agile dogs excel at, though that doesn't mean they are the only dogs who can do them. So long as your dog is physically mature and doesn't have any joint issues, you are essentially teaching your dog to join you on an obstacle course race that requires not only speed and athleticism, but coordination and hyperfocus. The sport is often dominated by herding dogs, but we have seen Spaniels, Huskies, Chows and even Shar Peis win agility titles.

Lure coursing

This is definitely targeted at sighthounds like Greyhounds, as the dogs must chase a mechanically operated lure or toy. But in fact virtually every dog will enjoy this sport, as it is essentially the fastest, most elaborate flirt pole you could think of – and it's the closest thing to chasing a rabbit without the moral or ethical concerns.

Dock diving

This one's very popular in Australia: it's possibly the easiest sport to understand and certainly one of the most entertaining to watch. It's essentially long jump for dogs into a giant pool! If your dog loves water, jumping and toys, she is bound to love dock diving. Trust us, if you ever hear a dock diving event is happening near you, go and check it out.

K9 Nose work

A terrific sport for every dog, but particularly popular for people with dogs who don't like to socialise or perhaps don't have the desire to work in one of the more high-energy sports. The dogs get to work in relatively low-distraction environments and use their noses to find things! Nose work starts at a very easy-to-understand level where the dogs learn to engage their noses to find treats. Then they work up to much more complex tasks: performing vehicle searches and learning to 'indicate' or 'alert' to a specific smell like birch or anise.

Gun dog trials

Again, the name gives it away. There are a variety of gun dog sports that test out aspects of how dogs might work, alongside doing tasks like finding, pointing, flushing and retrieving. As you might expect, these sports are dominated by Retrievers, Spaniels and Pointers.

Herding trials (aka 'sheepdog trials')

Truly one of the most awe-inspiring sports to watch, these vary from country to country, but in general they test out the dog's ability to work with the farmer and move, stop, direct and problem-solve herding livestock. Go now and google!

Tracking

Tracking tests the dog's ability to follow a scent trail. It is one of those sports that may seem overly difficult or complex from the outside or at a glance. That's because we humans can't necessarily see the scent trail, whereas most dogs working with a good coach will pick it up and progress quite well in their first couple of sessions. This is a very natural instinct for most dogs: all we are doing is harnessing it into a specific game with rewards.

Bite sports

Schutzhund (or IGP), Protection Sports Association, Mondioring and French Ring are all examples of what are commonly referred to as 'bite sports'. Yes, biting a 'helper' or 'decoy' is part of the sport, but complex obedience and tracking are normally part of these sports as well. Broadly speaking, these sports give owners a taste of what it might be like to handle a police dog or a military dog in a controlled setting. Bite sports are dominated by German and Belgian

Shepherd dogs. They don't turn dogs into killers; in fact, if done correctly, the dogs understand this is a game that is only to be performed under a specific set of circumstances. In our opinion, giving the dogs an outlet to perform these tasks and learn such high levels of obedience makes them safer than dogs who don't participate in similar activities.

Earth dog trials

These are dominated by the shorter-legged canines like Dachshunds and little Terriers. The dogs work their way through man-made tunnels to act out what they were initially bred for: hunting, flushing or bailing animals like rats, mice or badgers.

Sled dog trials

Of course, when we talk about sled dogs we think of Huskies and Malamutes – but we've also seen Pitbulls and Rottweilers do incredibly well at this sport, particularly when it isn't snowing!

Dog Parks and Off-Lead Areas

A chapter about play and exercise wouldn't be complete without a discussion of dog parks. They're places with the potential to be divisive and there is a spectrum of different dog parks. Where we grew up there were a handful of dog parks that were quite simply total and utter chaos: overcrowded, poo everywhere and nobody had control of their dogs, which meant fights were a daily occurrence (sometimes even fatal) and disease transfer was always a possibility. Owners were distracted with their phone while the dogs mimicked scenes from *Lord of the Flies*. That is often the norm and it really shouldn't be. The fact of the matter is, not all dogs are suited to the typical dog park.

Misconceptions about socialisation

In the last 20 years, humans have propagated this idea that all dogs need to run together and rumble and play every day with a bunch of random dogs. That is largely a false idea.

Some dog breeds, like those that fit into the gun dog category (Retrievers and Spaniels), are naturally more social and are often what we would call 'close talkers'. Others, such as Terriers and herding dogs, are either more task-orientated or owner-orientated, and just prefer to ignore other dogs or give them a polite nod from 10 m away. If you have a Labrador and all you do from day dot is encourage him to loosely socialise with a bunch of other out-of-control dogs and neither engage with you nor utilise his retrieving instincts, you will create a social monster. Many owners with dogs like this consider their dog a 'cute social butterfly', when in fact from the perspective of other dogs in his presence, he is the dog equivalent of the sweaty, sleazy dude at the pub who spits on you while he's talking.

What's more, most mature dogs don't actually need or want to socialise with unfamiliar dogs on a regular basis, particularly not off lead in a highly aroused state. Dogs are social creatures, but meeting a couple of dogs who belong to family members or friends and saying g'day to a couple of the neighbourhood dogs while on their walk is honestly all they require. Friendships formed early on in life are likely to last forever, and even if they go months or years without seeing a dog they've formed a friendship with, they usually remember them.

Our dogs probably have about twenty 'friends' who are either family members' dogs or dogs who join them on jobs. All other dogs are pretty much ignored. It's not something we've had to actively work on, because our dogs love us and have a very fulfilled life, which means they don't want to drag us on lead to meet every dog they walk past and won't rush up to a dog they see off lead.

If you are an available, engaged and active dog owner it's likely you are fulfilling your dog's social needs. Have a look again at Chapter 6 on socialisation for some tips. There are important periods of the dog's life where she needs to be exposed to other dogs, but dog parks are never an essential part of that.

Ingredients for a good dog park

If a dog park has lots of space, all dogs who attend are well trained and the emphasis is on dog-to-owner engagement (not dog-to-dog socialisation), then it can be a great place. And these places do exist!

We have been contracted to help design and create rules for 'safe' dog parks and off-leash exercise and training areas. These parks have a lot of space and a plethora of dog–human activities for the dog and owner to do together, including obstacle and agility courses, a training circuit, swimming areas, spaces just for small dogs, and on-lead-only areas. They can work really well, and the dogs will get some socialisation with other dogs either at a distance or while engaging in another activity, which is how it should be.

And it's not just about the space itself, but about *who* is using it. The kinds of dogs who we suggest should be allowed at dog parks include:

- Physically and mentally mature dogs.
- Dogs with a perfect recall (i.e. a dog who would come to her owner's call while someone is riding past on rollerblades in 1980s fluro, singing the 'Nutbush', handing out free barbecue chicken and throwing tennis balls).
- Fully vaccinated dogs.
- Dogs who would prefer to ignore other dogs and play with their owner.
- Dogs with a high level of tolerance for obnoxious dogs who make mistakes.

The kinds of dogs who we suggest should not go to dog parks are:

- Puppies: They may get overwhelmed or learn poor habits from unruly dogs.
- Unvaccinated dogs: They may spread or acquire potentially deadly viruses.
- Bitches on heat: They could get mated or cause fights.
- Dogs who have recently been rescued or changed home: They aren't fully bonded to their family yet and their family won't understand their temperament yet.
- Dogs who value other dogs more than they value their owner: They are unlikely to recall to their owner when it is required.
- Dogs prone to getting grumpy or fighting: The dog park is the last place these dogs want to be!

Whenever we see a client whose dog is displaying abnormal, anxious or aggressive behaviour, we very early on ask about play and outlets. We might say, 'So what do you do with your dog for fun?' Most (but not all) anxious or aggressive dogs are not getting the right types or amounts of stimulation.

Minus the dog park, we usually try to implement as many of the above activities as possible and will focus more heavily on exercises that the dog is likely to excel at. We look at the genetics and personality of the dog, and with the help of the owner, we come up with a list of fun outlets that they can do together. Once the dog starts to feel good and is actually having fun with her owner, training is exponentially easier. Sometimes the play itself actually solves the behavioural problems.

An example of an outlet routine we trialled on a 1-year-old American Staffy who had just changed owners is on pages 229 and 230. She was overweight and poorly socialised, had never been exercised and had been given no training. Behaviourally she was anxious, aggressive and not bonded with her new owner. As a result, she would trash the yard, rip clothes off the washing line and be unpredictable with other dogs when on lead. It was very difficult to know where to start as there were so many issues. But first of all, we needed to make the dog feel good and feel satisfied each day, so we began with simple play. In cases like these, training behaviours such as walking on lead or staying on the bed aren't our first priority.

The owners stayed in touch throughout the week and parts of the plan were adjusted based upon every successful step and the overall evolution of the dog's behaviour. By the end of the first week, the dog was much less destructive and was demonstrating the ability to settle at home.

Sample outlet schedule

	Monday	Tuesday	Wednesday	Thursday	Friday	Saturday	Sunday
Morning	Fetch training (3 mins)	Tug training (3 mins)	Fetch training (3 mins)	Fetch training (3 mins)	Tug training (3 mins)	Nose work class	Day off
	On-lead sniffing in front of property (5 mins)	Flirt pole play (2 mins)	On-lead sniffing in front of property (5 mins)	On-lead sniffing in front of property (5 mins)	Flirt pole play (2 mins)		
	Flirt pole play (2 mins)	Practise loose lead walking around lounge room (10 mins)	Flirt pole play (2 mins)	Flirt pole play (2 mins)	Practise loose lead walking around lounge room (10 mins)		
	Scatter feed prior to going to work	Food puzzle prior to going to work	Scatter feed prior to going to work	Scatter feed prior to going to work	Food puzzle prior to going to work		
Afternoon	Fetch training (3 mins)	Game: find treats in back yard (5 mins)	Tug training (3 mins)	Fetch training (3 mins)	Game: finding treats in back yard (5 mins)		

	Monday	Tuesday	Wednesday	Thursday	Friday	Saturday	Sunday
	Practise loose lead walking around lounge room (10 mins)	Excursion to quiet location without any dogs for a sniff (10 mins)	Practise loose lead walking around lounge room (10 mins)	Practise loose lead walking around lounge room (10 mins)	Excursion to quiet location without any dogs for a sniff (10 mins)		
	Flirt pole play (2 mins)	Flirt pole play (2 mins)	Flirt pole play (2 mins)	Flirt pole play (2 mins)	Flirt pole play (2 mins)		
	On-lead sniffing in front of property (5–10 mins)	On-lead sniffing in front of property (5–10 mins)	On-lead sniffing in front of property (5–10 mins)	On-lead sniffing in front of property (5–10 mins)	On-lead sniffing in front of property (5–10 mins)		
Evening	Dinner in food puzzle or something similar the dog can trash or dissect	Dinner in food puzzle or similar	Dinner in food puzzle or similar	Dinner in food puzzle or similar	Dinner in food puzzle or similar		

So let's match some games with some dogs:

1. John has a 12-month-old Australia Cattle Dog named Chompy who has decided chasing children on bikes and popping their tyres is his favourite pastime. John doesn't know how to play with Chompy and is worried that if he does start to play with him, he might get bitten in the process. What kind of games should they start with? The flirt pole, for sure!
It's slightly removed from John so the chances of the dog getting overexcited and biting him are very low. John also knows a local farmer who conducts herding classes on the weekends. He's been considering signing up for a class, but didn't know if it would make Chompy even crazier. Not at all – he would benefit greatly from it.

2. Freya has a 9-year-old Beagle named Spot who has just been diagnosed with arthritis. He pulls like mad on lead, which makes his arthritis worse. Freya wants to give him some fun activities to do that don't exacerbate his pain. What should they do? Well, we'd suggest some scent-based games for Spot: this could be as simple as hiding treats in the backyard for him or taking him to nose work classes. Either way, they can be done at low intensity and in suitable environments that won't upset his joints and will give him a lot of fun.

3. Doug owns lots of luxury cars and has bought a Rottweiler, Mischa, to help guard his collection. Mischa is a great guard dog, but recently she decided to chew the spoiler of his Porsche. Doug suspects Mischa is under stimulated. What would we suggest for Mischa? Definitely some games of tug and even some behavioural enrichment she can dissect and destroy. Doug also lives near a dog club specialising in protection (bite) sports that meets every Friday night. We'd suggest Doug go there, meet some of the trainers, and consider signing up with Mischa.

4. Martina has a Cavoodle called Begby, who is a little anxious about the world and doesn't seem to know how to control his emotions outside the house. What should they start playing?

Well, complex games of fetch are likely to be fulfilling and good for developing self-control while aroused, and scent-based games will almost certainly help Begby feel good and calm.

Chapter 12

The Teenage Dog and Beyond

Until a dog hits emotional and physical maturity, he is constantly learning and developing his own personality and behavioural traits. This means continually investing in his training, providing outlets, bonding and nurturing is vital to helping him become the happiest, healthiest dog he can be. From 16 weeks until roughly 1.5 to 2 years, your puppy will go through several more important and influential developmental periods that will affect his behaviour.

Since you're nearing the end of your journey through this book, we are going to hit you with some detailed and technical explanations using more scientifically correct industry terms – particularly when we talk about anxiety, phobias and aggression. We think you're ready! But also, if you do diagnose your dog as having a serious behavioural issue, you will be able to talk to your vet or dog trainer using the correct jargon, which will mean a better and faster outcome for your dog.

In this chapter we will address the following topics:

- Independence spikes – why your dog might suddenly start ignoring you or running away.
- Secondary fear phase – sudden onset of fears and phobias.
- Aggression – property guarding, dog reactivity, human aggression and resource guarding.
- Separation anxiety – fear of being left alone.
- Thunderstorm and noise phobias.
- Wildlife avoidance – teaching your dog not to chase or harm wildlife.
- Continuing your training journey with your dog.

Independence Spikes

Like any teenager, dogs during the adolescent phase will have times when they want to exercise their independence. They might want space, run off, not come when called or decide they prefer to sleep outside.

Provided the dog isn't ever facing imminent danger, none of these things is a big problem. We've been through it so many times we now anticipate and don't worry about it.

The most common problem is a dog running off and/or not coming when called. This often catches the owner by surprise – their usually sensitive and attentive puppy that rarely leaves their side is one day suddenly following a scent trail of an animal or chasing another dog without any care or thought for you!

This will happen with almost every dog at some stage. So what do you do? *Don't chase the bloody dog!* If you do, he will think it's hilarious and will run faster than you can, further away, and will now likely repeat this event many, many more times throughout his life. Here are some things we do that you can try:

1. If we are in an area where we'd really prefer the dog didn't keep going away from us, we often make some high-pitched sounds like 'Pup, pup, pup' and run or jog in the opposite direction to where the dog is heading. We might even say something silly like, 'Oh my goodness, will you look at this!' Keep moving and keep up the excitement and silly sounds until the dog changes its mind. When the dog does change his mind, we usually praise, keep moving and throw the odd treat nearby to keep the dog in our proximity. It's important to remain cool when the dog is back and near you. If you show frustration, anger, or try to grab the dog he will likely bolt far and fast. So chill, keep moving away and encourage the dog to come to you for a pat or a few treats before you try to put the lead back on.

2. If we are in a safe area and the dog is just off sniffing something and we know he's a very confident dog, we might quietly walk away or even partially hide behind a tree.

Admittedly, this technique isn't for everyone, and shouldn't be done on very sensitive or anxious dogs. However, if you know your dog is safe and pretty confident, letting him have the realisation that you won't watch his every move or perhaps even that it is his job to keep an eye on where *you* go can be a real eye-opener. If you see the dog stop what he's doing and have that moment where he starts to look for you, then you can praise the dog, or help him realise where you are.

The Secondary Fear Phase

From 5 months onwards, we often see a sudden and opposing shift in a young dog's confidence. If the dog has been raised well and is normally pretty happy-go-lucky, this usually presents as mild fear towards a few specific objects, particularly objects that they don't see very often.

If you know how to deal with this phase it won't create any lasting effects, whereas if you get it wrong, you can potentially create long-lasting phobias.

Most commonly, we see a dog who suddenly, on garbage day every week (or second week), completely freaks out when he goes for his morning walk and notices garbage bins on the side of the street. Something like this is usually a clear indication that the dog is going through a fear phase, because he would have experienced bin day many times already throughout his life with no adverse reaction.

Other dogs may react to people with different features from their owners, such as facial hair, large hats, high visibility workwear and different ethnicities.

If you notice this happening with your dog, the best thing you can do is avoid making a big deal over it. Try to be upbeat and even talk to your dog or sling him a treat to help lighten the mood when you see him spin out over something that normally wouldn't be a big deal. Don't force the dog to get closer to the bin or the person they fear. If you force the dog closer to the object he fears, you are likely to make things much worse. Respect the fact that your dog needs a bit of space from the stimulus and some moral support from you.

The secondary fear phase isn't something you should lose sleep over. But it is important to acknowledge that it will happen, and it is a sign to you not to 'push' the dog. Don't try to get him to face new challenges or big changes during this time. It may only be obvious for a few days or might even go for up to three weeks. Anecdotally, if the dog has multiple stressful events during this fear phase, the spooked and nervous behaviour can remain for a lot longer. You don't need to wrap him up in cotton wool (or keep him locked in your house) but the message should be clear: don't try to make him 'get over it' during this time.

Keep in mind that fear inhibits learning, so your training may go backwards or just stagnate in this period. Try not to worry about it. Keep your dog safe, keep life cruisy and manage your expectations for a few weeks and your dog should soon be back to his normal self.

One common mistake that is made with young male dogs is assuming behaviours related to the fear phase have something to do with testosterone or disobedience, and therefore desexing will fix the behaviour. Sending your dog into an unfamiliar place to be put under anaesthetic during this phase will possibly make his behaviour worse. As we will discuss further below, testosterone is good for overcoming fear, so keep his plums for a little longer!

Aggression

Aggression usually starts to rear its head at some stage during the teenage phase, particularly towards the latter end. It is a super complex topic, and many trainers base an entire career and business on dealing with dog aggression, so it is important not to downplay it.

If you have a dog who is displaying aggression we suggest you engage with an experienced dog trainer prior to starting training. This chapter will help you recognise aggression in your dog, understand the science a little better and give you a head start on the techniques and strategies best used to combat it, but we don't encourage you to tackle this without a trainer.

The triggers for dog aggression are often layered, nuanced and multifactorial, but we usually try to put them into categories to help us, which also helps our clients break it down and digest what we are dealing with.

The categories are:

1. **Fear** – towards dogs, people of certain appearances, vehicles, animals, children, groomers.
2. **Territory/Property** – guarding the house, yard or a vehicle.
3. **Resource Guarding** – guarding toys, food, bones, people, beds.
4. **Prey** – towards cats, pocket pets, small dogs, children.
5. **Frustration** – often seen in young dogs who were previously allowed to play with every dog they saw, but are now suddenly being restricted or not used to being on lead.

As mentioned earlier in the book, 'dominance' does exist, but it is certainly not one of the most common reasons we see aggression in domestic dogs.

What are the most common reasons aggression develops?

1. Lack of appropriate experiences in the critical development phase (first 16 weeks)

Often people assume a dog who has come from an unknown background (such as a rescue or pound) must have been beaten because of the way he reacts towards certain people, particularly men. We usually find out that this dog wasn't beaten or abused by anyone, but rather he just didn't have enough pleasant experiences with different people during the first 16 weeks of life.

On the other side of the spectrum, there are cases when people overdo the experiences during the critical phase. For example, they want their 8-week-old puppy to love kids so they take him to a children's party for 4 hours. The pup gets overwhelmed and then develops a dislike of kids!

Prevention: It's all about the middle ground, exposing your puppy to 'enough' without overwhelming it or creating an obsession. Pleasant, short encounters with people, dogs and environments go a long way. Go to a good puppy pre-school with an instructor who has relevant qualifications, a well-socialised dog themselves and who promotes *controlled interactions* during puppy class. This is discussed in detail in Chapter 6.

2. Genetics and/or lack of understanding of a dog's genetics

If a dog and a bitch with high resource guarding tendencies are bred, chances are the pups will show these tendencies too. Behaviour is genetic, but we can certainly work on undesirable genetic traits if we know they are there in early development.

Remember, many breeds were deliberately bred for hundreds of years to display certain aggressive behaviours such as guarding property or stock, or to be assertive when challenged or backed into a corner. This extensive selective breeding will influence your dog's behavioural instincts no matter how glorious its upbringing was or how good a dog trainer you are.

Prevention: If you are buying a dog from a breeder, always insist on meeting the parents to see what their behaviour is like or, if you're getting a rescue dog, do your best to find out his breed history so you can understand the stimuli that might be a catalyst for aggression. (See Chapter 3 for detail.)

3. Single-event learning

'Single-event learning' means learning from a highly stressful event, often during puppyhood or the secondary fear phase. The most common type of single-event learning we see is usually caused at off-leash dog parks. For example, a young pup is taken to a dog park and bowled over, chased or barked at by larger, older dogs. The young dog usually seems fine for a few months, then seemingly out of the blue (often in adolescence) he starts to show aggression towards other dogs, particularly ones that look like the one that harassed him.

Prevention: Don't take a young dog to busy dog parks, do your best to prevent traumatic experiences (such as being chased, bowled over, barked at or attacked) in the early stages of life and if your dog does have a seriously bad experience, see a dog trainer as soon as possible.

If you suspect your dog has experienced a significant stressful event, don't attempt to 'get him back on the horse' and fix his fear by showing him it's okay. Give him 48 hours to decompress before exposing him to anything potentially stressful again. This is because we know his cortisol levels will stay elevated during this time and, until they drop, will make him more likely to perceive his environment as threatening.

Two significantly stressful events back-to-back are almost certain to create a long-lasting fear.

What are the different techniques used to treat aggression?

Now the tricky part: the methods and techniques that are used to help turn things around. Here we will explain the scientific terminology around the different techniques that are commonly used to treat aggression and the principles upon which they work.

We suggest that you should *always* deal with aggression with the help of a professional.

If you're not dealing with aggression, you may wish to skip past this, although the techniques used for dealing with aggression can be applied to a number of other behavioural issues.

1. Counter-conditioning

Counter-conditioning works on the principle of pairing two events: specifically, pairing a stimulus that has been triggering the aggression with a pleasant event. So the scary stimulus comes to predict the pleasant event.

For example, every time the dog sees (or hears) something that would usually trigger his aggressive behaviour, he experiences a pleasant event, such as a food treat. As a result he will eventually form a pleasant association towards the thing that previously caused aggression, which in turn reduces the aggressive outbursts. The emotions attached to the trigger have been changed and the emotion-driven behaviour also changes. Sounds lovely, doesn't it?

Counter-conditioning is a highly effective form of treating aggression but often people struggle with some of the finer details that make all the difference. Understanding how the scientific principle was discovered will assist in applying it effectively in practice.

Counter-conditioning has been around since the 1920s when researchers by the names of Mary Cover Jones and Ivan Pavlov were conducting their revolutionary work. Both of their experiments and publications had similar findings. Cover Jones worked with children and Pavlov's theories were directly related to dogs and more widely accepted, so we'll focus on his methods.

Also known as 'Pavlovian conditioning', counter-conditioning is a type of classical conditioning described by Dr Pavlov in 1927. He worked out that when he presented food to a dog, the dog would salivate. Then he started to ring a bell *before* presenting the food. At first the dog's behaviour did not change upon hearing the bell, but after repetition, the dog started to *involuntarily* salivate when it heard the bell, even before the food was presented.

Now if you are putting the pieces of the puzzle together, you might start to understand that counter-conditioning involves trying to teach your dog that the previously-scary stimulus (men, dogs, lawn mower etc.) is the bell. With successful classical conditioning your dog will eventually involuntarily enjoy the sight or sound of these previously scary triggers.

One of the aspects that is incredibly important when using this method is to ensure the dog is being given the food/toy/pleasant experience while *below* his 'aggression threshold'. This means your dog must not be displaying any behaviours associated with aggression. Barking, growling, lunging or even intent staring is usually considered over threshold.

How do you expose your dog to the scary stimulus and still keep him under the aggression threshold? When we talked about Pavlovian conditioning above, we said that the scary stimulus is the equivalent of the bell. But the difference is that the bell is a *neutral* stimulus, not scary. This is where distance comes in. Cover Jones noted that when conducting successful counter-conditioning on children, the scary stimulus must be presented at a suitable distance so as not to elicit fear. Throwing treats at a dog who has already lost the plot due to fear is a bit like trying to teach someone how to swim while they are already drowning.

Another common mistake, particularly in the early stages of counter-conditioning, is applying punishments or corrections in response to aggression from the dog. The aggressive behaviour has been displayed because the dog is over threshold – that's our fault, not the dog's! It's counterproductive to use punishment during this process, particularly if the dog hasn't yet learnt a positive association.

For success, you need to present the scary stimulus at a level where the dog will *definitely* observe it but not be triggered into aggression.

The intensity of the stimulus can be affected by its distance from your dog, its volume (if there is sound involved), the duration of time your dog is exposed to it and the type of stimulus. Additionally, physiological aspects can contribute to aggression e.g. the dog's current cortisol levels (how much stress he has experienced in the past 48 hours), motivation for rewards (he must be a bit hungry if we are using food) and energy levels (we don't want him too excited or exhausted).

Counter-conditioning can be difficult to implement if the dog has low food or toy drive, is highly frustrated, is more motivated by his stimulus or is in prey drive. That's because if you don't have any bargaining tools, or if what the dog is focused on is more reinforcing than your rewards, you can't create a positive association. An attempt to conduct conditioning with insufficient rewards or with a dog above his threshold will make the aggression worse.

For example, we know of a couple of cases of dogs who've had a lot of success killing and eating smaller animals. For these dogs, the sight of those animals even at distances of 50 metres or more was so arousing that they could not eat a treat. In this instance, trying to use treats to counter-condition the prey driven aggression towards the smaller animals was not effective.

A few key points to consider to make counter-conditioning successful:

1. You must be able to present the scary stimulus in a way that the dog notices it, but isn't triggered into aggression.
2. You must have a reward that the dog places high value on.
3. You need to do many successful repetitions in a variety of ways before it works.
4. You are trying to change an emotional response, which means unlike training a 'sit', it is unlikely to occur within minutes; it might take months to be reliable.
5. You should not attempt to deal with aggression unless you are under the guidance of a professional.

The overall idea behind counter-conditioning is that you are creating a new emotional association: from something that used to make the dog scared and subsequently display aggressive behaviour to something that leads to a pleasant experience and therefore makes him *happy*!

2. Operant conditioning

The other methods that are used during training a dog with aggression form part of what is called 'operant conditioning', which we've mentioned in various forms throughout the book. Operant conditioning is particularly necessary for dogs who are displaying aggression based upon frustration or predation.

B. F. Skinner is considered the 'father' of operant conditioning, which he first described in 1938. It works on two basic principles: if a behaviour is *reinforced* it is *more* likely to occur, and if a behaviour is *punished* it is *less* likely to occur.

What is important to remember is that operant conditioning works on the principle that the dog can choose his *behaviour*, not emotion. What does this mean? Well, you can't punish or reward emotion, only the behaviours the dog chooses to do. You can punish or reward behaviours associated with emotion, but you may not be dealing with the emotion driving the behaviour.

This is something we've raised before in the book, but it cannot be stressed enough. If you punish a dog every time he growls at a child for picking up his toy, the dog will probably stop growling, but that doesn't mean he is no longer *feeling* aggressive. What that dog might do is hide the growl and just bite the child when you're not looking.

That doesn't mean operant conditioning should be overlooked in dealing with aggression – not at all. It is incredibly important, and pivotal in training the desirable behaviours that help deal with and prevent aggression, such as basic obedience ('heel', 'come', 'sit' and 'stay'). If your dog knows these basic commands (and not just inside your home) you can prevent a lot of aggression.

Understanding operant conditioning also gives us an opportunity to ensure that the dog doesn't perceive that aggressive behaviours work for him or are 'reinforcing'. For example, if a dog barks and lunges on lead because he wants to get to another dog, then allowing him to meet that dog while barking and lunging will reinforce that behaviour. Taking your dog away from the other dog when he starts barking and lunging will punish that behaviour.

On the flip side, if your dog barks and lunges on lead because he fears a dog and does not want to meet him, and the other dog moves away because of the barking and lunging, then the barking and lunging is also reinforced because your dog got what it wanted (the other dog moved away).

It might sound a little confusing, but the aim of the game when using operant conditioning is to understand what the dog wants or does not want, and use that to shape behaviour that is desirable to us.

There are four types of operant conditioning:

1. **Positive reinforcement:** *Giving* the dog a reward to strengthen behaviour you like e.g. a treat or toy.

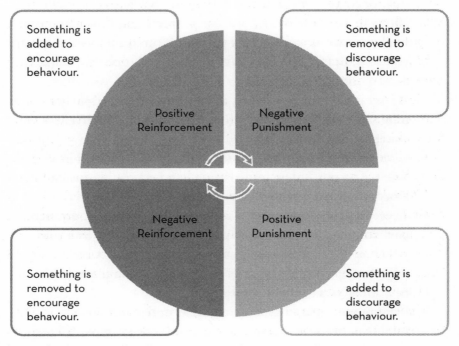

Operant conditioning: the four types

2. **Positive punishment:** *Giving* the dog something undesirable to weaken behaviour you do not like e.g. a tug on a leash, a whack on the butt. These are not techniques we suggest you use.
3. **Negative reinforcement:** *Removing* something the dog does not like to strengthen a desirable behaviour e.g. removing pressure from the leash, removing a 'scary dog', letting a dog go free.
4. **Negative punishment:** *Removing* something the dog likes to weaken an undesirable behaviour e.g. removing food, toys, or social attention.

Important points to consider when working with aggression

- Rehearsal is reinforcement. The more the dog practises aggression the more likely they are to use it in the future. For example, if you have a dog doing unwanted property guarding and you do five 5-minute training sessions a day, rewarding the dog for calmly letting people walk past your house, but then allowing him to bark and practise property guarding aggression while you are at work means you will be unlikely to see the result you seek. In fact, the aggressive displays will probably worsen.
- Send a consistent message to your dog of what you want. We set a plan for our clients to follow pretty religiously for a minimum of three weeks before reviewing its effectiveness or changing any techniques.
- Give the dog 'soak time' to allow things to be sorted in their brain. Too much new information can become confusing. Don't overload yourself or your dog!
- There may be times when a reduction in training is required, particularly if you have a young dog, a hyper dog or a dog who has had a particularly stressful experience. After a bad experience, a couple of quiet days in a row to recover is the best thing you can give your dog.
- Identify your dog's optimum exercise, outlet and genetic fulfilment needs to facilitate being calm. For example, all our dogs are high-drive working dogs so there is a certain level of

mental and physical stimulation they need in order to be calm. Our Spaniels need to search for things and our Shepherds need to bite things! But we won't let them search and bite all day, as they need to learn to chill out too. Think back to those favourite ways that your individual dog gets stimulation and fulfilment.

- Don't take the approach of 'I'll just let him sort it out'. You won't see results that way and it's not worth placing your dog or another dog at risk of physical or emotional injury.
- Remember that dogs are poor generalisers: what you teach them in one location or with one person does not automatically transfer to new locations or new people. You need to practise the behaviour in multiple varied locations once you've mastered the first.
- Focus on what you do want the dog to do, not what you *don't* want it to do.
- There is no such thing as a quick fix with aggression. It takes time and consistency to make your dog happy and reliable in a variety of environments.

The most useful behaviours to train a dog with aggression:

- recall/come when called (Chapter 9)
- go to bed/stay (Chapter 9)
- heel/loose lead walk (Chapter 10).

Separation Anxiety

If you haven't already, please read Chapter 7 on independence building and preventing separation anxiety. It is a complex issue and presents on a spectrum, from mild distress where a dog is restless when left alone, to extreme anxiety, where a dog can take dangerous actions like breaking windows in an attempt to find someone to be with.

Research suggests this anxiety is becoming an increasingly common and almost normal issue across a variety of dog breeds. We've owned a lot of dog breeds over our lives and none of them have presented with true separation anxiety, which we believe is due to their experiences during their critical phase as well as their ongoing fulfillment and management.

If we see a dog who's not comfortable in a particular setting, we work on it, we make it positive and we manage him accordingly until we have helped him gain the skills necessary. Some of our dogs are very comfortable in our dog pens immediately, while others take time. We know, for example, that Taylor and Connor (both working Spaniels) love our dog pens, and always have. They have a nice view and know it's the place they go and relax after a big day in the field.

Rafa, on the other hand, would prefer to be at the house. He sleeps as close as he can to the door and keeps a watchful eye on the house and property. He is a guarding dog, so we know that intrinsically he wants to look after the family. Rafa *can* stay in the dog pen if we need him to, but 90 per cent of the time we allow him to sleep up in the house, as we know this is his preference. However, if we are raising a new dog at home, we often need Rafa to sleep in a pen for a couple of nights here and there to allow the new dog extra space.

If we had always put Rafa in the dog run during his critical phase without sufficient fulfilment every day, he would probably display behaviours consistent with separation distress: pacing, struggling to settle and maybe even barking occasionally. Managing separation anxiety involves a bit of training, but it's also responsible management of the dog.

We believe that most dogs aren't suited to being left alone for 12 hours a day, five days a week, particularly working dogs. Admittedly, though, we've been there, and we've dealt with this situation successfully and ethically with two high energy Shepherds when we both worked full-time at the zoo. But our days were very carefully thought out. In the box below is an example of how an average day might look for us. But keep in mind our shifts were variable so we did our best to change the order of events and times where possible, so the dogs did not become dependent upon routine.

DAILY ACTIVITIES TO PREVENT SEPARATION ANXIETY

Morning

6 am: Wake up and nail a coffee!

6.15 am: Take the dog out for a walk for approximately 30 minutes (even in winter).

6.45 am: At home or at a park, do some training and games to exercise your dog's body and mind.

7.00 am: Dog comes into the house to hang out while everyone gets ready for work and eats breakfast.

7.30 am: Get enrichment and food puzzles ready.

7.45 am: Head out the door to work and give the dog access to the enrichment.

8.00 am: While you are on the road to work, your dog should still be burning off steam with the enrichment and getting some nourishment.

8.15 am: Your dog is probably finished with his enrichment, drinking some water, getting ready for a poo and a sleep.

Daytime

9 am – 5 pm: While you are at work, the dog should be sleeping and relaxing.

Evening

5.15 pm: Get home from work and have a relaxed greeting with the dog and hang out together.

7.00 pm: Take the dog for another walk or to dog classes such as obedience or agility.

8.30 pm: Feed dog.

9.00 pm: Cuddles on the couch.

10.00 pm: Quick adventure out the front of the property for a sniff and a pee.

10.15 pm: Bed.

If we knew we were going to be held up at work, we would often ask one of our friends or family to pop over and play with the dogs for a bit.

Obviously, everyone's daily set-up and routine will look different. However, for people who work long hours and own high-energy, high-intelligence, emotional dogs we'd suggest finding a daily flow a bit like this that will give them enough fulfilment and contact time with you to prevent the development of separation anxiety.

Now, what should you do when you have a dog with extreme anxiety who is busting down doors and windows whenever he is left alone even for a brief moment? Well, this may be one of the situations where we suggest a consultation with a veterinary behaviourist who is competent in prescribing medication. Having said that, medication shouldn't be the silver bullet, and there are plenty of other things that can be done to assist.

As with every consult, we look at management, training and outlets.

Management for an extreme separation anxiety case usually involves people staying home from work, hiring helpers or asking for favours from family, friends and loved ones to prevent the dog from being left alone while you are trying to implement a new training regime to address it. This isn't a long-term solution, but is an important part of the pathway to independence.

Training usually involves first identifying some minute base level of independence that you can work on. You need to find creative ways to mildly simulate the act of leaving the dog alone without him having a meltdown. For some owners this might mean allowing the dog into their bedroom. The dog is often so incredibly stoked to be allowed on his owners' bed that the owner may be able to leave the room for a moment, even close the door perhaps, and the dog, for the first time in his life, thinks, 'I might be alone, but I'm comfortable and still feel connected to the family'. Moments like this give you something to work from as a baseline. There are many other ways to simulate alone time but it's about baby steps and realistic goals. We are dealing with emotions, so this cannot be solved in a matter of hours or days; it takes weeks, usually months, of carefully planned steps of independence building.

The **outlets** component of the plan is just as important as the training, in our mind. Remember, outlets are exercises that are designed to make the dog feel good, powerful and confident. When the dog feels good about himself, is being appropriately challenged and is physically stimulated he is much less anxious in general, which can help us find those breakthrough moments in which he realises being left alone isn't the end of the world.

Thunderstorm Phobia

We have never seen a well-established storm phobia in an adult dog be cured. However, if your dog does have storm phobia, don't be too disheartened by that because there are plenty of things you can do to reduce the severity of the phobia and make your dog feel safe enough that he doesn't try to escape or get too concerned.

First, if you have a puppy and he hasn't experienced a thunderstorm yet, you need to be ready to make his first thunderstorm a fun experience (more detail on sounds in Chapter 6).

On the other hand, if you have an adult dog with established storm phobia you can create a safe place where you can hang out with your dog regularly when there *aren't* storms. Spending relaxed time in there is crucial: don't just look at a particular room and think, 'Yep, it looks safe, I'll pop the dog in there whenever a thunderstorm is on the horizon.' It will almost certainly upset the dog to be put in an unfamiliar space when he is already feeling distressed.

An ideal storm safe space should:

- have the ability to reduce the visual effect of the lightning e.g. thick curtains, something that covers the windows

- be as soundproof and low echo as possible – a few towels over a crate and furniture in the room work wonders
- have some additional hiding places within it e.g. a kennel, crate or even access under a human bed
- have some white noise available e.g. a fan, radio, music or television
- be warm and cosy but still have adequate airflow, as many dogs can heat up and pant during storms
- have plenty of water to drink
- have chew toys – some dogs will just like holding a toy in their mouth or chewing it when they are stressed
- be suitable for access by the dog without supervision. Some safe spaces might have doggie doors; others won't, so we advise our clients who normally leave their dogs outside while they are at work to give a couple of neighbours and friends keys to the safe space. If a storm is on the horizon while they're at work, they can contact someone else to let the dog in.

You may not be able to provide all of that for your dog, but even if you can facilitate something slightly better than what you currently have, you may find it creates wonderful results.

We advise you to regularly hang out in this space with your dog and use it as an affection and chill-out zone where sometimes the door is open, and other times it's closed. You'll be prepping this place for your dog as a suitable bunker. To keep the association positive, try not to let anything your dog doesn't like occur in this space (e.g. if your dog hates getting his nails clipped, don't do it in this room).

We know plenty of dogs who used to escape during thunderstorms and often hurt themselves in the process, but when we created and gave them access to a safe space, they started taking themselves into the safe space when a storm was approaching.

There are a variety of medications, pheromones, jackets and collars that may help settle your dog during storms as well. These can be useful, but in our experience a well thought-out safe space your dog has been conditioned to enjoy is without doubt incredibly helpful.

Living Alongside Wildlife

We are extremely lucky to have spent much of our professional career caring for and learning about the complexities of our rich and unique Australian fauna, from the iconic kangaroo and koala, to the lesser known potoroo and phascogale. Domestic pets, like dogs and cats, pose a major threat to our wildlife but there are things we can do to help native animals and dogs coexist and stay safe.

Together with the social marketing team from Griffith University in Queensland, we have worked on specialised community engagement programs around Australia to help prevent unwanted interactions between dogs and native fauna.

Regardless of where you live in the world or what kind of inter-actions your dog is likely to have with wildlife, there are a couple of basic rules and training exercises you can follow that will reduce the likelihood of any unfortunate incidents.

They are:

1. Bring your dog inside your house or into a secure pen at night. Statistically, most interactions are likely to happen in your yard with nocturnal wildlife. This allows any native animals to pass between backyards safely at night in search of food and mates.
2. Avoid regularly encouraging wildlife (by feeding them) down onto your verandah or deck where your dog has access.
3. Put your dog into a secure area with short grass (or no grass) when you are not home during the day (this will reduce reptile interactions).
4. Teach your dog to recall under distraction (Chapter 9) and consider incorporating into their recall training calling them away from stuffed toys or even scats (poo) from the animal your dog is likely to encounter. For example, we'll put a stuffed koala on a skateboard or on top of a remote-controlled car along with the scent of a koala (usually a few pellets of poo!) and practise recalling them away from this highly desirable moving object. Obviously, this is a very advanced step of the

recall training process and you will need to work towards it gradually.

5. Teach your dog how to walk on lead (Chapter 10). A lot of wildlife interactions during the day occur with dogs who are off lead in areas where they shouldn't be i.e. on bush tracks. Often the reason these dogs are off lead is because they are difficult to walk on lead and the owner now hates using one. Remember, walking on lead is safer for your dog, other dogs, other animals *and* humans. So basically, everyone is better off! If you want to give your dog a bit more freedom on nature walks, try a long line. This way, if your dog spots a kangaroo and goes in for the chase, you can hold him back, but it gives him extra freedom and length to peruse the smells of the bush without having to remain strictly by your side.

Protecting native wildlife is all part of being a responsible pet owner. If you are a dog lover, it's likely you are an animal lover as well, so ensuring a safe and comfortable home for all creatures big and small, domestic and wild is an area worth investing in.

Training Pages

If you are excited to teach your dog something new, but it currently feels like a big undertaking and you are not sure where to begin . . . get it out of your head and onto paper now. Write a training plan!

This is something we do with our dogs, our clients' dogs and the animals at the zoo. It's a great starting point and serves as a road map if there is more than one family member involved with the training of the dog, plus it can be a great reminder of how far you have come.

Fill in the following details and always remember, if you get stuck or are struggling on a particular step, return to the previous step and work on that for a little longer, in varying locations. We've provided some sample training pages for you to fill out in Appendix C.

- Ultimate goal: Insert behaviour you are hoping to achieve, like loose lead walking.

- Short term goals required to get there: This might mean some basic training beforehand such as conditioning the word 'Good'; training a 'sit' and 'free'.
- What rewards will you use: Make it something special and specific to the task.
- Who is responsible: Name the family members.
- What is today's date: Pop in the date as a reminder of when you started.
- What does my dog know how to do today: It might be nothing – that's okay!
- How much time is required for short-term goals: You might write something like five minutes a day, five times a week for two weeks, to achieve this.
- How much time is required for long-term goals: This may be something you estimate over a few months.
- What locations will you use for training, progressing successfully distractions: Decide on appropriate locations suitable to your dog's ability to pay attention with distractions. You might start in your lounge room for a few days, then onto your driveway, the street, and then somewhere exciting like a shopping strip or beach.
- Write out the order of steps (trainers refer to them as 'approximations' when writing a training plan) you want to work on and how many days and sessions it might take. If you were working on loose lead walking, for example, you may write:
  1. Condition the bridge: 'Good' with sausage (1 day, 3 sessions).
  2. Train 'sit' and 'free': (1 day, 3 sessions).
  3. Train the 'sweet spot': (2 days, 5 sessions).
  4. Work on straight lines in the loungeroom: (2 days, 6 sessions).
  5. Right-hand turns: (1 day, 3 sessions).
  6. Responding to pressure: (1 day, 2 sessions).
  7. Turning left: (3 days, 9 sessions).
  8. Figure 8s: (1 day, 2 sessions).

9. Putting it all together at home: (3 days, 9 sessions).
10. Taking it into the driveway: (3 days, 6 sessions).
11. Taking it onto our street: (10 days, 20 sessions).
12. Taking it into busy locations: (20 days, 30 sessions).

This is just a brief example, but if you feel at all overwhelmed by anything training related and you can't think of how you will get there, we suggest you write a plan! When it comes to writing the actual training steps, just think:

1. What does my dog know how to do right now?
2. What would I like it to learn over the time period?
3. What training steps do I need to take in order to get there?

The teenager phase for dogs can seem like a long and testing time period for many pet owners, but it is without doubt our favourite time with new dogs. It is when their sense of humour, personality and athleticism starts to shine through – you'll have more laughs with your dog in this time than ever. Those sudden and seemingly cheeky independence spikes are your dog's way of showing you he is becoming an individual and approaching adulthood. It's the best time to implement lots of fun and play into your dog's life and establish some really positive habits that will stay with your dog forever.

Chapter 13

The Tail End

Here we are, 13 chapters later, at the tail end of our book. Hopefully, we're leaving you inspired to dig deeper into your dog's genetics and experiment with what gets her excited and makes her feel good inside, and of course go forth on many training adventures together.

Raising a happy dog relies on an early investment into her emotional and physiological development. A dog doesn't hit maturity until anywhere between 1.5 and 4 years of age so supporting, training, and providing positive learning opportunities for this entire time is required to ensure you'll have a well-adjusted, lovely family pet long term.

We personally (along with the rest of the world) would love to see all dogs out of pounds so, where possible, adopting a dog is an honourable thing to do. But what we want even more than this is to educate people on how to choose and raise a puppy right from the beginning so a dog never needs to be rehomed or rescued in the first place.

It's worth remembering that prevention will always be better (and easier) than curing a behavioural issue. Preventing an undesirable behaviour relies on a combination of management, positive outlets and training. Hopefully, by now you will have plenty of ideas and options up your sleeve to help you prepare for the arrival of a puppy and plan for each stage thereafter. And don't forget to investigate the root cause of *why* a behaviour has manifested in the first place. By understanding the reason, you will be far better prepared to drive the right solution instead of barking up the wrong tree.

And above all else . . . have fun! When it comes to training your dog, *sure* – master the basics first, but don't stop there, get wild! Basics don't impress the relatives at family get-togethers. A dog who does parkour or finds your keys can become a *must-see* act and a great ice-breaker for the cousin's new girlfriend. Aside from this, your dog will honestly enjoy the new learning experience. Problem-solving keeps the canine brain sharp, happy and having a lot of fun.

If we had to leave you with one last piece of advice we would encourage you to offer something from each of the following categories daily for your dog to experience:

- MOVEMENT – Although each breed requires completely different amounts of physical exercise, every dog needs movement every day to stay fit and healthy.
- PLAY – Experiencing this together tightens your bond and makes you both feel good on the inside!
- FOCUS – Training new behaviours and continuing to teach your dog new things throughout her life, not just while she is a puppy, offers opportunities for your dog to focus and problem solve. Focus includes outlets as well. Think of activities that get the blood pumping and the brain thinking at the same time. Fetch, with rules! Tug, with rules! Agility, obedience – the possibilities are endless.
- SNIFF – Dogs were born to use their nose. With a nose at least 10,000 times more effective than ours, all dogs should experience some form of scent game every other day.
- REST – Rest and relaxation are such important factors in raising a content and happy dog. And a young puppy needs anywhere between 18 to 20 hours of sleep a day! Teaching your dog the skill of 'switching off' is equally as important as training and socialisation. As with humans, sleep really does promote sleep. Provide your dog with opportunities to practise 'mindfulness'.

The relationship between humans and dogs has evolved and strengthened more than ever in the past decade. In almost every second home, a family hound is curled up on a couch. More and more pubs, bars and cafes now market themselves as 'pet friendly' to accommodate the growing number of people whose dog must be included in all family affairs. Most department stores have a section for dogs as big as their section for kids! And let's face it, any clothing line would be crazy to release matching family Christmas outfits and *not* include a dog option as well.

In the last decade, we've seen dogs be trained for almost everything from conservation to therapy support. One of the greatest projects that exists today is coordinated by our good friend Steve Austin and facilitated through the Defence Community Dog Program. Steve hand selects dogs who need to be rehomed from pounds and rescue organisations and pairs them with the inmates at Bathurst Correctional Centre. The dogs are then trained by the inmates to an assistance dog level during their rehabilitation time and once trained, the inmates hand over the dogs to returned war veterans as PTSD support dogs. An extraordinary journey for all involved, including the dogs!

Some of the greatest leaps forward for dogs have been in the burgeoning field of scent detection, where much of our work currently lies. Dogs are widely used to protect human lives through the detection of infectious diseases, viruses (most recently COVID-19), explosives and people in need of search and rescue. In the realm of conservation, dogs are on the front line in many projects preserving species and habitats, detecting invasive, endangered and (previously believed to be) extinct plants and animals. A dog's nose is fast becoming well known for saving time and resources across many industries: finding underground water leaks, termites, truffles – the list goes on.

That being said, a dog's ability is limited only by the imagination of her trainer. Once you unlock this relationship with your dog, the sky really is the limit when it comes to what you can both do together.

Dog training has come a long way in just the lifetime of our 14-year-old Shepherd, Hugo. Imagine what dogs will achieve in the lifetime of your new puppy!

Appendix A

Harmful and healthy food for your dog

Harmful

Never feed your dog any of the food items on this list:

- apple seeds
- avocado
- baking powder
- chocolate
- fruit pits
- garlic
- grapes
- mouldy food
- mushrooms
- nuts (particularly walnuts, pistachios, macadamias, pecans and almonds)
- onions
- raisins
- food containing xylitol (many products advertised as 'sugar free' contain xylitol, particularly sauces, spreads, baked goods and chewing gum).

Note: this is not an exhaustive list. If you're worried about whether you should feed a particular food item to your dog, you can also check the RSPCA website for more information or contact your vet. If you are concerned that your dog has consumed something toxic, call your local vet immediately.

Healthy

Some food your dog might enjoy:

- apples (not the seeds)
- beans
- blueberries
- broccoli
- broth
- carrots
- celery
- chicken
- coconut
- corn (shaved off the cob)
- cucumber
- eggs
- lamb
- leafy greens
- mango
- parsley
- papaya
- peas
- potatoes
- pumpkin
- raspberries
- sardines
- sweet potato
- yoghurt (plain)
- zucchini.

Appendix B

Toxic plants

Here is a list of some of the more common plants that land dogs at the vet:

- avocado (fruit, leaves, bark, seed)
- azalea (all parts)
- cycads (seeds)
- daffodils (all parts but especially bulbs)
- foxgloves (leaves, seeds, flowers)
- lily of the valley (all parts)
- macadamia
- Morning Glory (seeds)
- nightshade (all parts)
- oleander (all parts, including dead leaves)
- rhododendron (all parts)
- tulip (bulbs)
- Wandering Jew (leaves, stems, sap)
- wisteria (seeds, pods)
- Yesterday-Today-Tomorrow, also known as *Brunfelsia pauciflora* (all parts).

Food (see Appendix A) and plant poisoning are common reasons why dogs end up being rushed to the vet. Toxins affect multiple body systems – neurological, liver, kidney, heart and gastrointestinal. Clinical signs include:

- vomiting, diarrhoea, decreased appetite
- increased thirst

- lethargy,
- increased heart rate
- shallow/rapid breathing
- dribbling urine
- drooling
- tremors, coordination issues, seizures, coma.

If you are concerned that your dog has consumed something toxic, call your local vet immediately.

Visit the ASPCA website's animal poison control page for a comprehensive list on toxic food and plants.

Appendix C

Training Pages

HOW TO TRAIN YOUR DOG

Date: _____

Ultimate goal:
Short-term goals required to achieve ultimate goal:
What rewards will be used:
Person responsible for this training:
Start date of training:
Level of training the dog understands today:
Number of training sessions per week required:
Date you hope to achieve your short-term goals:
Date you hope to achieve your long-term goals:
Location(s) you will use for training:

Order of training steps (this is your actual plan and should take up at least 10 steps):

HOW TO TRAIN YOUR DOG

Date: _____

Ultimate goal:

Short-term goals required to achieve ultimate goal:

What rewards will be used:

Person responsible for this training:

Start date of training:

Level of training the dog understands today:

Number of training sessions per week required:

Date you hope to achieve your short-term goals:

Date you hope to achieve your long-term goals:

Location(s) you will use for training:

Order of training steps (this is your actual plan and should take up at least 10 steps):

HOW TO TRAIN YOUR DOG

Date: _____

Ultimate goal:

Short-term goals required to achieve ultimate goal:

What rewards will be used:

Person responsible for this training:

Start date of training:

Level of training the dog understands today:

Number of training sessions per week required:

Date you hope to achieve your short-term goals:

Date you hope to achieve your long-term goals:

Location(s) you will use for training:

Order of training steps (this is your actual plan and should take up at least 10 steps):

Date: _____

Ultimate goal:
Short-term goals required to achieve ultimate goal:
What rewards will be used:
Person responsible for this training:
Start date of training:
Level of training the dog understands today:
Number of training sessions per week required:
Date you hope to achieve your short-term goals:
Date you hope to achieve your long-term goals:
Location(s) you will use for training:

Order of training steps (this is your actual plan and should take up at least 10 steps):

HOW TO TRAIN YOUR DOG

Date: _____

Ultimate goal:

Short-term goals required to achieve ultimate goal:

What rewards will be used:

Person responsible for this training:

Start date of training:

Level of training the dog understands today:

Number of training sessions per week required:

Date you hope to achieve your short-term goals:

Date you hope to achieve your long-term goals:

Location(s) you will use for training:

Order of training steps (this is your actual plan and should take up at least 10 steps):

Further reading

Austin, Steve, *Working Dog Heroes*: *How one man gives shelter dogs new life and purpose*, HarperCollins Publishers Australia, Sydney South, 2016.

Donaldson, Jean, *The Culture Clash: A revolutionary new way of understanding the relationship between humans and domestic dogs*, 2nd ed, The Academy for Dog Trainers, Washington, 2012.

Dunbar, Ian, *Before & After Getting Your Puppy: The positive approach to raising a happy, healthy & well-behaved dog*, New World Library, Novato, 2004.

Hennessy, Kathryn (ed), *The Dog Encyclopedia*, DK Publishing, New York, 2013.

McGreevy, Paul, et al, 'Behavioural risks in male dogs with minimal lifetime exposure to gonadal hormones may complicated population-control benefits of desexing', *PLoS ONE*, vol. 13, no. 5, 2018. https://doi.org/10.1371/journal.pone.0196284.

Pryor, Karen, *Don't Shoot the Dog: The art of teaching and training*, Simon & Schuster, New York, 2019.

Starling, Melissa, & McGreevy, Paul, *Making Dogs Happy: How to be your dog's best friend*, Murdoch Books, Sydney, 2018.

Tillman, Peggy, *Clicking with your dog: Step-by-step in pictures*, Waltham, Sunshine, 2001.

Acknowledgements

We would like to thank:

Steve and Vicki Austin – two of the world's most influential and skilled dog trainers and teachers. They are our mentors, friends and even parental figures in our lives. Without their continued support and guidance, we would not be where we are today.

Our TATE team – Kate McDonald, Claire Chiotti, Stephen Dalleywater, Simone Popp and Sammy Truswell.

Our vets – Sarah Short, Tim Barton and Michael Ferguson.

Amy Smith – Amy's puppy pre-school and the Soundproof Puppy Training app.

Mike and Kath Burling – The Dog Father Dog Training Townsville.

Taronga Zoo and Taronga Western Plains Zoo – we wouldn't have met half our friends or each other without these two places.

Discover a
new favourite

Visit **penguin.com.au/readmore**